Love Matters

For Psychic Transformation

Love Matters

For Psychic Transformation

A Study of Embodied Psychic Transformation
in the Context of BodySoul Rhythms®

Maja Reinau, M.D.

fisher king press

Love Matters For Psychic Transformation
A Study of Embodied Psychic Transformation in the Context of
BodySoul Rhythms®

Copyright © 2016 by Maja Reinau
First Edition
ISBN 978-1-77169-031-7 Paperback
ISBN 978-1-77169-032-4 eBook

Published in the United States of America by Fisher King Press. For information on obtaining permission for use of material from this work, submit a written request to:

permissions@fisherkingpress.com

Fisher King Press
109 E 17th St, Ste 80
Cheyenne, WY 82001
www.fisherkingpress.com
fisherking@fisherkingpress.com
+1-307-222-9575

Many thanks to all who have directly or indirectly provided permission to reprint their work. Every effort has been made to trace all copyright holders; however, if any have been overlooked, we will be pleased to make the necessary arrangements at the first opportunity.

Front cover Sprouted Oak image © is from an original photo by Mary Jo Hofmann.

www.stillblog.net

*The conscious feminine
gives us the courage
to love an acorn
without knowing
what an oak tree is.*

—Marion Woodman

Contents

Acknowledgements

First and foremost, I would like to thank the women who willingly and with great openness have shared their experience of the BodySoul Rhythms® (BSR) work with me. The interviews and their stories have been deep and moving, and an unexpected gift in my research for this book. The laughter and the tears shared in these moments are written into the words in this work. I would like to thank Ann, Mary and Marion. I am moved with gratitude for having been, and for continuing to be, a part of the BSR work and for having been in the presence of three such wise, embodied and loving women: three women, who have had a deep impact on my path and whose work I hope to do justice to in this book. And I would like to thank all the women I have met on the BSR journey: it has been richness beyond measure. In the process of getting the book published I am indebted to the Special Project group of the Marion Woodman Foundation who have granted me a sponsorship, thus making this publication possible. I am moved beyond measure for this support. I would like to thank John, my analyst, for being there unfailingly, for welcoming and receiving the soul, and for standing up for the soul again and again. I would like to thank my mother who deep in her heart knows the mystery of the soul and my father for teaching me the perseverance to follow my path. Several people have been immensely encouraging and helpful in the process of making this book a reality. I am deeply grateful to Daniela Sieff for her encouragement and helpful comments, to my brother Niels Reinau for giving me the encouragement to proceed being the first reviewer of the very first drafts and his immense and patient help with the layout, to Vernessa Riley Foelix for the artwork and creative comments – including her enlightenment in how to understand the symbol of the acorn, and to my publisher Mel Mathews with whom I share the love for the soul. Finally, I would like to thank my husband Benny for his love and encouragement.

Foreword by John Hill

Maja Reinau's book *Love Matters for Psychic Transformation* serves as an excellent introduction to *BodySoul Rhythms*[1] (BSR), a method created by Marion Woodman, Ann Skinner, and Mary Hamilton. BSR has been immensely successful, transforming the lives of many women who have participated in its programs. Maja Reinau's book elucidates the gems that structure this creative method.

The author received her training as a Jungian analyst at The International School of Analytical Psychology, Zürich, and at the same time completed her training in psychodrama. Having undergone intensive personal analysis, clinical supervision, course work on theory, and the experiential method of psychodrama, one might ask why did the author undertake a further training in BSR? Maja Reinau's book provides ample answers to this question. BSR has been a second home for the author. It is her passion that draws together several loose ends of a rich, multi-faceted personal and professional life. With focus on the psyche-body connection, which includes Jungian theory, dreams, myths, body movement, voice work, mask-work, and artwork, BSR adds a feminine dimension that protects, structures, and provides communal solidarity in the face of challenges arising from a patriarchal culture that engenders disconnect. Maja Reinau notes that at first BSR work had to be open to women only, simply because it was too difficult to hold the container for mixed groups in view of the deep wounds of intimacy generated in cross gender relationships. Eventually it intends to include men in all its programs, in fact this is already taking place in many of the workshops today.

The book skillfully outlines the space-time rhythms of an intensive BSR week. Usually it takes place in a beautiful landscape, which in itself nourishes soul work and activates inner landscapes. It would be beyond the scope of this foreword to describe all the activities of an intensive week, but let me mention a few that strike me as outstanding. Breakfast begins in silence, followed by a ritual dance, the reading of a poem, and a short meditation. The morning ends with a presentation on some specific theme, often connected with Jungian psychology. The afternoon is centered on body and voice work, adding an experiential dimension to what has been already activated through nature, dreams, meditation, or the morning presentation. The focus of the first evening is on providing a positive mothering exercise, the following evenings on the making of masks, and the final evening on an ending ritual.

---

1 Throughout this text The BodySoul Rhythms® will often be referred to as BSR. For more information about the BSR see www.mwoodmanfoundation.org

After having described the basic dynamics of BSR, Maja Reinau interviews six women who have completed the BSR training program. With great skill and confidence the author has documented the transformative moments that take place in BSR intensives. As each story unfolds, one feels one is moving with these women in the river of life. One story speaks about a shamed body gaining presence in the loving gaze of like-minded women. Next we learn about a participant who discovers she can explore a different feminine body that is free from the judgments of the brain and a culture that tells women how they should look. Another narrative tells us how the darkest, shut-off parts of a woman's soul finally could be met through the eyes of another. Through mask-work one woman faces a rigid defense system, learns to trust what happens in the moment, and discovers that her psyche finds nourishment and new life through listening to myth and poetry. In another case we read about a dramatic occurrence of rebirth that brought healing to an original birth trauma. In the final interview we witness an immersion in a common field connecting body, soul, and group members in a holistic experience that stimulates the imagination in a playful, loving way.

The interviews portray in the most vivid, detailed way what actually happens in an intensive week. Elaborating on this material, Maja Reinau launches into an in-depth theoretical discussion on the key issues that have been activated in each individual participant during a BSR intensive week. She draws upon the findings of Jungian theory, neuroscience, and developmental psychology, but is mindful that theory can never be reductive and certainly not replace the subjective lived experience of the participant, which always has the last word. Nevertheless theory helps weave fragmentary events into a pattern that can serve as a guide for future development as well as a means to communicate the meaning of the BSR method within a larger collegial context.

As Maja Reinau concludes her description of BSR, one has the impression that one has witnessed the essence of women's mysteries within a modern context. Process, presence, and paradox become the essential ingredients of those mysteries. Each participant has the opportunity of gaining awareness of the creative potential of the psyche, a sense of being truly present to oneself and to the other, and an acceptance of life's contradictions, especially the realm of the shadow. This salutary brew nourishes the soul when stirred under the auspices of an archetypal feminine triad: the mother, the virgin, and the crone, symbolizing loving containment, pregnant creativity, and the wisdom of age. For Maja Reinau, love is the final transformative factor that brings healing and renewal. This kind of loving is a highly differentiated blend of mirroring, containing, empathic attunement, and resonating with the life energy of all who undertake this daring journey. As one peruses the pages of this book, one cannot but feel the inspiring presence of Marion Woodman, Ann Skinner, and Mary Hamilton. Maja Reinau's book pays ample tribute to their pioneering endeavor in bringing hope and renewal to the lives of all who have undergone a BSR experience.

Aim and Structure of this Book

It is the aim of this book to provide the reader with an insight into what really matters for the soul to feel received and to start to unfold – an insight given through the accounts of the subjective, lived experience of psychic transformation as it is referred to in six interviews with women who have done the BSR leadership training. In addition, it is the aim to link the BSR approach with the new neuroscience and developmental theories in order to show how much the BSR approach has to offer, not only in the Jungian field but also in a broader field of approaches. It is not the aim of this book to give a detailed account of either Jungian theory or the work of Marion Woodman. For that, I refer the reader to the work of the C.G. Jung and Marion Woodman.

The book is structured in three parts. Part I is a description of the BSR work as such and descriptions of the values shaping the BSR approach. Part II is the six interviews. Part III is reflections on the material, weaving together the essence of the interviews with the theory, integrated with related reflections from modern neuroscience and developmental psychology and creating one potential image of what matters for psychic transformation and for the soul to feel received. I hope it will inspire the reader's approach to the soul.

Introduction

In 2002 I embarked on a rich journey to the inner world. The journey took place within a seven-day intensive course called BodySoul Rhythms®. This intensive was facilitated by Ann Skinner, Mary Hamilton, Marion Woodman and their apprentices. Based on the theories of C.G. Jung, and the work of Marion Woodman on the feminine and the psyche–body connection; this intensive combined Jungian theory, dreams, myths, body movement, voice work, mask-work and art work in a very creative and powerful combination.[1]

Actually my journey had started two years before this, when I went to Zurich to begin my analytical training. Throughout my analytical training in Zurich, I kept coming to these intensives every semester because of their profound way of enhancing deep psychic work. It gave me a precious, lived experience of inner work and it taught me about the type of environment that supports, nourishes and encourages the soul to express herself. It became immensely important to me, and I feel it is the cornerstone of my analytical training, together with my personal analysis.

What I have learned in the BSR work has shaped my way of being an analyst and my perception of the analytical encounter, and it is deeply incorporated into my way of practicing. It seemed a natural progression for me to write about it.

The writing of this book has been a process in itself – a process that in many ways reflects my own journey with the work. It has had several working titles: 'The neuroscience behind the BSR work,' 'Receiving soul,' 'The impregnating art of listening,' and 'The wise old uterus,'[2]

---

1 The BSR work applies to men and women, the development of the conscious masculine and the conscious feminine being equally important in both genders. However, up till now, the BSR leadership training has been open only to women. This has not, however, been to exclude men from this type of work. Marion Woodman explains that in the pioneering days of the work they found it too difficult to hold the container with mixed groups in a way that allowed for and could hold the deep work. As the approach develops and the collective becomes able to hold and contain both the wounded masculine and feminine and the sexual energies that can be constellated in deep work with mixed groups, it is the intension to move the work forward and include both men and women in the group (source: Marion Woodman speaking on the theme at the annual renewal in October 2006).

2 The symbol of the uterus as 'life-giving vase': C.G. Jung, Visions - Notes on the Seminar Given in 1930-1934, Volume I, edited by Claire Douglas, p. 328. The vas is analogous to the life-giving chalice in the legend of the Holy Grail and the vas in alchemy.

and, finally, 'Love matters for psychic transformation.'[3] The change in working titles reflects the development along the way.[4]

Upon setting out to write, I was determined to try to explain the power of the BSR work and the different aspects of it, wanting to relate the intuition, body wisdom and deep sense for soul work held by the three women who developed the BSR approach, with modern scientific findings in research of the development of the human mind, and of the importance of how we are met and mirrored in the forming and reforming of the human brain's neuronal networks.

From my medical background, I have an interest in the developments in neuroscience and developmental psychology. I feel a great enthusiasm about the expansion in neuroscience, as this field is coming to meet psychology in a mutual understanding.

When I started reflecting on this book, I was filled with knowledge from Allan Schore and his theory of right brain-to-right brain interaction and repair of the self; Daniel Stern's theory of "now movements," attunement, vital background-feelings, and the inner world of the infant; Antonio Damasio's work on the feeling of what happens and the role of body perceptions and feelings as basis for core consciousness, and his emphasis on inner images and feeling stages related to these images; Sue Gerhardt's work on infant–mother observation and why love matters in the development of the self; Margaret Wilkinson's work in her book "Coming into Mind" on the early dyad in therapy. I had also heard Bessel van der Kolk describe his program of working with trauma through dance, singing, group-work, and deep relaxation at the Trauma Center, at the Justice Resource Institute, Brookline, Massachusetts; and I had read the concepts of working with different emotional parts of the personality when working with traumatised clients as described by Onno van der Hart. I had been deeply engaged in Pat Ogden's sensorimotor psychotherapy and theory on trauma and the body; Peter Fonagy's description of attachment patterns and human relationship; and also the deep well of Jungian writers' wisdom collected from years on this journey.

I have to confess that theories alone never have been able to convince me, if I could not relate it to a lived experience, or feel some kind of resonance with living reality.[5] Since I first read Jung's autobiography *Memories, Dreams, Reflections*[6] I have been conscious of a deep

---

3 I have been deeply inspired by Sue Gerhardt's work and always felt that a loving and encouraging relationship was important, not only for the newborn but for all development and transformation.

4 For the meaning of the word love in this work please read post-script.

5 I find the link between the subjective feeling experience and the objective theoretical structure a vital place of exploration. A lived experience is a 'global experience' in the way Daniel Stern uses this phrase, and something is always lost when it is conveyed to the verbal sense of self. There is a danger in all theories that they can lose touch with the lived experience.

6 C.G. Jung, *Memories, Dreams, Reflections*, MDR refers throughout this publication to *Memories, Dreams, Reflections*.

interest in the subjective lived experience of psychic transformation. Theories are interesting, but subjective lived experiences 'of what matters for psychic transformation' are fascinating. They open up to the beauty of each individual we meet, and to his or her process.

Pondering on my own process and my own experience, I knew that for anything to transform it had to be alive within. And whatever wanted to express itself had to feel received. What enhanced that process? How do we encourage that inner life to step forward and move with us?

These questions were indeed very alive and I knew this had to be a focus of my writing. As I pondered on how I could shape this work to contain some exploration of how psychic transformation was experienced subjectively and what mattered from the soul's perspective to support that process, I decided that I would supply my own thoughts, lived experience of the BodySoul Rhythms work and my background theoretical knowledge along with interviews with women who themselves had done both analysis and BSR work.

I ventured out to gather the stories, visiting each woman in her home country. These interviews turned out to be much more than I expected; they were profound meetings. The quality of deep listening, the depth of the women's thoughts, and their willingly sharing of their lived experiences around the BSR work was very moving.

From the very first interview, I found myself shifting my approach, leaving aside my planned list of detailed questions about the BodySoul experience and simply giving space to each woman to voice what had been important to her: letting her story unfold, rather than directing it. Each interview took its own form, amplifying this question and voicing a journey that often had not been voiced before, and giving us a sense of something taking form or coming into being as we talked and listened. I hope the reader will feel this, as he or she reads each interview, and that it will not only describe a woman's story but also the process of coming into being, and a growing sense in the individual of what we in the Jungian field would call a growing relation to the Self.

The interviews are in themselves living symbols or amalgams of psyche's journey. Each interview is reflecting the individual woman's story. They are accounts of what moves the soul, what makes it dare to trust after a long time in hiding. While typing the interviews, I realized that these were gem stones. I decided that these interviews like raw natural stones had to be left untouched and I therefore offer the interviews in their entirety. My theoretical accounts are what links these stones together in an attempt to give the reader an understanding of the jewel of the BodySoul Rhythms work, but the individual stones have been left in their natural beauty.

I realize it is very much in line with my deeper belief: the soul can never be captured in a theory. This, too, is at the core of the BSR work itself, since its emphasis is to provide the container and the space for each participant to tend to her inner life and to let it come forth in its 'uncut' form, in its own expression, and to experience that fully first before one starts to analyse it. To allow the inner reality to have space for its full expression, and a space for the process of relating to it, gaining conscious understanding, letting it influence our attitude and become an integrated part of the patterns of who we are in the world. This does not indicate in any way that theory is not required, but it always holds a risk of blurring our eye for the natural beauty of the inner reality. To cultivate our senses, to tune into just taking in that level of the soul's expression in its many forms, is, in my opinion, crucial, since we are living in a culture where hardly anything can be allowed to come forth and just be given its space, holding the space for it and seeing its beauty.

With the impact of the beauty of the nature in the interviews, my approach shifted. The neuroscience stepped into the background. It became the technical background knowledge needed to refine the work. And the new neurobiological findings do give us a new layer of understanding and particularly sharpens our awareness of the importance of how we receive and welcome the inner life, and as analyst, the whole nature of our analysands. The 'how' is crucial and makes all the difference when we accompany the soul on its journey.

The journey itself, like Jung's description in *Memories, Dreams, Reflections* was what called me to my love for analytical psychology; the trust in the descent [the 'drop' or 'dropping'] and the exploration of the world, following the energy; following psychic life as experienced from the inside – unfolding and coming alive in the encounter.

Attending to the soul's needs becomes like a walk in nature; it stabilises and brings us 'into' or 'back to' ourselves. Equally a walk in our 'inner nature' seems to carry the same possibility. To relate to that inner nature and to feel joy and curiosity in its landscape, spending time there, is adding depth to our lives.

I hope to convey to the reader the BSR approach's capacity to enhance psychic transformation and an understanding of why the elements in BSRs approach are so potent.[7] I hope too that in the process of reading, the reader will feel invited to reflect on his or her own thoughts regarding the question 'How do we receive soul?' – a question that brings us to the depth of this work and often is subtly influenced by our own experiences. When does your soul feel received? And most poignant of all – how do you receive your soul? I would like to end the introduction by sharing a personal experience I had within my own analysis. I was in a situation where I was blocked, trying to make a decision. I had laid out small object on the floor in the office of my analyst, showing the crossroads I felt I was looking at. I was totally captured in this conflict whether I should do this or that, struggling deeply, giving voices to the two

---

7 I am aware that some of the material is presented in what at times may come across in an idealized tone. This is not the attitude intended but is merely the result of trying to describe the approach as clearly as possible, excluding all the nuances that surface in the reality of the work.

sides. I turned to my analyst and asked what he thought I should do. He replied; "I have no idea, but look at the picture you have made, it is truly beautiful!" I was baffled by the reply which took me to a total new level of looking at life and all the obstacles it made. It all created a picture that was actually beautiful. To have the eye for this kind of beauty – the beauty of a soulful life created under the pressure of layers of 'peat.' To see the beauty in that changed the perspective. It moved from the ego being caught in the opposites to a deeper perception of the beauty of a soulful lived life. Someone was witnessing and it all made sense – even the pressure and the obstacles. 'Someone' being simultaneously both the analyst and a deeper aspect within, that is the Self. The soul found again itself encouraged and I knew how to walk forward. John O'Donohue speaks to this style of presence in *Eternal Echoes*:

> Styles of presence - The encouraging presence helps you to awaken your gift
>
> There are people whose presence is encouraging. One of the most beautiful gifts in the world is the gift of encouragement. When someone encourages you, that person helps you over a threshold you might otherwise never have crossed on your own. There are times of great uncertainty in every life. Left alone at such times, you feel dishevelment and confusion like gravity. When a friend comes with words of encouragement, a light and lightness visit you and you begin to find the stairs and the door out of the dark. The sense of encouragement you feel from the friend is not simply her words or gestures; it is rather her whole presence enfolding you and helping you to find the concealed door. The encouraging presence manages to understand you and put herself in your shoes. There is no judgement but words of relief and release.
>
> Encouragement also helps you to engage and trust your own possibility and potential. Sometimes you are unable to see the special gift that you bring to the world. No gift is ever given for your private use. To follow your gift is a calling to a wonderful adventure of discovery. Some of the deepest longing in you is the voice of your gift. The gift calls you to embrace it, not to be afraid of it. The only way to honor the unmerited presence of the gift in your life is to attend to the gift; this is also a most difficult path to walk. Each gift is different; there is no plan or programme you can get ready-made from someone else. The gift alone knows where its path leads. It calls you to courage and humility. If you hear its voice in your heart, you simply have to follow it. Otherwise your life could be dragged into the valley of disappointment. People who truly follow their gift find that it can often strip their lives and yet invest them with a sense of enrichment and fulfilment that nothing else could bring. Those who renege on or repress their gift are unwittingly sowing the seeds of regret.[8]

---

8 John O'Donohue, *Eternal Echoes: Celtic Reflections on Our Yearning to Belong*, pp. 62-63.

Part I

Description of the BodySoul Rhythms®

This part of the book will be describing the development of the BSR work, the BSR work as such, and underlying values shaping the BSR approach. It serves to give the reader knowledge of this approach as well as a context for the interviews in part two.

The BSR*—Founders, Foundation, and the Programs

The BodySoul Rhythms work was developed and founded by Ann Skinner, Mary Hamilton and Marion Woodman. Marion Woodman, LLD, DHL, PhD, is a Zurich-trained Jungian analyst, teacher and author and co-author of eleven books. She has practiced in Toronto and London, Ontario in Canada. Marion Woodman travels extensively, lecturing and conducting workshops for women around the world. A visionary in her own right, Marion Woodman has worked with the analytical psychology of C.G. Jung in an original and creative way. She is the Chair of the Marion Woodman Foundation. Her writings include: *The Owl was a Baker's Daughter*; *Addiction to Perfection*; *The Pregnant Virgin*; *The Ravaged Bridegroom*; *Leaving My Father's House*; *Conscious Femininity*; *Dancing in the Flames* (with Elinor Dickson); *Coming Home to Myself* (with Jill Mellick); *The Forsaken Garden: Four Conversations on the Deep Meaning of Environmental Illness* Marion Woodman, Ross Woodman, Sir Laurens van der Post and Thomas Berry, edited by Nancy Ryley; *The Maiden King* (with Robert Bly) and *Bone - Dying Into Life*.

Mary Hamilton, MEd, is a graduate of the National Ballet School of Canada. She is a former professor at the University of Western Ontario where she taught modern dance, improvisation, and choreography for 20 years. In 1980, she began working with Marion Woodman, combining creative movement with dream imagery. In 1991, Ann Skinner joined them, and together the three created and taught the BodySoul Rhythms® program. Mary Hamilton is a member of the Canadian Group Psychotherapy Association, and is one of the authors of the book *Leaving My Father's House: Journey to Conscious Femininity* and the author of *Under the Horse's Ass: A Love Story Human and Divine* and *The Dragonfly Principle: An Exploration of the Body's Function in Unfolding Spirituality*.

Ann Skinner is Head of Voice Emerita at Canada's Stratford Shakespeare Festival and formerly Head of Voice at the National Theatre School of Canada. From her clown- and theatre-training with Richard Pochinko in the 1970s, she adapted the process of working with masks to her exploration of the origins of the letters of the alphabet, and to the psychological process in the creation of BodySoul Rhythms®. Her work has taken her across Canada and to the UK, Europe, and the USA.

Marion Woodman, Mary Hamilton, and Ann Skinner have worked collaboratively for more than three decades developing the BodySoul approach. This work is based on the understanding that psyche and soma are inseparable, and must be worked on together for us to become more conscious. The integration incorporates working with dreams and imagery together with body and voice while honoring the uniqueness of each individual. In the intensives, the facilitators create a supportive space where each participant can access and use her own individual dream imagery to discover her authentic self and express herself with her own freed voice. The roots of the work are a deep respect for dreams, the theories of C.G. Jung, the wisdom of the body, and Marion Woodman's commitment to articulate and deepen the understanding of the conscious feminine and the embodied soul. Recent scientific discoveries regarding specific neurobiological processes affirm the transformative power of this work. These findings in the field of interpersonal neurobiology confirm the concept in the BSR that the perceived and perceiver are one and are continually interacting with and affecting each other.

Within the BodySoul program it is a continuous aim to keep integrating the scientific, the psychological and the creative as the work evolves.

In 2002, the Marion Woodman Foundation was formed. It is a non-profit organization founded to ensure the work initiated in BodySoul Rhythms intensives continues and flourishes. It offers intensives, a leadership program and affiliated workshops. Intensives are programs of seven days that offer a chance to engage in a deep process involving the core of the work. They are held in a retreat setting. The format is intensive with morning, afternoon and evening sessions. Phase 1 intensives are designed for women who are new or relatively new to this particular work. They concentrate on individual experience and can be taken as many times as desired. Requirements are completion of at least 50 hours of Jungian analysis or therapy and at least 50 hours of bodywork. The required bodywork is that of using imagery and/or conscious attention such as yoga, Tai Chi, Authentic Movement, Feldenkrais. Phase 2 intensives take participants deeper into the work, include more theory and begin to train participants to conduct the work. The BodySoul Rhythms® Leadership Training is a three-year program that includes six BodySoul intensives (three Phase 1s and three Phase 2s), six leadership seminars, and apprenticeship with the faculty at an intensive. Participants can experience BodySoul work deeply themselves and then learn to incorporate the approach in their own professional work. Shorter workshops and seminars, as well as affiliated workshops, are also offered. Affiliated workshops are conducted by women who have completed the BodySoul Rhythms® leadership training.[9]

The Structure of the BSR Work

In the following, I will give a description of 'such stuff as the BodySoul Rhythms are made on.' That is, I will describe the structure of the BSR work. My aim is to give the reader a clear

---

9 This introduction is aligned with the text from the Marion Woodman Foundation's website and the brief biography in Spring 72, *Body and Soul: A Special Issue Honoring Marion Woodman*. For more information please visit www.mwoodmanfoundation.org

image of the structure of the intensives. This is important as background knowledge to hold in mind, reading the interviewed women's stories.

It describes what we are doing while that deeper process takes place, in Daniel Stern's[10] sense of this, or to explain the form of what happens in this way of working that allow for what feels 'like a modern Elysian mystery,' to use one of the interviewee women's wording. It is explained with respect for the founders and for their wisdom, intuition, sensitivity and deep insight into soul work.

It is important to clarify that the descriptions and reflections of the BSR work in this book are an account of what I have received implicitly and explicitly through the teachings and through my own lived experience. It is reflected in the light of my readings, my analytical training, participation in the BSR leadership program, psychodrama training and my interest in developmental psychology, body memory and soul work. It's intended to make the reader reflect on how we are meeting and receiving the soul, the importance of love for the soul as a quality of the container for psychic transformation, as well as deepening the insight of the body-soul connection and how that applies to our work. It is not in any way written with the intention of giving the reader instructions as to how to conduct BSR work, which would be a lack of respect for the difficulty of conducting psychic work: a difficult skill that certainly requires training.

When I refer to my own experiences, this refers to my participation in the first European leadership training program conducted mainly in Grimstone, in the United Kingdom, over a four-year period from 2001 to 2005. Over these years, approximately 30 women met once or twice a year and thus shared the journey together. The group consisted of women aged between 26 and 76, coming from approximately seven different countries. They shared the link of being interested in the BSR work and having fulfilled the entrance requirements, but apart from that they all came from a variety of backgrounds: culturally, religiously and occupationally. Some were young mothers, others were grandmothers, and some had no children. Many were themselves working within the therapeutic field. The group is still connected, linked by an internet group and are offering their work in Europe.

After completing the leadership program I have continued to attend the yearly renewal in Canada: an intensive for women who have completed the BSR leadership training to continue deepening their work. Here, new profound groups were meeting, again with a variety of backgrounds. Three of the women interviewed are from this group. All three of them are deeply involved in offering BSR workshops or intensives.

I recall reading Helen Luke's biography: *Such Stuff that Dreams are Made On.* In her writing she uses a beautiful image that has been resonating with me since I read her book; she

---

10 Daniel N. Stern, *The Present Moment in Psychotherapy and Everyday Life*.

calls her outer life's happenings the consonants of her life, which is the structure that gave it form and cut it into different separate phases or elements. She calls her inner life; her dreams and her relation to the Self, 'the vowels'—the underground stream that continues to flow, giving meaning, sound and depth to the world of the consonants—and which enabled them to be made into words, into her story. Thus the structure of the intensives is the consonants that provide structure and form for the underground river—the inner life of the soul—to be known and tell its story.

THE STRUCTURE OF THE WEEK

The intensives have a structure, a rhythm and a form that provides participants with a space that allows them to tend to their inner life for a continuum of seven days.

The seven days contain ritual, poetry, dance, movements, conscious space for the spiritual dimension, teachings which include the theories of C.G. Jung and Marion Woodman's work on the body and the feminine, dream work, movement to free the body, voice work, mask-work, deep relaxation, and various specific exercises including embodying the symbolic material and working with the energy in the body, giving it form and taking it into some kind of expression, whether in words or art work. These elements are woven into a daily rhythm of BodySoul work.

The week of the intensive has a rhythm too. A rhythm that invites the participants to tend to their inner life and the unconscious. This rhythm is carried by the vehicle of the mask-work that becomes the condensed expression of what arises for the individual from the unconscious in these seven days. The symbolic material that comes forth is given space to be experienced, related to and gradually given a form so it can stay in consciousness as the week moves toward its end.

The beginning and the end of the week are marked by a ritual opening and closing to emphasize the boundaries between the life the participants are coming from, the week-long temenos, and the life the participants are going back to. The metaphor of the rhythm in fairy tales can be used here, where the hero or heroine set out on a journey leaving the known; encountering whatever element they need to face in their development, and then bring the treasure back home.

The schedule of the week has a rhythm of arrival, a descent with receptivity to the unconscious, and an ascent—a coming back up from the descent and allowing for reflection—distillation and integration and preparing for the end of the week and the transition back to the participant's outer life, leaving the intensive. This flow is outlined below, with more detailed explanation of the details included later.

The intensive starts on the first night with a gathering, the opening of the altar, and a round of presentation, sharing feelings, expectations or questions. On the first full day, the morning will start with the morning ritual, followed by dream work and teaching. The afternoon is dedicated to arrival for the body, with body and voice work. The evening includes the *positive mothering* exercise. On the second day, the morning again will be as for the first day, the afternoon will be a body and voice warm-up which will initiate all afternoon sessions. This is followed by the *dance of three*. The evening will be dedicated to starting the mask-work. The third day will continue with the mornings and afternoons as described, followed by the *symptom in the body* exercise. The evening will be dedicated to mask-work. The fourth day will continue with mornings and afternoons as described, with the exercise *symbol in the body*. The evening will be for decorating the masks. The fifth day will be with mornings and afternoons as described, followed by relating to the mask for the first time. The evening will be for wearing the mask and interacting. The sixth day will be mornings and afternoons as described, working with the mask in triads, coming to an 'I am' and distilling the essence of the week. In the evening there will be the *ending ritual*. On the seventh morning the final closing takes place.

GENERAL ELEMENTS OF THE WEEK

The BSR intensives unfold in a three-layered container: nature, the venue, and the scheduled work.

Nature

> Nature has lost her divinity, yet the spirit is unsure and unsatisfied. Hence any true cure for the neurosis would have to awaken both spirit and nature to a new life. The relevance of this theme for us today may be that it is a problem we are still trying to solve on too personal, psychological a level, or on a purely cultural level without realizing it is at bottom a religious problem and not psychological or social at all.[11]

The intensives are held at venues surrounded by nature. The access to nature and the possibility to spend time in nature outside the daily program and at times within the exercises is a deep recognition of the importance of nature for the soul. Within the Jungian frame nature is the archetypal mother, the earth body. Spending time in nature is a holding and rejuvenating experience. Nature or the landscape around the BSR work becomes its container and mirror as well. Thus the outer nature is reflecting and containing the inner nature and being held by nature when one is doing such deep inner work opens up to the possibility of

---

11 Joseph L. Henderson, *Shadow and Self,* in Meredith Sabini (Ed.) *The Earth has a Soul: C.G. Jung on Nature, Technology and Modern Life*, p.279.

a deepening of one's relationship with nature. As described with examples in the interviews, often the space of nature becomes the place of deep transformation in the context of the BSR work. Being in nature when one is open to the inner world and perceiving one's soul seems to parallel one's openness and receptivity to nature and the oneness of the two is sensed in this reflection. Thus the inner and the outer landscape start to communicate and are experienced as being attuned and resonating. The access to nature also becomes the place for islands of solitude or introversion, areas to integrate the work and to be with oneself or go for shared walks. Nature is a sanctuary. The attitude to the outer nature parallels the attitude to the inner nature. The work, with the deepening of the relation to the outer nature, parallels the work with deepening the relation to the inner nature and strengthen the sense of belonging.

VENUE

Space for Silence and Creation

The venue differs according to where the intensive is held. Usually it is a venue without too many outer disturbing factors. The venue itself is chosen so that quiet rooms, and places for retreating are possible. The meals are served and eaten together, and special dietary needs are met. Often there is access to a swimming pool or other possibilities to tend to the body. The main working room stays available at times outside the schedule for yoga, movement and meditation.

SILENCE

Every morning the silence is kept to respect the need to tend to the inner life and to give space to meditate on dreams at the time where the veil between the unconscious and the consciousness is thin. Cultivating room for silence is cultivating our capacity to listen and be receptive to the inner world. Thus breakfast is shared in silence as well, and the silence is kept until the shared opening of the morning session.

ART WORK

> To the extent that I managed to translate the emotions into images—that is to say, to find the images which were concealed in the emotions—I was inwardly calmed and reassured.[12]

---

12 Jung, *MDR*, p. 201.

As a result of my experiment I learned how helpful it can be from the therapeutic point of view to find the particular images which lies behind the emotions.[13]

Throughout each intensive, a space set up for doing art work with crayons, paint, finger-paint, paper of various sizes, and clay. Art work is encouraged after several exercises but the access to use it stays available all the time. All art work in the BSR context is related to as a medium for the soul's expression. It is a way to give form and color to the energy in its broadest sense, and thus the art work becomes a container as well. If intense inner images or feelings arise, there is the possibility to give them some kind of form or expression that enables one to relate to it and reflect upon it from a more neutral stance, rather than feeling overpowered by it.

Like a dream series, a picture series can express the gradual evolving and transformation of the symbolic material. The participants are encouraged to hang their pictures on the wall of the work room and, as the intensive moves along; the transformations are mirrored back by the pictures that gradually are taking up the space on the walls. Furthermore the pictures are expressing the energies, themes and archetypal symbols that are constellated in the group reflecting them back, as they are worked with, and holding that living dialogue present in the work.

To have the art materials available and to have a rich variety of them is encouraging. The art materials at the BSR intensives include big sheets of paper in white, black and various colors; different types of crayons, charcoal, pastels, wet paint and finger paint, things to glue onto the paintings; as well as clay and paint that can go onto the clay. Often one apprentice will be responsible for the art room and can offer support and guidance in the use of the materials. For people who feel insecure to use the stuff or are held back or blocked, a guiding helper can encourage them. Often the inner impulse is held back because of performance anxiety or the fear of making an imprint on the outer world; the gentle support, patience and encouragement can help to overcome the fear and create the first spark of that new life. This process and its meaning are very vividly expressed in one of the interviews.

All the art work is treated as soul material; that is, it is treated with great care. It is not commentated on, or talked about using evaluating phrases. The attitude is that, in the end, it is only the painter herself who knows what it is about. If one wishes to share one's picture or talk about the content one is welcome to do this. The approach towards all the symbolic expressions that the participant is creating has some parallels to Winnicott's description of the relationship to the transitional object. The symbol can never be reduced to the transitional object, but I find it relevant to include Winnicott's point here, because it conveys a respect for the object that, in my opinion, is very important to hold for the symbol as well. In summary,

---

13 Jung, *MDR*, p. 202.

Winnicott describes the following characteristics about the quality of the relationship to the transitional object:

> The infant assumes right over the object. The object is cuddled and loved. The object must never change unless changed by the infant. The object must survive instinctual loving and hating. The object must seem to the infant to give warmth or something that seems to show vitality/ reality of its own. It comes from without in our point of view, but not for the infant, neither does it come from within. It is not forgotten and it is not mourned—it loses meaning—it becomes diffused (spread out over the whole intermediate territory between 'inner psychic reality' and 'the external world as perceived by two persons in common' (that is from the whole cultural field).[14]

In many ways I have found that symbolic expression emerging from soul work seems to be infused with the same type of energy as the transitional object; and the approach and attitude held by the BSR leaders are intuitively aligned with the approach that Winnicott describes. To understand this specialness around the symbolic expressions gives the understanding not to act with an intruding approach. The new life emerging from the inner work is young, as is the infant, and the receiving of it draws many parallels with the receiving of the infant, as does the need for its gradual development.

THE STRUCTURE OF THE DAY

The daily schedule starts at 9 a.m. with gathering in silence around what is named as 'the altar' (usually a table with a cloth, flowers and a candle). Marion opens the day with a ring of two chyme bells saying an invocation to Sophia (but always voicing the encouragement to each individual to use this moment to attend to what she finds meaningful to direct this moment to, if 'Sophia' does not feel right for her).[15] In Jungian terms, this is to open one's receptivity to the Self. What name or image that we as individuals find meaningful to use for that, which is bigger than our ego-consciousness, can be the direction of the attention. (I deliberately formulate this very loosely, since I am of the opinion that what we attend to is, by nature, undefinable and deeply individual). This ritual is followed by the morning dance. That is a ritual dance originally created at Findhorn, but adapted by Mary Hamilton to the BSR work. It is a circle dance, danced in a slow rhythm, shoulder to shoulder, holding hands

---

14 M. Davis, & B. Wallbridge, *Boundary and Space: An Introduction to the Work of D. W. Winnicott*, pp. 58-59.

15 Sophia (Greek for wisdom) is a central term in Hellenistic philosophy and religion, Platonism, Gnosticism, Orthodox Christianity, esoteric Christianity as well as Christian mysticism. Marion Woodman has never explicitly linked her use of the word to any specific tradition but uses it in the context, as the name that feels right for her, to refer to the feminine aspect of the divine.

in a meditative rhythm. The rhythm is carried in such a way that it can be danced with closed eyes, if wished, and the dancing creates a strong sense of the circle held by the group containing what is shared. Standing in the circle at the end of the dance, one of the leaders, often Marion, will recite a poem. A poem that often will provide the note for the day, striking the theme of the day in its symbolic expression or in other ways that reflects where the process is in the continuum of the week. This is followed by a short meditation, often guided by the apprentices who give it a form that resonates with them. This can be a piece of music, a dance, some movements, or shared readings of a poem. The opening enhances the supportive group feeling, gets one in touch with one's body, fosters mindfulness, and opens one to listen to the inner world (to be in a receptive state). After this opening of the morning, the group gathers for Marion's teaching and dream work.

At all times in the scheduled work, all the leaders and apprentices will be present. Whoever is guiding or teaching will be speaking, but the others are just as active with their presence —sitting on the edge of the group, containing and holding the floor, and holding the one speaking in an atmosphere of encouragement and love. They hold an open awareness of the energy in the group as such, of where it is going, and of the single individuals, and of where these individuals are in the moment. This type of holding, named containing, is one of the key elements of the work (to be described in the section on the Dance of Three).

THE ELEMENTS OF THE DAY

The Morning

The morning will be a combination of Marion speaking about a specific theme, teaching C.G. Jung's theories and often connecting the theme to a current issue in our culture. Often a myth is told during the week and becomes the point of reference and a reflector for the personal stories and the themes discussed. Through her teaching style Marion continually weaves and links the personal stories with the cultural happenings and the archetypal dimension.

The Afternoon

The afternoon work is centered on bodywork and voice work. This includes working with the energy from the morning and the dreams, bringing this energy into relationship with the body's reality. Each afternoon also includes a specific exercise. The afternoon is initiated by a demonstration of the exercise to be worked with that particular day, followed by a thorough warm-up of the body and the voice through movement, deep relaxation and voice work aiming at freeing, relaxing, enjoying, opening and expanding the body-soul to move into the work.

The Evening

The evenings have a special atmosphere because of the intense work throughout the day. During the first evening, the work will be the positive mothering exercise, then the following evenings are spent making masks, as they slowly come into form and find their expression in the mask-work. On the last evening, there will be the ending ritual.

The Space Between

After the morning session there is a long break for lunch and free time. In the spaces of free time in between sessions, the group leaders or the apprentices make themselves available if some of the participants wish to talk one-to-one. Within the group of leaders and apprentices there is a general care and awareness concerning how each participant is doing. This is experienced as a caring way of getting in touch and asking how one, as participant, is doing. There is equally a great care taken to be aware of where participants are, and to sense if anyone should need some attention. It is my sense that it is this care, relying on a highly developed feeling function in the leaders, which makes it possible to work so deeply and intensely with material that often triggers quite intense emotions in the participants, including potential preverbal trauma locked in the body.

Allan Schore describes, that if traumatized parts of a person's psyche have been triggered emotionally, and that person cannot self-regulate and come back into what he calls 'the window of emotional tolerance,' but instead they are 'going off' either into hyper- or hypo-arousal, they need the 'self-regulating' other to support them and help that participant come back into a state of tolerance and regain emotional balance.[16] This awareness as to how participants are doing, helps the leaders to sense if anyone should reach the point where they are in an emotional state outside their window of tolerance and then the leaders can offer support (i.e. support, broadly defined) to help them regain emotional balance.

Allan Schore at his lecture 'Body and the Trauma' Conference, London, UK, September 2007 described these dys-regulated stages and said that the hyper-aroused stage is not easily missed. It is the hypo-arousal response, where the person shuts down, withdraws and retreats, that calls for highly emphatic skills from a caring other, because that person's "automatic functioning-mode" (dissociated stage) disguises their feeling state. (Allan Schore's work will be described in detail in part III of this book.)

In the intensives, both as participant and as apprentice, I have seen how important it is to have these empathic skills and to be attuned to all the participants. I recall Mary telling us how she often has gone to 'check-up' on someone who had said she was 'all right,' and that she 'just felt tired,' and Mary had found her in her room coiled up in a bundle of silent tears. One

---

16 Allan N. Schore, *Affect Dysregulation and Disorders of the Self.*

participant shared with me how she had been in this situation and that it was the first time in her life that someone apparently, as expressed from the state of this deprived child, had cared to come and comfort her and rock her back to a place from where she could integrate this. The value of this empathic attunement for the process of healing[17] is illustrated further in the interviews.

The Content of the BSR Work

In the following I will describe what opens to the 'playing of the deep tunes.' That is, I will describe the general content of the BSR work: the teaching of Jungian theory; the dream work; the inclusion of the archetypal level in the form of myth and fairy tales; movement; voice work; breath work and body-soul movements—with a focus on working the energy in the body. Specific content and exercises will be described in the next section.

TEACHINGS

Teachings of the Theory of C.G. Jung and the Work of Marion Woodman

> For in the long run it is absolutely indifferent whether one has a sort of illusion or imagination, or whether it is a fact—it has ruled one's life in either case. Therefore the fact that rules my life, or that influences my life to a great extent, is the psychological fact, whether it is true or not in an objective way, whether the vision one has had is an actuality which can really be seen or whether it is a hallucination. That simply does not matter.[18]

The Jungian theory and model of the psyche is the theoretical foundation and frame for the work; it provides the theoretical container for the understanding of the processes worked with in the intensive (both inter- and intra-psychically). The work of C.G. Jung is considered in the BSR work, particularly Jung's writings on the body-soul connection.

Marion Woodman's work in particular elaborates on some of the deeper issues of our time: the repression of the feminine principle and its effect on our attitudes towards nature and the physical body. In her writings she works with the development of the conscious feminine, the conscious masculine and the inner marriage between the two; the spirit in matter and the psyche-body connection.

---

17 By healing I refer, generally, in this book to the subjective experience of moving into a greater sense of wholeness.

18 C.G. Jung, *Visions: Notes of the Seminar Given in 1930-1934 by C.G. Jung*, Vol. 1, p. 297.

The depth and width of the theoretical foundation, including incorporation of new theories of the BSR, is what enables the level of transformation that can be 'midwifed' through this approach. It is the instrument on which the music can be played; it is also the level of consciousness held by the leaders' containing that allows for the depth of this work.

To facilitate the participants' understanding of the theoretical background, readings are assigned to the intensives, and Marion Woodman teaches in the mornings. The teaching includes Jung's model of the psyche; the dream theories; the theories of the individuation process; and the theories on the masculine, the feminine and the divine marriage; the healing through the archetypal level and the body-soul connection (as well as other aspects depending on the context). The readings include the works of C.G. Jung, especially *The Structure and Dynamic of the Psyche*,[19] and *Nietzsche's Zarathustra: Notes of the Seminar*,[20] work by Jungian writers; and Marion Woodman's writings especially *Addiction to Perfection, Leaving My Father's House, The Conscious Virgin, The Ravaged Bridegroom and Dancing in the Flames*.[21]

The theory enables the participants to bridge their lived experiences with conscious understanding. It provides a framework to assist the individual to understand her inner processes; the value given to the reality of the psyche and the reality of the body, to the unconscious, to the dialectic relationship between consciousness and the unconscious; and an understanding for the symbolic approach and the archetypal level of the processes. It too, provides a framework for understanding the dynamics constellated inter-psychically in the group, where complexes and shadow material are evoked; and how to work with this, understanding projections and integrating aspects of one's shadow. And, finally, it gives indispensable background knowledge for the participants who wish to facilitate the BSR work.

In her teaching, Marion links her theoretical teachings with the content of the workshop connecting what manifests in the work with a conscious understanding of it. She facilitates the sense of interconnectedness and continuity in the process by weaving the work of the afternoons and evenings into the teaching and active reflections in the group.

The whole theoretical background for the BSR work is quite expansive, and new theories keep being incorporated. What will be emphasized, in my description of it, is the body-psyche connection and how that influences the approach to the analytical work and how it parallels understandings, theories and hypotheses in neuroscience and developmental psychology.[22] Jung's theory is based on the reality of the psyche. What Marion Woodman stresses is the equal reality of the body. Jung saw psyche and body as being two aspects of the same

---

19 C.G. Jung, *The Structure and Dynamics of the Psyche*, CW 8.

20 C.G. Jung, *Nietzsche's Zarathustra: Notes of the Seminar Given in 1934-1939 by C.G. Jung.*

21 For a full list of Marion Woodman's work please see the list of references at the end of the book.

22 For a complete account of the theories and work of Marion Woodman, the reader is referred to her writings.

thing—a hypothesis that Marion Woodman has at the core of her work. One could say that the BSR approach is rooted in the reality of the body-psyche.

For readers not familiar with the theories of Jung and the work of Marion Woodman, I will briefly outline aspects important to emphasize in the context of this book.[23]

In relation to developmental psychology and from a Jungian perspective, the individual development continues throughout life and the development-supporting responses from another continue to facilitate this spiralling process. The development taking place is less schematically defined than it is in classical developmental psychology. Instead the emphasis is more on the unfolding process, which is propelled by the Self and described as the individuation process.

The growth of the personality is not completed by the growing of ego strength, but one continues developing one's personality, capacity to relate to the inner world and the unconscious and the outer world including one's fellow human beings, one's creativity, one's capacity for responsibility, one's values, one's capacity to hold the opposite, to meet life's challenges and phases, and to relate to the spiritual dimension. The individuation process is aiming at one's 'becoming what one is' and living a life that is aligned with one's whole nature. In this process the ego's position is relativized by the influences from the Self[24] and the individual experiences a feeling of being guided by deeper aspects within oneself as the process is unfolding.

In the BSR there is an emphasis on the development of the adult woman described in the archetypal process of moving from unconscious maiden in symbiotic relation to the mother, through ravishment by the masculine, the mothering aspects of grief and the growth of the conscious feminine: the conscious virgin. The relation of the mother and the virgin is balanced by a third aspect of the feminine; the crone who is the wise old one.

According to Marion Woodman, the seedbed for the conscious virgin is the conscious mother. If one has not experienced conscious mothering on the personal level and has not internalized the conscious mother, the healing can happen through the archetypal level. The

---

23 I have chosen not to include an in-depth discussion of the aspect of the masculine and the feminine in this book. For readers interested in this perspective, I refer you to the work of Marion Woodman.
24 The Self is an archetypal image of the individual's fullest potential and the unity of the personality as a whole. The Self is the driving force behind the individuation process. The Self is the unifying principle within the human psyche. It is not only the center but also the whole circumference which embraces both consciousness and the unconscious. It is the God-image within. (Jung refers to the Self as an empirical concept, and according to the development in his writings he stresses different aspects. These descriptions are not exhaustive. In this work, the Jungian concept of the Self is written with a capital 'S' as is customary in Jungian writings to distinguish the Jungian concept of the self from other contents has to be exchanged with definitions.

work is to have a lived experience that can constellate an inner representation of the conscious mother, which can cherish and support oneself and the new life. This lived experience can come from a lived experience with another, who embodies the conscious mother, who carries the projection of the positive mother archetype[25] or through the active encounter with dream images of the positive mother.[26]

The conscious virgin is the authentic feminine within. The word 'virgin' is used in the sense of 'un-trampled upon,' like a virgin forest; it is the aspect of the feminine full of potential. Esther Harding describes it in the following way:

> [T]he woman who is virgin, one-in-herself, does what she does—not because of any desire to please, not to be liked, or to be approved, even by herself; not because of any desire to gain power over another, to catch his interest or love, but because what she does is true.[27]

The crone is the aged conscious feminine who has met life's challenges and is matured through the lived life. She is beyond personal agendas. She carries wisdom, has certain toughness, and is in many aspects close to the archetype represented by Hecate, the Greek goddess of the crossroads.

These three aspects of the feminine expressed through the three symbols—the mother, virgin and crone—give meaning and orientation to the process, yet they are still open enough to allow other representations of the feminine archetypes to constellate. There are equally metaphors connected to the development of the conscious masculine in the woman—a masculine which can relate to the feminine. It is through the gradual development of the masculine and the feminine that the enriching connecting between the two can evolve—a connecting that opens for the possibility of meetings—what Marion Woodman refers to as the divine marriage. The psyche is not static and thus moments of meetings—of feeling whole—are preceded by new levels of conflict, new aspects calling for integration or new developments in the different aspects.

As for all symbolic representations of psychic developments, it is important that the symbols stay open enough to allow for the individual content to 'shape' them.[28] To illustrate, I refer to two quotes from Jung (which are to be read with the historical context of his time in mind):

---

25 In developmental psychology this is referred to as 'Internalization of the good mother.'

26 Antonio Damasio refers to what he calls "bypassing the body loop"—resembling to great extent what happens in active imagination.

27 Esther Harding, *Woman's Mysteries,* p. 125.

28 I, personally, don't like the same word being used for a long time to describe something, because we then can start to think that we know what it is—and can pin the energy down to a defined concept.

The Great Mother means to a woman Mother Nature, the great mother principle in her. One cannot designate such principle in a definite intellectual way because all the original primitive ideas—the most important ones—are universal ideas of extreme vagueness. As soon as one tries to formulate them too definitely, they lose their meaning and their value all together; for then one could say it was just that and nothing else, whereas it is many other things at the same time. This account for the great power of such ideas: the Magna Mater is an idea of extraordinary wealth. One is probably closest to its meaning when one calls it Mother Nature or the feminine principle itself; any attempt to formulate it more closely gets farther away from it.[29]

Jung continues:

What is woman's nature? You see, women prefer not to mention it, and man does not dare to speak of it, or if he dares he will most probably be accused of violating the most sacred values of women and so on. It is hidden with the utmost care and it needs a woman of quite unusual consciousness and personal courage to speak about it.[30]

There is a paradox for the logical mind in the symbolic approach. The symbol can never be fully described, yet the trying to understand and describe is what builds the relationship to the symbol and what creates relation in the 'talking about' the symbol. This includes the relationship that builds up between the one who talks and the one who listens.

It is the tendency of the conscious mind—especially the left hemisphere of the brain– to want to know, to define, to categorise: a way of building order into chaos. The creative approach balances on the fine line between the two—the known and the unknown—holding the still point in the mist of despair, being in the space between the conscious and the unconscious where the third can emerge. This is the space of the living symbols.

Concepts are needed to give structure and to describe the theory without losing the aliveness and capacity to resonate with the individual. Concepts, when "sloppy" enough (to quote Daniel Stern's use of the word[31]) can give us some kind of language that reflects enough of the individual experience and enough of the shared experience, so that it is possible to find moments of meeting and mutual understanding of what is being experienced. This breaks the isolation of the lived inner landscape and opens up the possibility for shared walks on sharable ground. (See the discussion of the symbolic approach and moment of meeting in the third part of this book.) Marion Woodman in her work follows this symbolic way of describing the inner process and the concepts of her way of working.

---

29 Jung, *Visions: Notes of the Seminar Given in 1930-1934 by C.G. Jung.* Vol.1, p. 329.
30 Jung, *Visions*, Vol.1, p. 329.
31 Stern, *The Present Moment in Psychotherapy and Everyday Life.*

DREAM WORK

> The dream is a little hidden door to the innermost and most secret recesses of the soul, opening into the cosmic night... All consciousness separates; but in dreams we put on the likeness of that more universal, truer, more eternal, man dwelling in the darkness of the primordial night. There he is still whole, and the whole is in him, indistinguishable from nature and bare of all egohood.[32]

The dream work is done in the group, where participants are invited to share a dream that then is gently looked at in relation to the dreamer and her inner life (the personal unconscious: unique for the person; and the content shaped by her story and life-experience) but mainly opened via the symbols to reflect the archetypal dimensions (the collective unconscious: what is typically human; that which is shaped by humankind through our history). In this sense, the symbol connects the individual and the shared experiences in the group, and ensures that the individual is not exposed in the group. Thus Marion in her capacity as teacher holds a fine balance between the individual and the general, never leaving too much tension with one individual and with the aim never to humiliate or expose one person's psyche in any way. If a dreamer brings up something where Marion senses the dreamer or the dream should be protected, she will offer to work with the person later in a one-to-one session. If other participants become engaged in saying what they think the dream is about, she will refer the issue to that participant and bring it to a deeper reflection in the group asking everybody to consider what that would be in them. There is a craft involved in working with dreams in groups. It takes great skill to open the dream so the group engages in it without exposing the dreamer and robbing the dream of its symbols and energy. There is a very delicate balance in showing deep respect for the dream, and conveying that attitude with such an impact that it is perceived in the group. It is Marion's capacity for linking, connecting, elaborating, amplifying and inviting ponderings in the group, which gradually enables the participants to internalize the integrating reflective capacity themselves. It is the facilitator's capacity to hold the symbols; to weave in the archetypal with the personal, with the energy in the group and relevant current world-issues that might link to the context brought forth by the dream, which makes this way of doing the dream work so profound. This sensitive approach makes it a gentle yet very powerful way of working with dreams in a group. The aim is to leave enough space so that the dreamer's own assimilation of the dream can happen in an unforced way. Each symbol in the dream has, in a way, to have been opened up enough for the dreamer to connect to it and make her curious about knowing more, yet not so much so that she stops being somewhat puzzled and reflective. Marion, in her dream work, seems to deliberately leave the

---

32 C.G. Jung, *Civilization in Transition*, CW. 10, ¶ 304.

interpretation as an open question, allowing the energy to be alive. By reflecting questions back and opening up the symbols to the archetypal level, the dream images touch others in the group and become points of shared reflection.

MYTH AND STORIES

The Archetypal Container

> What we are to our inward vision, and what man appears to be sub specie aeternitatis, can only be expressed by way of myth. Myth is more individual and expresses life more precisely than does science. Science works with concepts of averages which are far too general to do justice to the subjective variety of an individual life.[33]

In each intensive, an archetypal story or myth is told or enacted by the facilitators. The themes of the myth are related and referred to throughout the week with emphasis on how to understand the material in reference to the individuation process. Marion will weave in her reflections on the conscious feminine, the conscious masculine, and their archetypal development, using the figures in the myths as archetypal representations of different typical aspects to be encountered on the individual's journey.

This way of weaving in the archetypal stories illustrates one of the real potentials in analytical psychology: namely, the telling of stories, myths and fairy tales both as teachings and as archetypal containers. Many native healing traditions use the remedy of storytelling. Stories with an archetypal core open our imagination, extending it into the future, and provide models of behavior that spark our own potential. The stories give us seeds for new behaviors or new attitudes in our 'old story' of living our lives. As one of the interviewed women speaks about, she could use the told-myth as a reflector for her own life, knowing or identifying when she acted towards herself as one of the characters in the myth. Having the development of the myth as a potential solution to her conflict, she could use the characters in the myth as models for her own attitude towards herself and how she could act in her life. Marie-Louise von Franz, a student of Jung's and a well-known Jungian analyst, said:

> .. the hero [or heroine] is an archetypal figure which presents a model of an ego functioning in accord with the Self. Produced by the unconscious psyche, it is a model to be looked at, and it is demonstrating a rightly functioning ego, an ego that functions in accordance with the requirements of the Self.[34]

---

33 Jung, *MDR*, p. 17.
34 Marie-Louise von Franz, *The Interpretation of Fairytales*, pp. 62-63.

The symbolic inspiration and possible ways of dealing with constellated psychic difficulties hold immense potential. The symbol or the metaphor speaks not only to the mind but also to the body and the imagination. In the way the myths are worked with, in the BSR context, their prospective aspect is emphasized.[35]

In reference to the individuation of the feminine in men and women, the power of fairy tales and myths can be especially valuable in a Christian culture where women, as Jung pointed out "have no metaphysical representant in the Christian God-image."[36] Marie-Louise von Franz comments that due to the lack of general archetypal role models for the modern women, the modern woman is in search of her full feminine identity. Mary, as represented in the Catholic faith, only represents one aspect of the feminine. Representations of other aspects of the feminine are to be found in myths and fairy tales and can provide role models for the lost aspects of the feminine that call to be experienced and integrated in the individual woman (or man).[37] This supports the often, in my opinion, too-neglected side of the power of archetypal stories as providers of role models for the development of the individual identity, and shows how the telling of constructive stories provides great teachings about the aspects of the feminine and masculine that have fallen out of the conscious collective mind in our modern world.[38] The power of the myths inspires the individual to reflect on her personal myth and kindles the process by which the individual aligns herself with acts that are in accordance with her own deep truth. This movement is often reflected in what must be sacrificed in the ending of the intensive to make room for new ways of acting in the world.

From a developmental perspective, the stories hold great potency as well. The infant learns by imitation—observing procedural activities and then enacting them.[39] No research, within my awareness, shows that the adult does not rely on this way of learning new ways of enacting and being as well. By imagining the characters in the myth or even better—by seeing the myth acted out, which gives you a body memory of the lived character—your body knows how to live that action and you can apply it to your own reality. Imagine yourself being Perseus beheading the Medusa who can turn you to stone. This immediately shifts your body posture, your feeling, and your body chemistry. The motion of the body combined with the images in the mind create accompanying emotions and the body-psyche can imagine the 'act

---

35 Jung saw dreams as having both a causal and a prospective point of view. That is that the dream on one hand can indicate what caused the present state of the psyche and on the other hand can indicate the future development—where the unconscious life is leading the person. The latter he called the prospective aspect of the dream.

36 Marie-Louise von Franz, *The Feminine in Fairytales*, p. 1.

37 von Franz, *The Feminine in Fairytales.*

38 Or refers to the shadow.

39 J. Bauer, *Warum ich fühle, was du fühlst.*

of doing' to change the situation. What is stressed here is that, if one only works on the psychological changing of a situation but the body itself cannot enact the actual change (that is, the body's reality is not aligned with the conscious insight), then the body cannot act out the action. This is often felt as a betrayal from the conscious viewpoint but is in fact an expression of the lack of coherence between the reality of the body and consciousness. Realigning the two, enables the act of change.

MOVEMENT

> Movement, to be experienced, has to be 'found' in the body,
> not put on like a dress or a coat.
> There is that in us which has moved from the very beginning;
> it is that which can liberate us.[40]

The body warm-up is conducted by Mary. She has an infectious love for her own body and playfulness in her moving that in itself has a transforming power, and soon the dancing bodies start to explore with delight the marvellous possibilities of movement. In her attitude and entire approach to the bodywork, Mary's skills are felt. Her choice of music, the metaphors she speaks in, her way of moving and caring for her own body, her playfulness combined with deep knowledge of the pain that can be carried in the body, and her radiating love for the bodies she meets in the room all weave into this experience. The type of metaphors she uses, speaking about the body seems to keep resonating long after the exercises are done, leaving the body more open, more welcoming of its own reality, more appreciated, more playful and freer to express its delight. A particular set of emotions creates a certain body posture and way of moving. Equally a new way of moving evokes a certain field of emotions. Being in this field of playful exploration, finding movements of delight and joy is a 'body-lived' resource; and this opening up in the body to one's living-moving-space spreads out like rings in the water. Also, in her way of conducting the group, Mary invites in the 'trickster' and the humor that melts rigid patterns both psychically and bodily. Relating in such a focused way to the body's reality and embracing it with care is so devastatingly missing in our culture, so it is like water on dry earth: bodies are just revivified in that space. The body warm-up thus opens to the awareness of the reality of the body and it opens to connecting to the resources in the body. This connection to the resources in the body is important for the work.

The resources in the body become an anchor and a source to rely on in the further work. The BodySoul work, due to its opening to the body's reality, can potentially evoke preverbal

---

40 Mary Whitehouse, "Physical Movement and Personality," in P. Pallaro (Ed.), *Authentic Movement: Essays by Mary Stark Whitehouse, Janet Adler, and Joan Chodorow*, p. 51.

trauma held in the body. If such traumatic memories surface, the access to the body-anchored resources is important. A connection with body resources helps to balance and re-stabilise the person if overwhelming unconscious material surfaces. The body awareness helps to pace the unblocking of unconscious material locked in the body so it can be contained without overwhelming the ego. Working with the unblocking of bodily-held trauma (including preverbal trauma) can easily become re-traumatising in the hands of untrained people, so skills for working with trauma as leaders is very important. The pacing of the process and the containment of what is released is crucial. Naturally, deep individual trauma work is not the aim in the intensives, but the work can evoke previously unconscious traumas, so there must be skills to recreate stability. This is also why there is a requirement for intensive participants to be in ongoing analysis or therapy.[41]

The body warm-up is like a baton, taken over by Ann who leads the group through an equally transforming sequence of deep relaxation followed by voice work.

VOICE WORK

An essential part of the BSR work is the voice work. Again, the aim is to free the voice and open the participants to express themselves. The voice channel is the organ that we use to express ourselves verbally in the world. As with all other kinds of expression this can be blocked, locked, or molded unconsciously or consciously. The voice is very often influenced by the way our expression was received in our early environment and by the kind of adaptations we made to be heard or not to be heard too much or to sound a particular way that would be more liked. There are 21 muscles in the voice channel; some under conscious control, others influenced by the autonomic nerve system mostly the Vagus nerve.[42] There might be contradictory contractions or relaxations in these 21 muscles (for example, the autonomous parts influenced unconsciously are constricted and the voice has to be pressed out by will—that is by the muscles under conscious control—or there may be tensions so that the person does not use the resonance of their lower chest and abdomen, thus giving them a high pitched voice, reflecting the tension between consciousness and the unconscious in verbal expression). In the voice work the focus is to free and open the voice, to relax tense areas, to use the whole

---

41 For trauma work and the body see Rothschild, Babette *The Body Remembers: The Psychophysiology of Trauma and Treatment*, Donald Kalsched, *The Inner World of Trauma: Archetypal defenses of the Personal Spirit*, P. Ogden; K. Minton; and C. Pain, *Trauma and the Body: A Sensorimotor Approach to Psychotherapy*, Peter Levine, *Waking the Tiger*.

42 The Vagus nerve carries sensory, motor and parasympathic fibers. It is connected to the voice-channel, the ear, the heartbeat, the breath, the diaphragm, the digestion system, the kidneys and the involuntarily muscles related to posture. The Vagus nerve also plays a central part in survival responses to threats to the organism: responses such as fight, flight, freeze and collapse.

space where the voice is formed and thus to move from the adapted voice to a more authentic voice. In the work with the voice channel the whole body is participating and the voice work is initiated by a deep relaxation. The relaxation is so inviting and comforting that it is not only the muscles influenced by consciousness that are relaxing. The whole body is brought to such a state of deep relaxation that the involuntarily muscles also relax. In this state of deep relaxation, the breath is attended to. The participants are encouraged to invite breath into every part of the body: working with expanded, deepening, opening, softening, relaxing, letting go, warming and melting the tissue. From the deep relaxation, the sounds of the breath are invited in. Guiding the work along, Ann brings awareness towards the mouth, the lips, the tongue and their movements and how the sounds change when playing with the lips, tongue and mouth.

Gradually movements of the body are included. In a rhythmical wave-like pattern, Ann guides the floor of women to let the movements of their body to open, expand and then become smaller and more subtle, and then open again to expansion. The voice work follows this rhythm as well: opening, expanding and then growing more quiet and soft, and then opening up again. Often, Ann guides the floor to work or rather play the child's sounds, attending to an inner awareness of the sounds and playing with one's sounds as infants do before they start to speak. This is an exploration into one's own sound with the playfulness that children show when they feel safe and secure to expand their world curiously. From this state, gradually, the voice is raised by bringing the body to a standing position. All the guiding is in a soft, deep, inviting voice to hold that space of a non-threatening, safe environment. Often, even unconscious feelings of threats contract the voice. Gradually, more and more voice or sounds are added, expanding it from an inner experience, continuing, sound by sound to reach out, letting the voice reach out and resonate in the room and to bring it to further expansion by letting the voice resonate in the horizon. The level of self-consciousness that often blocks the voice is reduced by the amount of other sounds in the room and by the playful attitude of the instructor. The influence on this work on the voice is remarkable. The amount of sound that the group is able to make, without effort, simply by freeing and expanding what is already there, is vibrant and the depth of the voices and volume of their expression are highly impressive. Once the room or the group has opened this often blocked channel of expression and freed it, the sounding quality in the group shifts. Not only the quality of the voicing shifts but also the content seems to come from a deeper more authentic place in the participant. Also, it is as if the fear that usually holds people back from giving sounds to their movements evaporates and they can allow their sounds to be expressed, accompanied by body movement. As the expressions are freed, the floor work often opens to a lot of deep forgotten sounds accompanying the other exercises. There is a feeling of being more free, more relaxed, more able to express as result of the voice work. Any resistance towards opening the voice is often a fear of opening to one's true voice and letting the 'me' come out. Through the voice work this 'me' gradually finds its expression through its own authentic voice.

BREATH WORK

Listen, are you breathing just a little, and calling it a life?[43]

A vital part of the voice work is tending to the breath. Feeling the natural involuntary impulse to breathe and the rhythm of the inhalation—exhalation—pausing—waiting for the new impulse to inhale. This "waiting for the new impulse" is crucial metaphor for all the different areas of the expressive work done in the BSR. This natural pause before a new impulse—the 'gap between' an ending impulse that has come to its completion and the rising of a new impulse, the natural rest in a cyclic rhythm, is often not brought to consciousness in our daily life. Instead we fear the gap, afraid that no natural impulse will come and therefore impose one though our will. To learn (again) to trust that a new impulse arises in the pause and attune oneself to a natural inner rhythm, the resting being before a new creation, is encouraged by the guidance of Ann in her voice work. Both in the context of the BSR and in my own experience and work, I have noticed a need to re-learn to attend to and to trust the pause. Reflecting on the cause for that, I suggest both a cultural and a developmental perspective.

BEING IN THE CULTURE

Over the last 3000 years we have moved culturally and religiously from a cyclic cosmology, often found in native mythologies, to a linear mythology and from that to philosophy of positivism. The general loss of the trust in the pause, in every cyclic rhythm could be influenced by this development, causing a change in our attitude to the natural pause. By living in a culture whose value system is based on constant progression, a pause in itself seems to evoke the fear of a stop, a feeling of standstill, or even the experience of potential death. Also our connection to the rhythm of nature has changed. Because of technology, we are no longer impacted by the shifts in seasons, and the rhythm of nature influence us to a lesser extent. In many ways, we are losing touch with cyclic rhythms. It is not my aim here to evaluate whether this is good or bad, but to point out that we cannot assume that people have a trust in the natural pause, and we need to be aware of the potential fear evoked by pausing, the urge to do something, or to give up, that this 'being in the pause' may create. Therefore, helping participants gain a growing trust and confidence in the pause is an immensely rich contribution that they can bring with them into many areas of their lives, rebalancing or complementing

---

43 Mary Oliver in the poem: *Have You Ever Tried to Enter the Long Black Branches?* p. 61.

the linear progression attitude so prominent in our culture. (This focus on 'being in the pause' is also taught in the tradition of mindfulness).

BEING IN A DEVELOPMENTAL PERSPECTIVE

Looking at the developmental perspective, our capacity to drop into a pause and resting in our being as a source for nourishment and renewed impulses for creativity is related to our early relationship. (Re-)learning to hold the pause, validating the pause, trusting the waiting, and resting is often especially difficult for the un-mothered child who has not experienced enough holding and therefore has not felt the state of 'beingness' as a resource, a place to pause in for re-generating or being nourished before a new impulse arises and move them. Rather, this pause is felt as a gap where nothing is holding them and where they therefore fall into 'nothing' (rather than falling into their own beingness). This may feel as an abyss or evoke a frightening and overwhelming feeling of emptiness. Working on a deep body level (the preverbal self, founded in infancy), re-learning to be in the pause, and through the perceptions of the body finding it a place of relaxing and a place from where something new will emerge, is therefore a profound healing. A new experience rooted in the body perceptions can gradually grow to complement the early experience. Little by little, through working with the pauses on this body level, a growing new trust in the body and in the now is created, and as the individual's capacity to hold the pause and allow the gaps, the space in between the beingness in life is strengthened. Gradually trusting the pauses opens to "being in life."

The pause itself is often pregnant with the new, the seed already inside. For the pause itself to be fertile it needs the same holding as the unborn child. This includes listening to signals that indicated the readiness to come forth, and holding the focus. This way of holding the 'not yet born' with deep awareness and participation without pushing, nor pulling, but by being there, is another elementary key attitude in the BSR work that will be discussed later.

BODY-SOUL CONNECTION

Body-Soul Movements—The Working of the Energy in the Body

> The body is merely the visibility of the Soul, the psyche; and the soul is the psychological experience of the body. So it is really one and the same thing.[44]

Having described the dream work, the voice work, and the movement work that continuously complements each other in the BSR approach, I will continue by describing some of the

---

44 Jung, *Nietzsche's Zarathustra: Notes of the Seminar Given in 1934-1939 by C. G. Jung*, Vol. 1, p. 355.

specific exercises of the intensive. These are the positive mothering exercise, the 'symbol in the body,' the 'symptom in the body,' the Dance of Three, the mask-work, and finally the ending ritual. As an introduction to the description of the exercises, I will dedicate a paragraph to describe the background for the embodied work, for the mirroring, and for the containing. The value of working with embodiment, the non-verbal sharing and symbolic language from the neuroscientific perspective will be described in Part Three of this book.

Throughout the description of the exercises, the words 'mirror' and 'container' will be used. The most comprehensive understanding of the concepts within the BSR work is obtained in the description of the exercise, 'the Dance of Three.' If the concepts are completely new to the reader I suggest reading this section first, since I have chosen to explain the exercises in the order in which they are conducted during the intensive to give the reader a feel for how these exercises build on each other and gradually deepen the work, allowing the participants to gradually extend and widen their capacity to express themselves authentically, and to mirror and contain each other and themselves.

To understand the BSR approach it is important to comprehend the core view that the body and the psyche are one. That body-psyche mind functions in one coherent organism. Dreams, art work, active imagination, body movement and body symptoms are different ways in which the soul can express itself. These are different ways of expressing the energy and all of them are worked within the BSR. If we can connect to the energy and allow it to be expressed, it can move. By bringing it to consciousness, change can happen—whether the change is in the conscious attitude, in unblocking what was blocked, or a transformation of the way that energy was expressing itself.

> When we bring images from dreams, movement, visualization, drawing or other forms of creative expression into consciousness in our bodies, we can experience the transformative power of the psyche.[45]

In particular working with the body and bringing the energy into connection with the reality of the body, and allowing it to express itself, plays an essential part in the BSR work. Working consciously with images, symbols, symptoms and feeling stages, letting this energy express itself in the body and voice, letting it develop and transform is the focus enhanced in various forms in the different exercises, which all, in different ways, facilitate this process.

In most of the exercises, one person will work and one or two partners will facilitate—being the 'mirror' and the 'container.' The partner will be what Marion calls the 'soul-mirror,' mirroring what is expressed back to the person working. Often the soul's expression has not been mirrored in our childhood, it was not seen and it was not heard, or we have lost the

---

45 Marion Woodman, quoted from the website http://www.mwoodmanfoundation.org

connection to our soul later in life for various reasons. If the parents failed to mirror the soul, this is most often because they had their own agenda as to what they wanted the child to be, how they wanted he or she to act or speak, and, therefore, they could not really see the child. The mirroring of the child might have been the mirroring of what they wanted the child to be, not what the child really was; or perhaps the child had to mirror the parents rather than being mirrored by the parents. In the latter case, the parents used the child as self-object. In both these types of early environment, the soul of the child went into hiding or it was never really born. In the BSR work, one tries to reconnect with what went into hiding (which might be named the soul, the soul-child or the inner child depending on the individual). The *mirror* tries to do the mirroring that the parents were not able to do. This includes seeing what was has not been seen or has not dared to truly express itself. Thus the key-role of the *mirror* is to facilitate the soul in expressing itself. The key obstacle is if the woman being the *mirror* starts to have her own agenda or is frightened by the soul's expressions and thus starts to influence the person working to find her soul's expression.[46] When the process of mirroring goes well, gradually, by being given space, being met and being encouraged, the authentic expression of the person working comes more and more into life. Facilitated by the presence of an attuned and encouraging other, the soul grows into trusting its own expression. Gradually, the attitude of the *mirror* can be integrated, so that one starts to meet oneself with the eye of the *mirror* encouraging the soul's expressions with growing courage and living in a way that is more aligned with one's true nature. There are vividly described examples of this process in the interviews.

Description of the Specific Exercises

> When the soul wishes to experience something
> she throws an image of the experience out
> before her and enters into her own image[47]

The next section will be devoted to describing the following concepts of the BSR work: the positive mothering exercise, the symbol in the body exercise, the symptom in the body exercise, the Dance of Three exercise, the mask-work and the ending ritual.

The concepts are both parts of specific exercises and form the backbone or spine of the BSR work, forming ways of being, attitudes to inner work, ways of thinking about each module, ways of perceiving and meeting each interaction and relation, thus forming the

---

46 In Daniel Stern's perspective, the mirror moves from attunement to misattunement.
47 Meister Eckhart quoted in Marion Woodman's, *Bone: Dying into Life,* p. 221.

containing attitude and the structure of the work. I would ask the reader to hold this in mind when reading these sections and taking in the impact that this way of being and thinking about the structure reverberates through the whole BSR approach on the different levels.

I will describe the exercises here and elaborate more on the spine forming part in a later section where other vertebra's such as present, paradox, and process will be presented, thus aligning the full spine in the BSR work.

DESCRIPTION OF THE POSITIVE MOTHERING EXERCISE

The 'positive mothering exercise' is done on first night of the intensive. Each woman is asked to bring her comb with her. The evening is introduced explaining the background behind the exercise, giving a demonstration of the mothering exercise, followed by a short body- and breath-tending exercise before the participants are asked to pair up. Each woman in the dyad, in turn, gets to be both the mother and the child. Between the two of them, they will agree upon who takes which role first. The one going to be the mother first places herself comfortably supported by pillows sitting against the wall on the floor. It is important that the 'mother' is comfortable so that she is able to tend to the 'child.' This image is just as important for the therapist, who is often in the role of the positive mother. If the 'mother' is not comfortable, she cannot give her full attention to the 'child.' Before entering the exercise, the two women are consciously connecting with their "adult selves," taking breaths together and making eye contact. After the exercise they are again consciously connecting soul to soul as two grown-up women. In this way the entrance and the exit of the 'mother or child-part' of the roles are consciously marked and none of the women is left in the role as either child or mother. During the exercise the lights in the room are dimmed, and voices are kept soft and low. The leaders and apprentices are holding and radiating the overall atmosphere of presence, acceptance and love—being very aware of what goes on in the room and in the individuals. If needed, they are there to help; and after the exercise they are also there to help, if one of the participants has something that is too difficult to handle or contain alone. After the exercise the participants are encouraged to go quietly to their rooms and have an early night, paying deep attention to their dreams. Almost always the unconscious responds deeply to this exercise and the dreams will reflect deep patterns around the theme of 'mother.' The next day's sharing of dreams is held in the light of the exercise. The dreams might contain very potent images of the archetypal mother or personal mother. They might also show the negative polarity of the mother archetype. If the woman has had a positive experience in the exercise, the dream might reflect the negative aspect as an expression of the enantiodromia, swinging from the positive pole of the mother archetype to the negative. The sharing of the exercise and the dreams widens and strengthens the container of the group and is consciously establishing the positive mother both in the group and in the individual. This has a crucial impact on the attitude, with which the new life that comes forth during the rest of the intensive is met and received, both in the individual and in the group. Consciously constellating the positive pole of the mother archetype makes the group and the individual more prepared to meet and hold the still point when the negative pole of the mother archetype constellates and to be able to bring that to consciousness as well. Examples of this are given in the interviews.

The reflections and sharing of the exercise and dreams often results in the sharing of mother-daughter stories in many variations. Often the dream images are reflected in the telling of the myth of the Demeter-Kore-Persephone by Marion, thus bringing in one expansion of the archetypal ground of the mother-daughter relation. Through this work the personal-archetypal axis becomes the reference point in the group, holding the possibility of healing of the personal story, through the collective level in the group and the archetypal level of the myth and dreams. The healing of the personal stories by the relations and sharing in the group is a positive richness in the BSR work, but maybe not-so-often-voiced. By hearing the many stories shared—and that is both stories of deep and nourishing mother-daughter bonds or grandmother-mother-daughter-sister bonds as well as stories of wounding—the potential is opened and the individual is provided with new ways of looking at her own relationships or possibilities for her own reactions in her relationships. This touches on Yalom's list of the therapeutic potential in group work.[48]

The Healing Potential of 'The Positive Mothering' Exercise

While going through the exercise, two levels of awareness are activated. One related to the actually lived 'now,' with the women receiving or giving the encouragement, the loving gaze, the soft toned voice, and gentle rocking of the body. The other level of awareness is related to what Stern calls "the activated past" or what in Jungian terms belongs to the mother complex or child complex. That is our past memories of receiving or giving in relation to our mother or child and the feeling tone connected to that. These memories are stored in the body and by paying attention to our reactions, feelings and body-states; these memories can be brought

---

48 Therapeutically, factors in group therapy according to Yalom, include that good group therapy has the capacity to: 1. Install hope; the participants meet others who have been through the same experiences; the therapist holds the hope. 2. Install a feeling of universality, which breaks the isolation: 'not only me.' 3. Increase altruism: it fosters skills in 'caring about.' 4. Impart or share information of 'how to deal with problems.' 5. Provides the participants with corrective emotional experience; re-program or imagine a more supportive response, visit surplus reality to create that, and become co-creating. 6. Develop socialization techniques. 7. Modelling—picking up healthier behavior. 8. Interpersonal leaning. 9. Group cohesiveness: give a sense of belonging with all one's uniqueness 10. Provide the possibility for catharsis—emotional release. 11. Existential issues can be shared—life is shared—you walk alone but others can walk with you. (Irvin Yalom, *Theory and Practice of Group Psychotherapy*, pp. 1-117.

to consciousness. If the past experience has a high negative charge and is forcefully activated in the now, the past impairs the perceiving of the now and the old pattern keeps being relived as the subjective experience. Becoming aware of these patterns makes it possible to start questioning their actual reality in the now. And I think most importantly within the context of this exercise, a repairing lived through embodied experience of positive mothering is possible. An experience stored both in consciousness and in the body-memory—a new lived experience can be formed.

The reflections after the exercise helps to understand what one perceives, both when one is mothering and is being mothered. How one is mothering the other person, how one is mothering oneself, how one is receiving oneself and one's own matter—the body. If there are any contradictory patterns or feelings of ambivalence, this can be brought to awareness and worked with. And finally to be aware of what one needs to feel received on this deep level and potentially to ask for it as well as to start to provide it for oneself—consciously constellating the positive mother for the inner child.

We cannot work with material that for various reasons has never dared to come forth before, if we are not working with the attitude by which we will receive it. Unconsciously, we often receive ourselves and others as we were received ourselves. How we receive new life is influenced by how we were received as new life. In the exercise, one therefore consciously pays attention to this level as well, being aware of body memories, attitudes, feelings, needs, silent agendas, and patterns of adaptations not corresponding with one's true feelings—all which are evoked both as one receives and gives.

By doing the exercise in this meditative way, with dim light, soft voices and in the evening when the body is more relaxed and open to receive, the content of the lived experience is more likely to extend beyond the cognitive level, thus reaching the emotional subconscious and somatic unconscious level as well. The body can take in the experience of being held, cherished and attended to in a loving way. This experience roots itself deeply in the body-memory. The body remembers and can later draw on this experience. For some women whose body—that is whose core—being has not had this experience of being received. Being in a state of 'being' and being held, this exercise can have a huge impact. Some will experience old memories of fear, rejection, adaptive patterns, dissociation, grief and sadness. Because the experience is done with another woman, who is relatively unknown, whatever is perceived in her eyes will often evoke what was perceived in the eyes of the mother. Likewise in the role as mother, how you tend to the child, and how you react emotionally towards the child, and what feelings the child evokes in you, will often be close to the attitude of your own mother or compensatory to that. Thus, on a deep level, it is possible to bring these feelings and attitudes to consciousness and work with them.

The exercise, finally, has an impact on the group and on the whole level of being in the intensives. Because positive mothering is consciously constellated and the individual's attitude towards new life is consciously tended to, the amount of constellated negative mothering towards one another in the group is lessened or dealt with in a much more conscious way. There is a conscious awareness of how we receive one another and the extent to which this influences the new life that is trying to come forth and is trying to find the courage to do so. There is a conscious awareness of the enormous effect it has on the work, when one has the feeling that one will be received, if one tries to work with parts of oneself or behavioral patterns that in the past meant rejection or criticism stored in the body's tissue.

What it means to actually live this rather than to just talk about it, is that the words do not reach the parts of the memory system concerned with this primary experience of being received in our core being. This is developmentally perceived preverbally through the senses in a global experience including touch, tone of voice, smell, expression of face, the gaze and the rhythm, the feeling of the breathing and heartbeat of the other.

Through the positive mothering exercise there is the potential to consciously give the body, or the core being a new lived experience that can balance, counteract or complement the personal mother-child complex (see the later discussion on RIG and repairing lived experiences in therapy).

For this exercise to have positive healing potential, the intensity has to be deep enough to make a lasting impact—to provide a new experience of self-with-other. Since it cannot be small-intensity long-term interactions as in ongoing therapy, it has to be high intensity or highly emotional charged to be stored as significant in the body's memory system. The individual may find that she holds various defences towards opening herself to the experience. This must be fully accepted and received with an attitude of total acceptance. No resistance stored in the body may be forcefully removed. It is only by slowly growing the trust, safety and security on the body level that the defences can gradually soften. The degree and amount of this softening is individual. What can be allowed in is a balance. What is important is the process of working with what feels right for the body to take in. Here the body is very precise (see later in the interviews).

All exercises, but especially the mother-child exercise, are therefore introduced. The introduction includes talking about potential resistance and inviting people to be respectful of their feelings and perhaps explore why they feel the resistance rather than trying to repress it. The women are invited to voice their needs so 'that something that seems not possible could be partly possible.' It is also stressed that none of these exercises are fixed. The exercises vary slightly, depending on where in her personal life the individual woman is, what is particularly constellated in her and in the woman she works with and in the field between them.

To illustrate, I would like to share one woman's description of the positive mothering exercise. She describes:

> At one intensive I recall having an experience where I, when going into the role of the child, just could not face my 'mother.' I had the feeling that her gaze would completely invade me, because I would have to react to her needs of seeing a 'happy' baby, which I did not feel. I therefore could only, on the body level imagine doing the exercise sitting two metres away from the 'mother' with my back to her. Only in this position could I take in her loving attitude and the holding that I knew the woman I was working with was sending out. Facing her gaze and seeing her eyes would be too confronting and just trigger the past. I knew I could not do it otherwise without betraying myself and 'giving' her 'the smile' that I projected onto her that she expected and 'needed' from me. Now this became a huge healing experience for me, mainly because I knew that all these feelings had nothing to do with the actual woman I worked with. Actually knowing her gave me the courage to feel what I felt, because I knew she could take it. My personal mother could not handle my 'rejection.' If I turned my head away from her and did not react to her with a smile she would fragment. Knowing I could trust that my 'exercise mother' would 'hold,' I could allow my body to feel what it felt and trust it, and work with it and 'reject' 'mother' and see and feel that she was still 'holding.' This is very early stuff coming up in the body memory that I could never have accessed through words. Yet this body memory had a huge impact on my behavior around 'mother' and whoever carried the projection of 'mother.' To work through it, in this way, created immense healing because my body received a lived experience of being 'allowed' to express itself and its needs without being 'rejected.' On the contrary it was being held and contained. 'Mother' was there.

This was obviously a high-impact positive mother-child exercise that this woman had, out of several in the intensive. Not only was it a new lived experience, it was also, on a metaphysical level, a lesson that the past experiences and patterns of relating can undergo transformation. She experienced that new ways of interaction were possible and, if she could find ways to explore that, her body could gain new types of memories of interactions that were good and nourishing for her.[49]

Because she had listen to her deeper perceptions of the 'mother' she worked with, feeling she could trust her enough to open to her body's request and live it through, she gained an increasing trust her own body's perception of people. She could increasingly use her body's feeling of safety as rudder, guiding her into much more fruitful attachment patterns.[50] She

---

49 Through this experience and insight the possibility for the process that according to attachment theory would be called 'learned secure attachment' was opened up. (For a description of attachment theory see Fonagy, Peter; Gergely, György; Jurist, Elliot; Target, Mary *Affect Regulation, Mentalization, and the Development of the Self*).

50 Attachment theorists talk about how this learned secure attachment is provided in therapy (see Part III for the attachment theory perspective).

did not have to separate herself from her core-body perceptions in connections, but could be there with all of herself.

It seems to be implied, on the basis of increasing evidence, that this level of transformation is not easily addressed through the verbal sense of self.[51] The core sense of self must be reached in some preverbal way though body perceptions; the loving gaze, the voice, the radiating attitude of acceptance and possible non-invasive touch.

The BSR approach reaches the preverbal as well as the verbal sense of self. In terms of Stern's developmental model, it reaches multiple senses of self and all the time the work implies bridging and making connections between them, creating a greater coherence among domains.[52] In terms of the Jungian frame it connects the mind, the body and the imagination, giving rise to the growing experience of wholeness.

DESCRIPTION OF THE 'SYMBOL IN THE BODY' EXERCISE

The work with the symbol in the body is an essential part of the BSR work. According to Marion Woodman the soul lives on symbols or on metaphor, and soul work is an act of the imagination. By soul she means 'embodied essence.' Esse is Latin and means 'to be.'[53] She quotes Blake: "Body is that portion of the soul perceived by the five senses."[54]

---

51 See for example: Sue Gerhardt, *Why Love Matters: How Affection Shapes a Baby's Brain*, Ogden, Minton, & Pain, *Trauma and the Body: A Sensorimotor Approach to Psychotherapy*, Schore, *Affect Dysregulation and Disorders of the Self*, and *Affect Regulation and the Repair of the Self*, Stern, *The Interpersonal World of the Infant: A View from Psychoanalysis and Developmental*, and *The Present Moment in Psychotherapy and Everyday Life*, Van der Hart, Nijenhuis, & Steele, *The Haunted Self: Structural Dissociation and the Treatment of Chronic Traumatization*, Wilkinson, *Coming into Mind: The Mind-Brain Relationship: A Jungian Clinical Perspective*.

52 Stern, *The Interpersonal World of the Infant*.

53 Marion Woodman, *Conscious Femininity—Interviews with Marion Woodman*, p. 71.

54 "Psychology means the science of the soul. The terrible irony is that many psychologists think of themselves as a scientist who does not believe there is such a thing as soul" Woodman, *Conscious Femininity*, p. 71.

By 'psyche' Marion Woodman refers to "the presence of the observer in the things observed; a presence that changes what is observed. She explains that when we see something "out there," we see an image. This image is constructed at the perceptual center of the brain. The psychical object does not enter the eye. What enters are the light waves (or the sound waves in the case of the ear) which become electrical impulses that the brain [visual cortex] converts into images. "The consciousness of those images as images is what I mean by soul. Soul is not the physical external thing but the immaterial image of it, which may or may not have an identity with the external thing. The soul is not restricted to making a copy. The world the observer constructs from the things observed is always other than the things observed." Woodman, *Conscious Femininity*, p. 40.

According to Marion Woodman our images and the images evoked through bodywork are pictures relating to our soul. Dream work and bodywork are similar in the way that the body gives rise to metaphorical images and messages from the unconscious as do the dreams. In the BSR the images are worked with as the bridge between psyche and body. By taking the time to listen to the body and tending to the images the meaning can be revealed. Marion Woodman says, "The point is we are flesh and blood and often we don't experience the reality of a psychic image until we feel it in our body."[55] The metaphors in dreams give us the picture of our psychic condition and how to change it.

Marion Woodman uses the word 'metaphor' interchangeably with 'symbol.' She explains that she "likes the word *metaphor* because it comes from the Greek for 'transformer' and that is what a metaphor is: it transforms one kind of energy into another."[56] When working with the symbols or the metaphors, the person is encouraged to take a powerful image (often from a dream) and to concentrate on it, perceive it, meditate on it and reflect on it. This objectifies the energy and thus transforms it. With psychosomatic problems one tries to concentrate on the symptom, or the energy in that symptom, and allow an image to arise. Again this opens up the way for a possible transformation.[57]

The work with metaphor is distilling the raw energy patterns of the unconscious into forms that can be assimilated into consciousness. This transforming function of the metaphor works similarly in fairy tales, literature and dreams. The metaphor affects the person on three levels: the mental level on which we interpret the meaning, the imaginative level where the actual transforming power resides and the emotional level connected to the feelings embodied in the metaphor.[58]

In the 'symbol in the body' exercise, participants work with an individual chosen symbol in the body. As described, the symbol arises in the body and becomes an image we can hold in our minds.[59] This exercise allows for an image held in the mind, to drop down into the body,

---

"The image as distinct from the thing is called, in alchemy and in like-minded traditions, the subtle body. It is not a thing in itself but the image of it constructed by the brain and reshaped or reconstructed in an infinite variety of ways by the imagination, the image-making power of the brain. Soul is the world of metaphor. We inhabit it all the time whether we know it or not... Most unconscious people don't know it." Woodman, *Conscious Femininity*, p. 41.

"Soul lives on metaphors. The soul wants to paint or sing or write or dance but it must have metaphors because metaphors bring the whole person together. That is where the healing is." Woodman, *Conscious Femininity*, p. 64.

55 Woodman, *Conscious Femininity*, p. 118.
56 Woodman, *Conscious Femininity*, p. 78.
57 Woodman, *Conscious Femininity*, p. 78.
58 Woodman, *Conscious Femininity*, p. 78.
59 See also the section on the neuroscientific for comments on the symbol in Part III.

and let the body move with the energy.[60] The participants are again working in pairs, taking turns to embody a symbol and to be the mirror and container. The person in the role of mirror and container holds the conscious reference point and supports the process through moving and sounding with the person working, attuning to her and resonating with her. Again the exercise is marked by the participants consciously connecting before and after the exercise by holding hands. When the person who is working with the symbol is ready, she moves to her starting position and tunes into the symbol. If she needs her partner to hold a hand on the body part, where the symbol feels most prominent, she can ask for this. Embodying a symbol is allowing the energy of the symbol to drop into the body and to move us by opening the body to being the symbol. One lets the symbol take over and express itself in the reality of the body, exploring the energy in the body and moving accordingly. Like in an embodied active imagination, the person allows the symbol to express itself and follows the energy in body movements. She follows the energy until it seems to come to its natural completion. Reconnecting to her partner she can then chose to speak and share reflections which further the process of consciousness. The mover is then encouraged to express the energy and the process either in art work or through writing. The partner keeps facilitating that. When it feels completed, the pair swaps roles.

As all archetypes have a positive and a negative pole, the energy of the symbol can express itself as a blend, with more or less dominance by one of the polarities that it contains. Naturally it is more difficult and needs more psychic strength to contain and work with the negative aspect of an archetypal energy. Depending on where the participants are in the process, their personal stories and their experience with psychic work, the work with the symbol must be adjusted to that. The leaders stress this point very seriously and also help the individual to try to anticipate to what degree one should stay with working with the positive aspect of the symbol, until one's strength grows and one's capacity to encounter the more negative aspects are developed. It is always stressed that the ego has control and should the energy 'flip' (that is, if an apparently benign symbol suddenly appears very negative to a degree that is more than the person can deal with at that time), and the participant starts to feel either uncomfortable or less in control, she can stop the exercise. Here again, the partner is there to help. The aim of the exercise is to try to mediate the symbolic energy, not to be overwhelmed by it.

DESCRIPTION OF THE 'SYMPTOM IN THE BODY' EXERCISE

The 'symptom in the body' is a parallel exercise but instead of a symbol, one works with a symptom. In this approach the symptom in the body is related to a blocked or locked energy

---

60 Pat Ogden uses the phrases 'top-down' and 'bottom-up' to apply to the approaches; in the bottom-up, one lets the body perceptions guide the work, (Ogden, Minton, & Pain, *Trauma and the Body*).

in a physical form. By relating to the symptom, working with it and allowing the images to arise, the energy can change.[61] The 'symptom' could be a chronic aching shoulder, a sore back, 'too big thighs' or a headache, etc. This is often a more difficult exercise because a symptom is often not met with the same degree of welcoming attitude by the ego. The attitude or feelings of the ego may be a mixture of trying to accept and being angry, feeling defeated or wanting to get rid of the symptom. These emotions are encouraged to be voiced. Also, the symptom often holds a pain constellation that longs to be voiced as well.[62] Again it is worked with as energy, giving it a voice and expression. Particularly in this exercise, placing the partner's hand on the place of the symptom helps hold the focus. Often, when tending to a symptom in this way, as a symbolic expression in a physical form, the ego's attitude and relation to the symptom starts to change. Compassion for what is hurting and for what that place of pain needs often seems to be the outcome. A deeper understanding may emerge and meaning or knowledge may be found within the symptom corresponding to a shadow part of oneself. As with the symbol in the body, the energy and the process are expressed in art work or writing when this exercise has come to its natural completion.

DESCRIPTION OF THE DANCE OF THREE EXERCISE

The Dance of Three integrates aspects of the former presented exercises, yet is moving into a more 'naked' or vulnerable exposing space of expression. The dancer is holding no symbol or image to let the expression move through or be centered on. At the core of the exercise is the concentration to hold the inner focus and express one's perceptions from this place in movements. Working in triads, the participants focus on enhancing and supporting the dancer's authentic expression. One is the mirror, mirroring the new life to the dancer; one is the container, holding both the dancer and the mirror in a safe space and radiating an encouraging loving attitude.

---

61 It is strongly emphasized that this is not a cure for somatic symptoms, which should always be examined by a doctor, but a way of working with symptoms belonging to the psychosomatic realm or as way of working with symptoms that are also treated in other ways to work on one's attitude and relation towards the symptom.

62 Mara Sidoli, *When the Body Speaks*, p. 115. Mara Sidoli speaks to the body as container and signifier: [when pain of the soul gets stuck in the body because the mother could not contain the psychic pain of the infant]…"the body becomes the container of pain, undifferentiated but concretely visible because as such it is attended to and relieved by a mother who understands suffering only in concrete terms. There is no room for invisible, impalpable psychic pain. The somatic symptoms become an expression, a dramatization of psychic pain which has the quality of mime rather than a play. It is a drama without words, through which the body sufferer will receive the primary care that will vicariously provide solace and comfort to the soul."

The triad of the dancer, the mirror and the container is a form that reverberates throughout the BSR work. It is the symbol for a potential internalized triad, where the individual can move between all three aspects as she continues to bring to life and live her authentic self. It is the triad held by the leaders; when one is teaching, the others are sharing the roles of the container and the mirror. The role of the holding mother and the mother mirroring the true self of the infant as it grows and develops, according to Winnicottt, is what forms a growth-facilitating environment. And finally, it is the described exercise that becomes an embodied "feeling voyage" lived and shared between the triad working together in the exercise.

Elaborating more on the three roles or three aspects forming the whole, the dancer is the 'doer' expressing the process unfolding. She holds the groundedness, and the unified field. She lives the "virgin self" as Marion expresses it. That is, she expresses herself from her own authentic ground, without performing and she is grounded in her own body.

The mirror is the one who energetically—that is, in movements and energy—mirrors back to the dancer what she is expressing. For example, when a mother mirrors her child, she mirrors back to the child, the child's own reflection (as opposed to the mother imposing her own wants or desires upon the child).

The container is the protector who sees and loves both the mirror and the dancer. She sees the relationship between the two and she sees the expressions without judgement, encouraging and welcoming what is expressed and making sure the space is kept safe so that the dancer is free to focus on the dance. The container does not push or pull, she simply holds with love—like a midwife encouraging what wants to be born to come forth. Like the conscious mother she is holding, cherishing and mirroring the soul.

This exercise holds the potential for the individual to ingrate the triad, holding all three parts of it in one's own psyche. The dancer is one's own authentic being, Marion Woodman refers to the dancer both as the soul and as the body. Other expressions for the dancer could be Winnicott's "true self" or in Jungian terms the part of the ego aligned with the Self, connected to the Self by the ego-Self axis.

The mirror is the part that can mirror oneself when the world is not doing so. That is, holding the self-reflecting aspect that has an encouraging effect on the creative or authentic dancing part of oneself—an internalized 'playmate' that reinforces one's own reality and encourages one to be free to live one's own life. The container is the protector for the soul, the eye of the deep heart. This protector shields the mirror and the dancer from harsh impacts from the outer world and/or from negative inner complexes.

This relation between the three is mirrored in the start of the exercise, where the triad connect by holding hands and tune into the space between them. The dancer gives the signal and starts her move, when she is ready, that is, when the impulse comes from her authentic self. The music is Chopin. According to Mary Hamilton, this music is chosen because of its capacity to create an atmosphere that invites one to authentic expression (the music has to be liberating and open for many types of expression, and not impose a particular mood on the dancer). Having the triad as an outer lived experience holds the potential to provide the individual with a new lived experience of how to receive both oneself and others. Through this exercise, (perceived by all the senses—seeing the 'demo' (demonstration) initially, living through all three parts as the triad takes it in turn being the different aspects and, finally, bringing the experience into reflection in art work), there is the possibility of forming new alternative sets of images, new ways of embodied being and new ways of receiving soul.

DESCRIPTION OF THE MASK-WORK

The mask-work moves like a thread through the intensives. Each participant makes a mask, spends time to decorate and paint it, and then moves into working with the mask. Working with the mask includes getting to know the energy, live it, interact with it and integrate it. This work is in many ways like working with the symbol of a big dream. The mask becomes an expression of what is constellated in the unconscious of the individual's psyche, which wants to come forth from the unconscious, expressed in a symbolic form. It could be said to be a piece of shadow or rather a piece of hitherto unlived life-energy crystallised into the mask. When I use the parallel to a symbol of a big dream, it is because the mask as symbol becomes alive—it is experienced as a living character and has its own world and its own way of being. It too, as a living symbol, keeps evolving and showing new aspects. The mask-work is intense work with symbolic energy, feeling oneself into it and becoming it, by wearing the mask and, hence, getting to know the world of this symbol. In the BSR intensives' Phase 1 workshop, the participants create and work with a mask. In Phase 2, the participants work with a previously made mask, expanding on the work with it. The masks are made of plaster of Paris added onto the face. The making of the masks is done in a meditative atmosphere, where the participants are grouped in triads, as in the Dance of Three exercise. As the plaster dries and is ready to come off the face, it feels like a birth process of a new previously unconscious piece of oneself that is coming into form.

All masks are handled as if they are personal dreams. That is they are never to be left unguarded or treated casually but kept safe, never to be worn by others, and never to be worn speaking from one's normal ego in the mask. There is careful preparation to create the right container before any mask-work is done; and, equally, every ending is marked, making sure that people are consciously stepping out of the role of the mask. In the decorating, the participants are encouraged to feel into the new life, to sit with it, to try to feel what the mask wants to express, letting the mask character come through, not having a project, but being open to let this new life come into its form.

Each work phase with the mask is initiated by a demonstration led by Ann. She unfailingly conveys with great skill the atmosphere of modelling how to start the relation to the mask and how to let it grow. When all the masks have found their form and have been decorated, the work moves into the wearing of the mask. Putting on the mask is proceeded by getting ready to allow the energy to be expressed. First, one works with a line or a shape from the mask, taking in the energy and letting the body move with that energy. The same is done with a color on the mask. Lines and forms are all part of our energetic character and this initial playful work facilitates one in using one's senses with the mask. You then place the mask on the body, breathing with it, allowing for an inner readiness to put it on. When the mask is on, there is some time for one to get into the feeling of the mask. This is followed by different small improvisations aiming at bringing out the character of the mask. For example, the mask has to find its home, showing its attachment capacity and environment, and its sense of belonging. Something threatening comes along and the mask reacts; thus showing the mask's response to threats—is it aggressive or frightened, and how is this enacted? And how does the mask react when the threat moves away again? Then the mask loses the thing it loves the most and, after a while, finds it again revealing the mask's capacity for relationship and feelings around intimacy—giving insight into the heart of the mask. Thus, slowly, the character of the mask becomes more and more alive.

The next phase of the mask-work moves participants into being more in the mask energy, starting to explore the world of the mask—or at least having the potential space for it (the mask might not like to move at all!) and letting the mask interact with other masks, again getting to know the mask more and more. Is it introverted or extroverted? Is it a being? Is it an element? Is it shy, bold, playful, angry? Is it highly energised or slow moving? Is it moving fluid in the world or more staccato-like? Does it have an age or is it ageless? What is it attracted to? All these details are gradually revealed. Participants are encouraged to write down their new gained experiences after each encounter with the masks. In the mask-work the leaders and apprentices are there actively interacting with the masks, thus helping to bring out the characters, playing with the masks and supporting the process in different ways.

When the world of the mask is more known, its expressions are explored further; this is done using the Dance of Three model. In Phase 1 the work is done in triads. In Phase 2 the work is done in dyads. In the dyads, the helping other holds both the mirroring and the containing aspect. As the end of the week approaches, the mask-work moves towards coming into expressing itself through the voice, finding its "I am...." The "I am..." is the essence of the identity of the masks. Depending on the mask character, the "I am" could be "I am bold and barefoot" or "I am wind moving with ease" or "I am black swan holding grief." The meanings of the expression stated in the "I am" are multi-layered. Firstly, it is a statement, arising from the mask energy, coming into consciousness, holding the essence of the mask and being able to come forth, expressing this essence in the world. Secondly, in voicing the "I am...," one is developmentally moving into the verbal sense of self, voicing and claiming one's identity, and, thirdly, it has remnants of poetic expression, where the essence of the goddesses were stated in long poems, starting each line with an "I am" declaring the essence of the goddess (see examples in the interviews). The process of coming into the "I am..." is worked with in dyads and through the help of the mirror, the mask energy is worked with towards some kind of integration. A step in this integration includes the holding of the mask energy, no longer wearing the mask, and being in the "I am" of the mask. This assimilation of the energy is supported by gradually taking off the mask, having it held by the partner, who all the time mirrors back to the one working with her mask, what she is expressing. Slowly, the identity of the mask becomes consciously integrated energy available for the ego.

DESCRIPTION OF THE RITUAL ENDING

As Marion stresses, often the new energy brought up and related to from the unconscious, the new insight and the consequences for one's attitude, like the treasure in fairy tales, is lost on the very last part of the journey. That is, it falls back into the unconscious and we proceed in our life without change. To bring awareness to this risk of losing the treasure, and to support that the treasure can be brought home so that the new energy and insight can be integrated in conscious life—this theme is worked with towards the end of the intensives. Marion stresses the necessity to consciously reflect upon the risks and obstacles that could hinder a person integrating the week's work into their home life. The end of the intensive is formed around bringing the treasure home. Every single participant is given time to distil for themselves what the week's work has been about for them, and what they need to let go of in their current life, to give room to integrate the new. Often, something has to be sacrificed to provide space for the new; it can be the letting go of an old pattern, an old way of being, an old attitude or way of relating. On the final evening everyone gathers and, one by one, each participant goes to the center of the group to share their essence with the group. A sacrifice can be made, or an intention can be voiced if the sacrifice cannot yet be made. The evening ends with a circle dance. Objects that have been left on the table with the candle, the symbolic holding center, are taken back, signaling that the week's end, and the official goodbyes are made.

On the last morning the silence is broken. There is a final gathering, the central candle is blown out and the final morning dance is danced. In this way, a very marked closing of the work has taken place, securing that participants are fully in their ego and ready to meet the outer world, after having been immersed in the inner world for a week.

Core Values in the BSR Work: Presence, Paradox, Process

Having described the structure of the BSR intensives, and the specific contents of the different exercises, I would like to end this part of the book summarising the core values behind the work that shapes the feeling quality of the container and the attitude of the leaders. This includes describing present, paradox and process and the three symbols: the conscious mother, the virgin and the crone. Furthermore I find it relevant to end with a paragraph on the shadow. A reflection on the value of the different exercises in the light of neuroscience and developmental psychology will follow in Part III.

As characteristic for the Jungian approach, the qualities or values behind the work are not given in any definite or exhaustive description, but rather conveyed in images or concepts perceived as symbols. A symbol, in its nature, is the best possible explanation of something relatively unknown and, when it is 'alive' it constantly reformates and recreates itself, allowing us to see it from a new perspective.

The underlying values for the BSR work are open concepts defined in a 'loose' enough way, so that each individual can find what resonates with her. These are defined by amplification, rather than by definite description.[63] This quality creates enough similarities to find a shared field, and yet they remain open enough to allow for an individual integrity. This types of definition goes beyond right or wrong and moves into a more synthesised way of perceiving theories. As will be visible in the interviews, each woman puts different emphasis on the different values and concepts and is mostly inspired by the parts that resonate with her own reality. These loosely woven concepts thus allow for shared ground. The plasticity allows for inclusion, and creates a container that is experienced as wide and open for individual ways of perceiving the world. This is in itself healing, as mentioned in the interviews. The women find a place where they can experience what it is to be 'part of' yet 'true-to-their-own-reality.' It gives a 'sense of belonging' yet 'respecting the individual,' and it gives each individual a possibility to grow or change within the belonging, without a threat of exclusion, because the container is flexible as opposed to rigid (a metaphor for this kind of container could be the uterus).

VALUES

I think we have to open our hearts and feel our collective wound.

---

63 See Stern, *The Present Moment in Psychotherapy and Everyday Life*. To use a word from the neuroscience there is 'plasticity' in the concepts—Stern, from the developmental field, speaks of the need for "sloppiness."

Through our own suffering,
our hearts are broken open in love for one another.[64]

Many of the underlying values[65] of the work have already been introduced such as: *receiving the soul with love, holding, mirroring, containing, active resonating, trusting the pause, staying with, being, attunement, holding the tension of the opposite*—the position referred to as the still point,[66] *commitment to the process, trusting the unconscious, allowing space for the unknown and not-yet-born, authenticity and being aware of one's own shadow as much as possible.*[67]

In my own experience, both as participant and as apprentice in the BSR intensives and from the interviews, what seems to be stressed continually is the overall feeling of having one's body-soul received with love. Accounts of what that means for the individual and their psychic growth will be revealed in different versions in the interviews. The last part of the book will explore the neuroscientific and developmental aspects of the impact of being received with love.

Here I would like to emphasize three symbols and three concepts that are deep influences from the BSR work: conscious mother, conscious virgin and crone; and present, paradox and process.[68]

The three archetypal images conscious mother, conscious virgin and crone[69] are symbols for the work, representations for the feeling values and tuning forks for the qualities that contain the work.

---

64 Marion Woodman, *Empowering Soul Through the Feminine,* Interview with Marion Woodman by Michael Bertrand, 1992, quoted from Marion Woodman's homepage: www.mwoodman.org.

65 For a more comprehensive description I refer the reader to the work of Marion Woodman.

66 Referring to part of T.S. Eliot's poem *Burnt Norton, Four Quartets*: "Except for the point, T.S. Eliot, (1952) Complete Poems and Plays: 1909–1950, p. 119.

67 I use the word 'shadow' in this context in its broadest sense: referring to everything that one does not own consciously and which is perceived as incompatible to the chosen conscious attitude and therefore denied an expression in life. Disowned shadow aspects have a tendency to react as "splinter personalities." Becoming conscious of these aspects and owning them as parts of one's self, integrating them into one's field of consciousness is part of the work in the process of individuation.

68 Readers familiar with the writings of Marie-Louise von Franz might notice the play with the 'P's here: "PPP." This abbreviation is contrasting what Marie-Louise von Franz refers to as "PPFF": the values that strongly influence the collective consciousness in Western culture and often drive the individual away from their own authentic life in order to be accepted within the collective. "PPFF" stands for: Power, Prestige, Fame, and Fortune.

69 These archetypal representations are thoroughly described in Marion Woodman's work. The short description here is based on notes from the intensives.

The conscious mother embodies the qualities of receiving the new psychic life with the attitude of a mother who supports, nourishes, protect, mirrors, holds and contains with love. She is attuned to the needs and expressions of the new life.

The conscious virgin or the pregnant virgin incarnates soul. Like a virgin forest, she is 'un-trampled upon,' untouched by projections, "she-is-who-she-is-because-that-is-who-she-is." She is authentic in her being and lives and expresses her own authenticity. She differentiates through feelings: deciding 'this is of value to me—this is not.' She is the carrier of the new life impregnated with potentials and she *is* the new life.

The crone is the wise woman who has gained her wisdom though 'the lived life.' She can hold both the darkness, the light and the tension between the two. She is stripped of senti-mentality. She is free of her own agendas and therefore truly able to attune to the soul. She is on the side of the soul, but not necessarily on the side of the ego, and she is not shattered by the protest of the ego. There is toughness in her that serves a deeper purpose—a deeper transformation.

PROCESS

In the BSR work the emphasis is on the process, as such, and less on the product. This focus opens to the now. Not being focused on reaching a product, the now becomes a place to be in more fully. The now has a complete value of its own with no need to rush to the next moment. Also, the awareness of the process unfolding links the now with the already unfolded past, creating a sense of continuity of the process, which gives rise to a trust in its 'future' unfolding. The tendency to be fixated on a product projected into the future steps into the background, and an awareness of a process unfolding steps into the foreground. This again allows for the spontaneity, the unpredictable new shape of the moment. The ego becomes a companion of the now as it unfolds, rather than taking control of it. This gives openness to impulses from the unconscious and a readiness to follow the soul process, which in its nature is unpredictable from the ego's viewpoint. It gives rise to a trust in following what might not make complete sense, but is felt only as a hunch. If we are focused on a specific outcome, it will occupy our minds and block what spontaneously arises or what seems to be hinted at. If the process in itself is the goal, we are called upon to be fully present in the moment as it unfolds. We are opened to follow the soul wherever it might lead us. Jung said that once you are on the path of the individuation process, you are at the goal. This opening of the now, of being fully present in the moment and open to whatever wants to come forth, leads to the next key concept.

PRESENCE

The concept of presence—of being present—to one's inner life and to the other in the moment, radiates quite strongly from Mary, Ann, and Marion. To be in the company of someone truly present—focused and *there,* influences us. Being aware that the perceiver and the perceived are one, that how we perceive that we are received by the other, influences our bodies, our feeling-state and our own capacity to be truly present to our selves. Examples of that are given in the interview. To illustrate the impact of what it means to be present or to be in the company of someone who is present, it may be helpful to give an example of the opposite: that is, to be in the company of someone who is absent—not absent physically but absent emotionally and psychically. Infants, whose mothers are present physically but absent emotionally either due to depression or dissociation, fail to thrive. Their development is impaired and their bonding patterns, less trustful and secure. Also, showing an infant a 'blank' face creates higher distress in the infant than showing an angry face.[70] Now these examples are extremes, and between the poles of being absent and present, is a whole range of degrees. We all know the place where we are only eighty per cent present in an encounter, but what might be not so conscious to us is how that influences the field, especially on the unconscious level. The impact of being met by someone fully present, fully there, is remarkably highlighted in the interviews. It seems, especially from one interview, that if someone is fully there, engaging in an accepting and open way, without expectations or judgement, it allows the person to fully receive herself. The unthreatening bond (a secure attachment) with the other opens to a deeper bond with one's self and with the other (no need to split-off unacceptable parts or parts hidden due to shame or fear of rejection). What we see in the gaze of the other is crucial. When we are in the company of someone truly present to soul, it works as a tuning fork on our energy. We become present to ourselves on a deeper level. Something inside us resonates with that 'presentness' in the gaze of the other and awakens us to be present to it in ourselves.

The whole BSR intensive is a long meditation in being more fully present to ourselves, to our inner life and to the other. Many of the exercises are designed in different ways to enhance the participant's awareness and capacity to be more present to themselves and the person they work with.

I have focused on the aspect of presence in time. Another aspect of presence is to be present to what one *is.* That is, to be present to what one is—not to what one wishes to be, tries to be, strives to be, or to feel something other than what one feels, but to be present to one's own human reality. This means to let go of an idealized image of oneself that prevents one from living or is fostering a split life between an idealized fantasy of what one is supposed to be, and the repressed shadow side. Being present in this context means to live as the human be-

70 Sue Gerhardt, *Why Love Matters*, p. 48.

ing that one is, including being present to one's shadow. To be present to one's shadow means to include one's shadow rather than deny, repress or project it. This aspect of presence opens to a fuller embrace of oneself and others, and gives rise to a more authentic way of being.[71]

PARADOX

The last concept I will mention here is paradox,[72] and holding the paradox. The word 'paradox' is well-known in the Jungian field. It embraces the capacity to hold two seeming contradictions in mind. To hold the both/ and. This includes to be with two seemingly contradictory opposite statements, identifying with neither, but rather holding both as equally valid—for example, the equally valid reality of both the inner and the outer world. Rather than identifying with the either/or, the Jungian approach puts emphasis on holding the conflicts, that is holding the tension. This holding opens to the possibility for the third to arise. Jung emphasizes the value of cultivating the capacity to hold the tension of the opposites—to learn to be and live in a world with paradoxes such as the inner and the outer world, the masculine and the feminine, etc. To hold the paradox means to be able to hold two mutually exclusive views of reality in mind at the same time. Holding the paradox opens to the possibility of living both.[73]

THE SHADOW—HOLDING THE STILL POINT

I think it is quite appropriate to end part I with some space for the shadow. The shadow belongs to being human and, where there are humans there are shadows. When we have an encounter with someone who tries to live without their shadow they appear superficial—appearing like 2-D stereotypes or like a cut-out doll. Encounters with our shadow give us depth and 'make us human' (see the interviews). Where there is great light there is a great shadow and there is no exception to this within the BSR context. One big difference in my experience is the aim and awareness among the BSR leaders to consciously relate to the shadow constellated in the group and be aware of integrating it into the whole, including addressing

---

71 See Marion Woodman, *Addiction to Perfection: The Still Unravished Bride,* for a full understanding of this split.

72 Referring to the post-Newtonian area of physics where light is at once both particles and waves. What aspect of the light one sees depends on the experiment used to determine its nature. This gives rise to the understanding that our subjective attitude influences what we see, and the absolute nature of things is relativized. This generates introducing the concept of both/ and (instead of either/ or) Marion Woodman, *Conscious Femininity: Interviews with Marion Woodman,* p. 51.

73 Since this manuscript was written, I have been introduced to Iain McGilchrist's work that gives a new understanding of living with paradox, see Iain McGilchrist, *The Master and His Emissary.*

it openly in the field and allowing it to be shared. The BSR work happens in a group context where the shadow is invited in and allowed its expression. The shadow itself contains huge energy and is often the fuel that brings the work to a much deeper level. It is often the fire that burn away sentimentality and the sword that can cut through what Marion refer to as "artificial love" (that in reality binds the other and thrives on "symbiotic sameness"). It is shown that women in groups tend to hold each other back and strive for "sameness." Sticking out in any way constellates "sister-envy." With the amount of gifts the women in the BSR context share it takes a great deal of shadow work to allow for the participants to blossom in their individuality within the group.

The awareness of the shadow and the unfailing constellation of shadow material, both in relation to the BSR as such, in the group, among group members and within oneself is invited to be voiced and attended too consciously. The idealization of the group leaders constellates the opposite—the shadow—and not to identify with either of the opposites, but to be able to hold the still point between the two, is stressed. Equally the humanity of the shadow is stressed, which makes it open to reflections and investigations, rather than denial. Envy towards other women in the group becomes a vehicle for taking responsibility for one's disowned sides or it might dissolve when the deeper stories are shared. Also all groups will create a shadow—aspects not accepted or appreciated in the group can easily make the group rigid and exclusive. Consciously attending to the shadow dynamics of the group, fosters a spirit in the group of staying flexible and inclusive. In the BSR intensives, shadow work is encouraged. There is a dialogue on the process of taking responsibility for one's own shadow and to work with it. This work is modelled by the leaders, voicing their shadow aspects and bringing shadow aspect to awareness openly in the group. Naturally, there will always be shadow material around, but the attitude towards it opens up the possibility of working with it and bringing it into consciousness as much as possible. Especially on day three of the intensives, when the energy starts to "cook" and dynamics in the group gets going, the facilitator's awareness and capacity to hold the shadow as well have a huge impact. Marion usually quotes the line from poet W.H. Auden:

> You shall love your crooked neighbor
> With your crooked heart.[74]

This usually drops the whole group into a deeper awareness. The consciousness around the shadow in relation to the leader/ apprentices is held in awareness as much as possible. The apprentices have meetings with the leaders to process and to learn. There is quiet awareness about group dynamics among the leaders. Naturally, often the leaders receive the idealized

---

74 W.H. Auden, from the poem "As I Walked Out One Evening," *Another Time*, p. 45.

projections, whereas the shadow stuff often will come out in relation to the apprentices or the owners of the residence. This happens naturally. One will go to the apprentices to confess what one is dissatisfied with. The whole difference is whether one is conscious of this dynamic or not. When one is, one can hold it with more consciousness and process it. It can be brought to consciousness and worked with. When done in the group as such, the energy released from the constellated shadow fuels into the work and becomes the heat that can take it to a deeper level.

Part II

Interviews: The Subjective Lived Experience

Introduction to the Interviews—
The Sound of the Underground River

In Part I, I focused on describing the structure and the form of the BSR work—the conso-nants in Helen Luke's metaphor.[75] I would like now to invite the reader to a journey into the world of the vowels—the deeper sounds creating the individual stories by including the transcripts of the interviews with six women.

They are all very gifted, deep and conscious women, who so generously have shared with me their deep thoughts and inner subjective experience of the BodySoul Rhythms work and their own process in relation to that.

Each interview has its own form and emphasis, reflecting my focus on trying to capture whatever had been unique for the individual I was sitting in front of and talking with. Each interview is a testimony of the soul's journey and an account of what moves the soul: what makes it dare to trust, and what seems to matter for psychic transformation and for the soul to feel received.

The six women interviewed carry wisdom reflected in their words, each contributing to this work with her rich and multi-faceted background and deep insights. They are an equal balance of introverted and extraverted, sensate, intuitive, thinking and feeling types. Their ages range from 41 to 64 years and they come from four different countries. They have all been in Jungian analysis for 6–16 years and are deeply committed to their inner work. They have all completed the BSR leadership training program.

Each woman has been asked how she prefers to be introduced and whether she prefers to appear anonymously or with her given name. The introduction of each interview is presented with respect to these wishes. Five women wished to include a more extended biography; these biographies are included at the end of this book. Also there has been a dialogue in the process of writing up the interviews, and each woman has approved the final form.

Each interview has been given a title reflecting some of its essence. Poems referred to or liked by the interviewee are added to the individual stories (some are repeated but, in respect for the interviewee, they are included). I ask the reader to receive the stories of these women with care and appreciation, hoping that you will be touched too, by their beauty and willing-ness to share.

---

75 Helen Luke, *Such Stuff as Dreams are Made On.*

LOVE MATTERS FOR PSYCHIC TRANSFORMATION

"Being Held in the Mist of Despair"

There is a kindness that dwells deep down in things;
It presides everywhere,
Often in places we least expect.
The world can be harsh and negative, but if we remain generous and patient,
Kindness inevitably reveals itself.
Something deep in the human soul seems to depend on the presence of kindness;
Something instinctive in us expects it,
And once we sense it we are able to trust and open ourselves.[76]

Introduction

This woman has asked to stay anonymous and will be introduced as 'Lynn.'

Maja: How long have you been involved in the BodySoul Rhythms work?

Lynn: I started back around 2000 so it is more than a decade now.

Maja: And what drew you into this work?

Lynn: I believe it was my unconscious. At that time I had just started as a student at the C.G. Jung institute in Zürich. They have a marvellous old library there. It is very tiny but the atmosphere was special. As I walked around, a book fell off the shell. I picked it up. It was Marion Woodman's book, *Addiction to Perfection*."[77] Now, if you are Jungian and a book falls down in front of your feet, you read it! I remember sitting in my study room turning page after page thinking "How could she know—this is just how I feel." It deeply touched something within me that I had never been able to put into words before. Here was someone who knew these things from her own experience and who had worked with it. I marked some especially moving pages and went to the students copy room to make a copy so I could bring them to my analysis. As I was copying a student entered the room. I could see she was under time pressure so I invited her to copy before me. She asked me what I was to copying. I told her about the incredible book by Marion Woodman. "Oh" she said, "Do you know that Marion Woodman teaches workshops too? I believe the next is going to be here in Switzerland." Somehow inside I knew that that was what I had

---

76 John O'Donohue, *To Bless the Space Between Us*, p. 185.
77 Woodman, *Addiction to Perfection*.

to do. So within a week I had signed up for the first BodySoul Rhythms Intensive. The synchronicity of the string of events still touches me today.

Maja: Do you have any memories of what words Marion Woodman said in her book that sparked your soul?

Lynn: I believe it was her images and her way of writing to the body. My struggles were connected to my body. I could speak about it for hours without anything moving, but here, in Marion's writings, my body felt heard. It was as if the body recognized what she described. For the first time my body felt heard and mirrored in its struggles, not just being wronged or neglected because it would not behave. There was a voice inviting my body to tell her untold stories and something made me believe that it was "perhaps possible" to do so without being shamed to silence.

Maja: From your telling, I understand you were in analysis at the time. What did you hope that BodySoul Rhythms could give you that were not possible within the frame of one-to-one analysis?

Lynn: It could give me a place and a space for embodiment and a possibility to share with like-minded women. I believe the community of women doing this work together, sharing with each other and supporting each other in the process is rather unique. It helps you step over a threshold you might never had dared to pass on your own.

Crossing that threshold to share the shamed parts of my body was something that I could not do in my own analysis. It felt so vulnerable. Sometimes I felt that if I were to let it out, it would not be able to be told within an analytical hour. In the BSR work you have the continuity of immersion. In a seven-day cycle the psyche can trust that it can go to its deepest places and still have the time to process and come back up again. You can touch themes so deep that without the soul time to digest and assimilate them would leave you fragmented. I think the soul responds when there is this continuous time. The intensives are unbroken concentration. But I want to stress that the one-to-one analysis is a profound and deep process too. I see the two as complementary to each other.

Maja: You mentioned the word 'embodiment' and the longing for embodiment...

Lynn: The longing for embodiment was a deep longing to live in my body, to feel myself present in my body and to love being me in my body. I longed to start to feel the love and joy I knew lived in my body. In my childhood my body had always been told it was too this, too that, and another thing and that it should be in another way. My body was seen as an object to be corrected. I longed to set my body free as a living being, a subject in its

LOVE MATTERS FOR PSYCHIC TRANSFORMATION

own right. I feel this is what the BSR work opened up to: loving who I am in my body soul in the present moment.

Maja: What was your first experience of the BSR like?

Lynn: It was very intense. My ego got me there but on arrival it was as if my soul took over. Something that had waited so long to have a voice found a place to express itself. I made a mask that embodied a deep cry from the neglected and abandoned part of me. She incarnated hunger—a hunger for love that was immensely painful to contain and therefore had been frozen down for decades. What was it that allowed this pain to dare to trust and voice itself in the workshop? It is hard for me to put to words because the answer lies beyond the words, but I'll try. First there was a sense that all the women knew these places, and were in touch with them and working through them. Then there was a sense of deep containment that allowed my body to begin to trust. It felt it could be held in all the chaos and despair that emerged from inside - held in a loving holding presence. Today I am so grateful for that holding. I wonder if all the stuff had come out anyway—because it wanted to—as a child being born. Potentially it could have been dropped on the floor. But it was not. There where psychic midwives who welcomed it gentle and held it.

Maja: After this first experience what made you go back?

Lynn: I just knew I had to. I have a rather strong intuition. And I just sensed I had to if I was to be true to myself. I knew this work was healing for me. I knew it was tough and hard and difficult, but I knew I had to go down that path. After the first workshop the conscious connection to these broken parts in me had been made and I went back and worked hard with it in my personal analysis. I had the sense that this rhythm of doing deep body soul work in the BSR intensives and integrating it over the next half year in my personal analysis was essential for me.

Maja: What you are saying is that your personal ongoing analysis, in parallel with the BSR intensives is very important?

Lynn: Certainly! My mind tends to be very busy with everyday stuff, planning, schedules, the whole realm of 'doing.' I feel the structure of the workshop creates a container for inner work. Through the deep immersion in the archetypal realm, the dream work, the movement through the body into the symbolic process, a frame is created that enables profound inner work. In the intensives I was immersed in the work for a week, deeply listening to the body soul. Going for an intensive is leaving the ordinary going into the extraordinary. Going into BodySoul space. You have nothing to do but to tend to your inner work. I am rather introverted so I loved to have the silence in the morning. I would get up early, spend an hour with my diary and then go for a morning run. In the breaks I would paint or sleep. I always went into a very concentrated introverted room in myself held by the loving containment of the group and the leaders. And it was all right. It can be rather troublesome to be an introvert in our extraverted culture. But here was a community where it was all right. It did not exclude you but included you. The introverted sides were not seen as odd, boring, slow or loners but merely as part of a spectrum balancing the other pole of the spectrum. So I felt included in my introversion. That was such a relief. I did not have to "play extraverted" and feeling exhausted afterwards. I could just be.

I think the sense of being able to follow one's soul and having mirrored that it is all right has been one of the most healing lived experiences I have received.

Gradually over the years I could internalize the accepting and loving holding and the encouraging mirroring. I still recall the deep love and encouragement from the eyes of Mary, Ann, and Marion in times of inner uncertainty.

Maja: I would like to go back to your first workshop. What else do you remember?

Lynn: I remember a meeting with Mary. The workshop was held at Landegg in Switzerland. There was a footpath right on the top of a mountain ridge. Along the ridge was a little simple chapel for the divine Mary. It was a very early morning in spring. The sun was rising and I was out running. I passed the chapel and stopped. I stood there, thinking about the divine feminine and taking in the peaceful atmosphere of the chapel. I was raised in an atheist family and had been working in my own analysis to find my relationship to the divine. Through my dreams and inner work there had been an opening to the divine feminine that felt as balsam in relation to a family story where the feminine had been very wounded and wounding. As I turned away to continue my run I saw Mary Hamilton in a distance walking towards me. I started to walk too. She held out her arms for a big embrace. She looked into my eyes with love, as if she was embracing me with her gaze. Because of the morning silence we kept silent too. Mary simply looked into my eyes and gave me a long hug, holding my hands and looking deep into my eyes again. That gaze was transformative. I saw a love and acceptance for who I am. It was as if her soul touched my soul and something changed in me on a deep level. I had always thought that I could love but not be loved. I had a tiny sprout of hope that I could lean into the divine feminine and find comfort and love. But at this moment I felt it was possible in the human realm too: that I could be met with love and acceptance. And it was unconditional you see, I had not done anything to deserve it except "being me." This morning I was embraced by unconditional love on a mountain ridge in Switzerland and things turned from "never possible" to "maybe—because I have tried it once!"

Looking back over the intensives there has been many of these transformative key moments. These were moments of meeting that has meant profound healing for me. Moments that went beyond the wounds healing them at the deepest level.

Maja: Would you like to share other such moments?

Lynn: Yes, I recall another workshop in Grimstone, England. I woke up early in the morning filled with some very horrifying images from my dreams. I went down to the painting room and painted them. I could hardly stand painting them. I was filled with horror, pain, fear and a wish to freeze, not feeling. But I knew it was important. I painted from 5 o'clock to 9 o'clock in the morning. When the morning session started, I was there, yet not really there. Somehow Ann sensed that and made her way over to me. I told her about the pictures and she asked if I would like to share them. We sneaked out from the morning session. I showed her the three images. The first was an image of a frozen uterus, the second of a bleeding and injured uterus and the third depicted a woman being raped by two men. The images were horrifying. I remember she just stood behind me holding me because I cried and cried and cried. I felt that she sensed with her body what my body was going through and she was just there - supporting, staying there, not trying to get ahead, to create meaning, to put it into words. She was simply there and she stayed. Many things where healing in these moments, but most important was the sense that she was not destroyed with what I shared, neither by my sadness. I sensed she would stay there with me which made me dare to stay with it too. I was not a burden to her because I contained all these horrible feelings. When there were no more tears and all the images had told their story I remember her saying: "Would you like to come with me into the main room again? You can sit close to me." I nodded and we went in. Together with the apprentices, she created a little nest of pillows and people sitting. And then she said a line that has stayed with me since: "You need some good mothering." For the next two hours during the morning session I just felt Ann's warm body and her hand on my back, I felt the woman holding my feet and another supporting my lower back. I lay there under blankets and something was just healing—I was maybe the two-week-old infant feeling safe and held. An experience I had not had when I was two-weeks-old.

Years later I discovered that the images were my mother's untold story. Somehow my unconscious had picked it up and held it. I feel her story has been held and enabled to heal together with mine, through the shared stories of many women in the BSR group and through the archetypal level that the BSR-work opens up to.

Maja: You shared that you have this very clear image and body memory from the BodySoul workshop of being held in the midst of despair. And you said you had never had that experience of being held in that kind of way before. What were the steps before that, what was it that somehow conveyed to you, that you could go there, how was it initiated? Is there anything that you can voice that led you to that kind of trust?

Lynn: The wound in me is a wound of neglect. That means that when something happens to me, as it did that morning, the first step of healing was that "someone held me in mind." Ann noticed and reacted to the fact that I was not all right. That place in me was "found." When she offered to see my pictures I sensed an invitation to share from this place that at the time did not know words. The sharing was a very bodily feeling because I sensed that she sensed the pictures in her body, and somehow she could contain that and therefore contain it with me—before that sharing it had felt uncontainable. She was there, beyond words—and she kept being there. She did not leave or became occupied with something else—she stayed making me feel that what was being shared did not disgust her away. And then it was as if she sensed the two-week-old baby's need to just integrate. Just to be. To feel safe, to feel "mother was there." It was a space that for all kind of reasons had not been there in my early childhood. But it was not only my story that was transformed—it echoed healing to my mother's story as well. And Ann's story too I sensed. So it was not just receiving something that has been missing, it was sharing the pain with someone who can hold it through her knowing of her own wounds. And it was also integrating the dis-integrated parts in me and learning to be a good mother for myself. It was a cornerstone in re-writing my own story.

Maja: What was your motivation to keep coming back into the context again and again?

Lynn: I had too. It was an intuitive feeling - I sensed that it was crucial to continue with this work. I never really thought about the Leadership training. It just happened as part of the process. For me the process itself was what propelled me. Also I felt a bond with like-minded women. I have always been drawn to the inner life and not always been at ease with the more extraverted sides of life. Here was a community with women sharing my interest and at the same time room for being introverted.

The experience of sharing life at that level in a continuous process throughout all these years with women from most parts of the world and with an age range between 28 years old and 78 years old is an invaluable gift. You are exposed to the diversity of the stories of everyone else. Just to share that . . . These women have opened my mind and heart for the beauty of the diversity of the soul.

Maja: We spoke earlier today about the mother wound and the personal mothers. In terms of the process around your own personal mother, what did it mean to you to be amongst other women, hearing their stories and sharing?

Lynn: Something in me was opened up by their sharing. On the level of mothers, daughters, and grandmothers' stories—I heard so many stories from all perspectives; sufferings, struggles and shared joys that I have more compassion now. I can see my personal mother's wounds and her story with empathy now. I think I feel my personal story has been linked to the story of all women. My mother has never entered therapy which has been a great pain to me. But sharing her story and mine in the group of women seems to have created a sense of tribal healing. It is very special to be part of generations of women who are sharing. Something I find that we sadly have lost in our western culture.

I recall an episode at a workshop during which there were bombings in Palestine. In our group we had both Jews and Palestinians. They started to share their pain, their losses, their fears and their grief. And then they started spontaneously to embrace each other and then the whole group, including many Irish women who carried similar pains from the civil war, started to connect in what seemed as one big embrace. We were all standing crying and comforting each other, sharing the pain of loss and grief through generations. That was a very moving experience. It was an experience that created hope for the possibility of communal healing.

Another important aspect of the sharing was that it eased the shame. Through the context of hearing the stories from others, I began to heal some of the shame about my own wounds. That was a profound thing for me. I did not have to sit there ashamed of my wounds. Shame maintains the wound; it feeds the internalized voices that carry on wounding, which then evokes more shame and guilt. My wounds, being in my mind, particularly dark in the way it revealed themselves—all of a sudden I could see the soul. I could feel the pain that my soul was actually going through. I could see that this is part of the human range, that it was the way that my body-soul tried to express the wounds that I had encountered.

That is also where the container, which resonates with what Marion, Ann, and Mary are holding, is felt so strongly. The container is held through the energy that they can contain. I believe that and it has been my experience on a feeling level. I think that Marion, Ann, and Mary, both in my projections onto them, but also who they are as human beings, are very containing.

Maja: Both Mary, Ann, and Marion do share their own wounds. What do you think that has done for you or to you? It is a bit unusual in an analytical setting with that openness on both sides.

Lynn: It helped me to respect my own wounds and to work with them as part of my individuation process. It enabled me to look at the grace of the new energy that emerged from the other side of the archetype or complex: the new positive energy. It reflects that the positive and the negative are two parts of the same process. When Marion, Ann or Mary share their personal story of their own psychic difficulties and especially because of the way they do it, it opens me to realize that this just is the human story. It is human.

When a story is shared on that level of the human condition the story is voiced in the present by one particular person but the relationship around the symbol can be reflected back and shared in the group, and it can enable transformation in others as well.

Maja: We have talked about the positive mother constellated. What about the negative mother?

Lynn: It is quiet natural that there would be a lot of negative mother constellated in this kind of setting as well. Both negative mother and sister envy. I think that is part of all women's group. The big issue is your attitude towards it and whether you deal with it consciously or not. From a Jungian perspective it is natural that when you engage with the positive mother, the negative mother is bound to be constellated as well. They are two parts of the same archetype. Accepting and respecting that you can then start to work with it consciously. In the inner process the responsibility starts when the negative mother gets constellated within yourself. Bringing it to consciousness, realizing what constellated the feelings and why, working with it is all part of the process.

And the same was true in the group. Working consciously in the group with the shadow aspects that where bound to be constellated.

Actually, it is the first time where I have been given an opportunity to be in a group sharing like that over years where the group dynamic could actually be worked on consciously.

Maja: Were there parts of you that felt sceptical as well, and if so, what was the scepticism about?

Lynn: I am a quite pragmatic person so my scepticism would come in when sentimentality or over-focusing on the positive aspects would be too predominant in the surfacing constellations in the group. To me it needs to be grounded in an authentic reality. And I have to say that I found the BSR-work and its leaders are very grounded. But there is a seductive force in such groups that want to make it fly. I think it is because we wish to get away from the shadow stuff, because it is so hard work. But when we stay with it, it is also where real transformation takes place.

Maja: Have you sometimes experienced that some of the more extraverted women would voice issues in the group where you, as a more introverted soul, would sit and think "that [experience] is parallel to mine."

Lynn: Yes, that is exactly what I meant by what I said previously. When something came up, voiced by someone in the group, I could reflect on where that was meaningful for me. Definitely, I think it takes many different types of energy for the group to flow, it can't all flow through extroversion neither through introversion, and I think there is always a balance in the BSR intensives. The other thing that helped me was my experience as apprentice. Throughout the process we are being emerged as participant in the group work. Then, during the apprenticeship, something really important changed for me. A completion was felt by seeing this other side. As such I was actually seeing how this energy works and learning by seeing how Marion, Ann, and Mary witness the energy flowing in the group. As a participant you don't see this. And if we did, it would be a distraction because transformation comes mainly from your subjective experience and you need to stay with that. But when we apprentice, we see how this dynamic works, not from a distance but from being engaged in creating the workshop. And we experience the inner wisdom of the rhythms of this soul work. You see where to put the emphasis, where to hold more, where to encourage more. It is a very good structured program in the way it works from the different stages of the intensive to the seminar and to the apprenticeship. It gives a real grounding in the body and an authentic voice. You get the experience of this rhythm working as apprentice.

Maja: You spoke about how your own process was enriched by hearing other women's stories. Do you feel that there is also a communal healing taking place—for the collective feminine?

Lynn: Yes I do believe that. As I have emphasized earlier I think those shared moments holding the shared pain are transformative. It gives a lived experience of a possibility for synthesis that can counterbalance the diatheses that often is the focus when we hear stories in the news. You see such moments create the hope. There is a bond formed. Your question reminds me of a story I was told by a friend. There was a conflict between the indigenous people living in an area and some white people claiming the land. They could not agree upon where the old boundaries were. The whole thing had escalated; there had been fights, threats and occupation of the land. The negotiation had broken down and the moment was critical. Then all the grandmothers from the indigenous tribe armed themselves with big mugs of hot coffee (it was freezing wintertime) and aligned themselves. Then they started to walk towards the frontier created by the other group. Slowly, like a big field they preceded forward, holding out the coffee, offering it to the other side. And miraculously the group of hardened men stepped down from their defensive barricades and took the coffee. And in sharing the coffee, they started to share stories about the land, the family stories, and they found what they actually had in common. Relating opened the door to transformation. The conflict found a solution but it took the courage of the grandmothers to create that possibility. Now back to the BSR-community I do believe that healing for the collective feminine is taking place through sharing our stories and creating connections.

Maja: In terms of how Marion, Ann, and Mary honor the feminine during the intensives, how do you see that honoring come forth? Where do you feel the feminine is honored?

Lynn: For me the feminine is alive when there is no pretending and when life is fully accepted. When all that is emerging through the work is welcomed and given space. I think the feminine… the way it is honored… is that whatever "she" … wherever that energy is in our bodies, it is encouraged to live. It is the aliveness. It is the life force itself. You get a glimpse of it in an uninhibited movement Mary would make. It is the honesty of the movement in the body, in the whole being, and it is the beauty. It is the rewarding feeling that arises, when that is witnessed and experienced as the feminine, then that becomes the lived experience of what that soul expresses in that immediate connection.

Another level is related to the mother issue—just to experience that whole spectrum of mothers in the group. That is one of the transformative experiences I have received too.

The sharing between generations and between bodies also expands the honoring and vision of the feminine too. I have witnessed the most courageous stories from a 77-year-old in our group who transformed her life… you see the cultural view on age is tragic. The value of the wisdom in lived experience and the sense that we stand on the shoulders of generations before us creates a sense of belonging that we dramatically are losing in our culture. Through the BSR–work I got a sense of belonging to a community of women searching to live their life as authentic as possible.

I mentioned age, and I want to stress bodies too. In my upbringing there was such a focus on the physical appearance, [as there is in our culture now, MR]. Many people only relate to their body as an object which is supposed to look this, that, or another way. To move into a deep acceptance of the journey of the soul in this body on this earth is quite something. It does not have to be judged in different phases as good or bad. It is just living in a body on earth. Through the BSR work I was exposed to the transformation of that complex, which I would never have been, had it not been for the BSR. I would have had met it in more diluted forms. In the BSR group there is a big amount of it: seeing the soul in every type of body that she wants to be in. Embodied soul and soulful bodies.

Maja: Are there any other moments that stand out from the ten intensives that come to your mind. A moment where something just shifted—maybe an insight, a special kind of movement, a painting, something said. Whatever comes to your mind whenever you go over that long line of workshops? Are there any such moments that you would like to share?

Lynn: I think it is the gaze of Marion. The sense of her holding what I was not yet able to hold. Through her containment my own capacity for containing my own feelings of loneliness, despair and sadness grew. She holds a presence that the tiniest bit of consciousness can refer itself too.

I recall a meeting I had with Marion. It was after a morning session and she came up to me and said she had been wondering how I was doing and asked if we should go for a walk. It was early spring at Grimstone, in Devon, England. The very first sun was out and I could feel the ground coming alive. Marion had injured her foot so we walked arm in arm up to a little bench. We sat down and Marion held my hand and just looked at me.

And there I was, with all my vulnerability, and injuries, and she just looked at me. Normally, I would have felt too naked to stay in that place. Normally, I would have covered myself in layers of smiling defences. But Marion just looked at me and somehow I could meet her eye and stay in her gaze. I could be seen without fading away in shame. I saw into her eyes.

And I found myself in her gaze. It was as though the true me that had been hidden for so long came alive in the gleam of her eyes. I did not have to please, to comfort or to mirror her. I could concentrate on daring to be seen. And in her gaze I found love for what she saw. It was as if her loving gaze enabled me to grow a loving gaze towards myself. I think I felt as one of the daffodils emerging above the ground for the first time. It's not easy to put into words because it all happened beyond words. It lives now in my body.

There are other moments too. I have one beautiful image that is like a poem in my mind right now. That is the image of Marion doing her blessing in the mornings and opening the altar. That holds me too. Jung speaks about the ultimate task: to find what holds you when nothing else holds. I feel that the opening to the space or place or energy greater than the ego has been such a shift and a relief in my journey. By relief, I mean that the ego did not have to hold it all. Though terrifying for an ego addicted to perfection there is a great relief in the surrender. To me, Marion enabled this opening by stepping into the space when she did her blessing in front of the altar. There is a great place of scepticism in me that does not easily rely on anything beyond the ego. But my soul responded to the opening knowing and feeling the connection. The opening and surrendering is a feeling in my body now, on a cellular level. It is difficult to describe but it is like a warm embrace that fill me with gratitude when it visits me.

In a way, all the moments by the altar have formed into a condensed feeling imagery—like a poem of all the many lived mornings of the intensives. A lot of the time, special moments appeared from something that Ann, Mary, or Marion would talk about or do and it would hold me. Moments where I felt a sense of being held so I could heal. It reminds me of a profound holding I experienced one time working with Mary. That was a key moment too.

Maja: Would you like to tell why?

Lynn: I had had a series of dream images about my body. At that time I carried a lot of shame about my body. I had made drawings of the dreams and Mary spontaneously volunteered to work with the dream-pictures with me. It was like shedding layers of shame. And I think it was only possible because I could sense Mary was with me. She stayed and stayed as my body shed layers of shame, arriving at the true body hidden underneath. A strong and vibrant body full of life. It was her presence that help my body learn to unfold itself without shame. My body learned to hold the images that were expressed in the dreams. I can't put more words to it. I have not got them. It was in the cells.

Maja: Can you reflect back on how she was when she worked on the dream with you?

Lynn: I feel an immense concentrated presence and then I see her eyes, and I think that is important—there is a containing in the gaze. I see her eyes and I feel her body. I feel the energy from her, just present. She is not blocking anything. That encounter has become a role model for me to work with.

Maja: And as you look into those eyes what did you see?

Lynn: I actually saw myself. I don't know if that makes any sense, but I could see myself—unthreatened.

Maja: And what did you receive from her body?

Lynn: Comfort, and a deep commitment to the soul. It is a deeply felt commitment that I feel in Ann, Marion and Mary. That is the true gift. To get the resonance of how seriously they takes the soul's life. It impacts you deeply. It is a gift to have worked around women like that.

Maja: You said how seriously they take the soul—what does that do to you?

Lynn: It makes my own journey worthwhile. There are so many times when I am working on some small thing connected to my own suffering, and I think, "Oh no not again. It is too much. I can't take it anymore." I have a counterpoint to those voices because Marion, Ann, and Mary and what they teach is an example of the counterpoint to that inner voice.

They have helped me to learn that every single thought and every image is worthwhile, and not to judge. I have been given a lived experience of a counter-voice from that encounter with the BSR work. I think that is what BSR has done.

Maja: You spoke about how Marion's opening of the altar holds you. It is a bit controversial to have a workshop with an altar in the middle where the leader starts the morning with a prayer to Sophia. Could you speak to that?

Lynn: I know it might feel controversial and in some ways it might be. But I think this type of work is bound to be controversial because it does not adapt to the collective but strives to give space to the soul. Somehow I think there is a collective longing to have a living relationship with what we in Jungian terms would call the Self. But it is a delicate theme to work with. There is a fine balance between New Age stuff and old doctrines. I love the line from Rilke's poem: 'They fed it, not with corn, but only with the possibility of being.'[78] I think that is the art. To create a potential space where the individual can open up to the Self and whatever images that is represented by for that individual.

If we take out our relationships to the divine, something else steps into the space. I feel mammon often has been what has taken up the space—at least in the culture where I grew up. I have sensed in myself a longing to reconnect to whatever we call that which is bigger than the ego. I believe the answer has to be found within us. Marion tending to the altar creates a possibility for us to tend to that inner place in our selves.

Not only that, but because that realm is honored so explicitly in the BodySoul group, it creates a community with whom I can discuss these issues. That has been tremendous important for me too.

Maja: How is the BodySoul Rhythms, and the work you have done in the intensives alive within you right now?

Lynn: It is alive through a deep love for my own body and soul. I live in my body now and I can feel the joy that is alive in a body that is loved. There is tenderness in the way I approach myself today. "It's all right sweetheart." There is more humor—humor that can embrace the sadness and struggles and still find the laugh.

There is a great respect for the psyche's profound way to heal itself if we dare to listen. The BodySoul knows where it needs to go. The surrender of the ego to that wisdom is a living practice in me now.

---

78 R.M. Rilke, *Selected Poems*, p. 69.

There is also the BodySoul community. All these unique women I have met and shared stories with across the world. That is profound. The world is now mapped with friendships and a shared interest in the BodySoul—and then, of course, all the key moments with Ann, Mary, and Marion. They stand as turning points, openings, and transforming moments in me as I live right now. The gesture to capture the essence would be eyes and arms wide open embracing the day in a fully alive BodySoul.

"Reclaiming the Rubedo"
Marlene Schiwy & Maja Reinau

I said to my soul, be still, and wait without hope
For hope would be hope for the wrong thing; wait without love
For love would be love for the wrong thing; there is yet faith
But the faith and the love and the hope are all in the waiting.
Wait without thought, for you are not ready for thought:
So the darkness shall be the light, and the stillness the dancing.[79]

Introduction

Marlene is a workshop leader and author, and does Jungian work with individual clients. A former professor of literature, women's studies, and creative writing, with a background in music and psychology; soul-work has been the essence of Marlene's personal life and vocational calling. She completed the first Leadership Training Program in 2004 and teaches Affiliated Workshops in Canada, the USA, and Europe. From 2005 to 2007 she studied at International School of Analytical Psychology (ISAP), Zurich. Marlene has had a lifelong love of creative process and finds great fulfilment in helping others to explore their own buried creativity and make contact with the deep archetypal images that carry their life energy (see Biographical background).

Maja: Would you like to tell us what drew you to the BodySoul Rhythms work?

Marlene: I had been reading Marion's work through the eighties [1980s] and early nineties. I think the first book I read was *The Pregnant Virgin* and I felt it was profoundly important for my life. I was resonating and vibrating as I read it. I think many of us had that experience and, although I did not always understand it, something in me knew it deeply and

---

79 T.S. Eliot, *Complete Poems and Plays: 1909–1950*, pp. 126-127.

LOVE MATTERS FOR PSYCHIC TRANSFORMATION

I felt it was true to my life. So when I was writing my first book, I thought about who I would like to have writing my Foreword and Marion was my first choice. I actually went to a one-day workshop that she did in Manhattan, called 'Women in the Second Half of Life.' I think they defined that as forty and I was probably just forty, but half of the women in the group were younger than that anyway. They just wanted to hear Marion speak. I did not want to bother Marion with my request then. However, I did ask if she would recieve a letter if I addressed it to her publisher in Toronto, and she said yes. So I wrote to her by way of her publisher and she agreed to write the Foreword.

At some point as we were speaking on the telephone she told me about the BodySoul Rhythms program and added, "This is something you might be interested in." I imagine she said that based on our conversation and on her reading of my book. So finally, in early 2000, I was able to get to an intensive. That was just before my husband and I were moving from New York to Vancouver, literally six weeks before we moved. But I knew I had to go and thankfully my husband felt it too, so I did go. And that experience opened up a whole new world. At that time I also asked her [Marion] if she knew of any Jungian training that was not based at a training institute and she said quietly that she, Mary Hamilton and Ann Skinner were just beginning a new training program. The timing was just perfect for me. This was where my soul wanted to go, and here was the perfect opportunity to enter in.

That first intensive was at Kripalu, Massachusetts, at the old yoga center. The one-day workshop in Manhattan had already had a deep effect on me. I remember my husband picking me up afterward and asking, "How was the workshop?" I thought, "I don't know how to answer that," and I told him, "It's not like any other workshop I have ever been to." It was amazing. There were probably 150 women there, but in the final dance we did, we were weaving around in such a way that Marion was able to make eye contact with every single person in the group. First of all there was a feeling that once you have been looked at by Marion you have really been seen. There is no hiding from that gaze. I found that beautiful and profound.

Also we did a short version of the Dance of Three. At that time she was using head, heart and body as metaphor, rather than mover, mirror and witness [or dancer, mirror and container, MR]. I just loved it, and I loved being with the two other women and that close trio of holding each other and witnessing a soul expressing itself, and being witnessed that way myself. That was already quite beautiful and made quite an impression on me. But the other thing that I felt was—I had actually invited an older friend and colleague of mine who taught with me—and she said it too, and she had not been familiar with Marion's work, nor read anything and she said: "You feel like she loves you, and you know she does not know you personally, so there is something else going on." I have never been at a workshop where I felt that kind of love and felt that I almost could not talk about it because it might just sound "airy fairy" or unreal. And I knew it was real. I felt it, I lived in it, and so I just tried to answer my husband's question as honestly as I could. I said, "I have never been in a workshop where I felt that kind of loving warmth and energy." It was really more than a human love in a way, because Marion did not know most of us personally, and yet there was that enormous personal sense of a bond, a sense of being seen, and a sense of being loved and accepted.

Maja: When you say "seen" and "loved"—can you say a little about what it did to your body?

Marlene: It already started with the first exercise that she had us do. She said: "Ladies, have you got mirrors with you?" Then she added, "Ladies you all have mirrors, we spend our whole lives fixing our lipstick so you must have a mirror!" So we ducked into our handbags and found mirrors and she asked us to look at our faces in the mirror and to note what we felt as we were looking into our own faces. I am trying to remember honestly what my response was. I do remember that the very way she encouraged us to do that invited kindness towards ourselves. I felt I was looking at myself with a kind of gentleness and maybe a lot less judgment than I would have had otherwise. I don't know if everybody felt that. Afterward she asked us to share our experience and there were people who said, "I could not believe what contempt I felt, or what self-rejection." I remember writing about it and that I was surprised because I expected to feel more dismissive toward myself. "This is my face in that mirror, what is the relationship to who I am?" And there was a lot of kindness and gentleness there.

Then Marion asked us to look into our mirrors again to see if we could see our mother's faces there and to note what that brought up in us. And again I did not feel the judgement of myself that I thought I would feel, and I am sure that was partly her influence. I also felt that so much of what I had read of hers was so alive in me, that the work was already going on before I met her. A lot of the work was alive in me even before I went to that workshop.

What did it do to my body? It's almost hard to remember, because I feel I am in a different body now than I was ten years ago. Not necessarily physically but it is a different body—it's a loved body—it is home in a different way—it is so hard to even try and put it into words. Maybe I can talk about the first intensive and then see how it evolved over the course of the following intensives. My experience was fairly compressed. Some people were working with her [Marion] in the 1990s. My first intensive was in 2000, although I had been reading her work for at least fifteen years and living with it so closely. I remember a lot of things. Feeling that this was really altered space, because Kripalu was in some sense the most restrictive of all the places. It was my least favorite of all the places. Strict vegan food and I thought, "How am I going to deal with no coffee?" I mean, I can deal without sugar but not without coffee—so I even smuggled in my coffee and felt like a criminal sitting in the back of the cafeteria with my coffee fumes around me!

But I remember the silence at breakfast, and feeling that once we met that first night we really were in a kind of liminal space and something was going to happen that week that I could not foresee that some part of me was probably terrified of. Another part was completely fascinated and curious and wondering how it would unfold, and then feeling so many mixed feelings. I remember the Dance of Three the first time and how profound that was. I'd probably always wanted to dance, but in my religious background that was considered sinful, so my body from early on did not dance but carried tremendous suppressed longing to do so. Then to dance the Dance of Three, which I might have thought would make me self-conscious; I just remember weeping with ecstasy all the way through it. And I remember how lovely that was and how my body felt seen and honored and free to move, and ecstatic. I felt like I had waited all my life for something like this to happen. For someone to hold me with that attention, and to be able to move that freely. I did not mind that tears were rolling down my face the whole time—I was just so happy. And of course I loved the Chopin (the Dance of Three is danced to the music of Chopin). I loved the whole experience.

After the intensive was over Marion asked me if I would write down my experiences, any feedback I had, and send it to her. And so I did. My overall impressions had to do with being immersed in loving attention. I remember that during the morning sessions, when Marion was talking and we were all gathered around her and doing dream work, I would look around the room and see Ann on one side, and Mary on the other and, in the middle, the three apprentices. Wherever I looked, somebody's eyes looked back at me with loving attention and usually a smile. Something warm. And I told Marion I felt like we were at kindergarten with all kinds of teachers there who loved us—no matter where we looked, somebody looked back.

Wherever I looked, there was 'Mother.' That was a big part of the experience.

I also felt myself beautiful that week. I felt radiant, like all my cells were alive. Oh, I want to make this as honest as I can, I just have to keep trying to find the words. There were some absolutely amazing and archetypal moments with a number of different women in the group; I had never experienced anything like that. For one thing they were introducing a new exercise. I did not know it was new but they told us they had never done it before. It was toward the end of the week when we worked with the masks that we formed a big oval and people with the masks on would move into the center and one or two other masks could feel free to join and to see what kind of dynamic would happen between those energies. The leaders said, "Nobody has to do this. It's an experiment so pay attention to how you are moved. It is not a requirement."

One after one, the women got up, and I was still feeling very self-conscious. I had made a gypsy mask. I love that mask. It was very hot and I was not feeling "pulled up." I was thinking, "Okay, I think this is not going to happen." At this point only a few of us had not been up and I thought, "I am not going to do this just to be a good girl." They say it is not a requirement. So I took the mask off because my face was all sweaty and hot and sticky. They had wanted us to keep the masks on, to keep solidly in that energy and I thought, "Well, I think it is just not going to happen and I just have to make peace with myself even if I am the only person who does not get up. I am not going to get up just to be a good girl." And then somebody got up.—And now I will say something very general in order not to betray the soul of what happened in that experience. Something about her seemed unbearably alone and lonely and before I knew it something propelled me off the floor and behind her in the middle of the group.... And then I knew that I could trust the impulse that said, "Don't get up until you are moved to get up." I understood that it was impersonal, something coming through the mask. The whole process was deeply moving. There were several other archetypal moments that had the same sort of feeling to them. There was no explaining what happened. You could say there was a lot of love there, and there were thirty women willing to open their hearts and souls, but none of it would explain the power of what actually happened.

Maja: Was there anything in the structure that felt difficult for you?

Marlene: I was not easily comfortable with opening the altar in the morning. I did not have a problem with it, but I was not going to pretend that I would do this on my own, because the whole concept of prayer, especially petitioner prayer, is something I am very allergic to! Asking a divinity, who, as far as I am concerned, should already know how to take care of their charges with love—that was not something I could resonate with. Now the opening dance I could completely resonate with—creating that circle and the sacred space—I just loved it right away.

Maja: How did you bear that—the opening of the altar—how did you do that—some people might have run out the first time? Did it change for you over time?

Marlene: Well, I think first of all, I went along with it. I was not terribly uncomfortable with it; it just did not feel native to me. But it was obviously true to Marion and to the other leaders as well, although she usually did the opening. I suppose you could call it prayer, but I don't like the word. Let us say the invocation to Sophia. I could certainly feel the symbolic resonance of what that invocation was and, as the intensives went on,

I became more comfortable, because I understood what it meant for me with time, to a point where it almost did not matter if it was the same thing as what Marion was evoking. It became for me more and more separate from what I had grown up with as petitioner prayer. I did not feel like leaving the room, but I did stand on the edge of the group, feeling "this is alright," but it's also alright that I don't feel fully engaged—and it was. I mean everything was alright. Sometimes it drove me crazy. I kept thinking: somebody is going to come along and say, "You are doing it wrong," but nobody did. They did not say, "You are doing it right" and they did not say, "You are doing it wrong." And I thought; "Well, how will I know?" I could not fully trust that they were not thinking, "Oh God, she is really not getting that," or "She is trying but her soul is not in it. We can see that, she cannot see it." It's a critical voice in me that had nothing to do with them. It took me the whole week to really start to trust that, but also to realize that something in me had shifted and I was looking at other people with the eyes of love. I realized that if I could look at those thirty women without judgement and feel whatever they were doing was true to who they were, maybe I could trust that they were looking at me the same way. And maybe I could look at myself that way a little bit more. To integrate that will take the rest of my life, but it is a possibility.

I can't remember if I made a sacrifice or an intention at the end of the intensive, probably an intention, because I took it very seriously. Marion said to us, "If you make a sacrifice be prepared to be called on it." I thought, "I'd better be really careful here! I want to be true to where I am, always." The whole experience was archetypal—it was an archetypal week. I do remember putting that gypsy energy—which had gone into skirts and which had sometimes gone into big gold earrings—to make that face. It was my face as that gypsy and I feel that this was some kind of deep soul part of me. To look at that and see how beautiful she was—the colors—and to feel that this was now seen in the group and accepted as part of who I was. I think I lived in that energy for a long time afterwards, always coming and going more and less strongly but it was very important. And I think the experience on the bodily level of the tenderness of the week, the care and the honoring of every touch, and the permission.

Some women have come and they had said it was a whole new life to them. It was not that to me, because I think in some way I have been a mother's daughter and the feminine, to a large extent, has been where I've lived. I mean within patriarchy and at some level that deepens, but in some ways I have always loved, been at home with, and felt loved and supported by women; so it was not a change of direction, it was a profound deepening and validation. And in some way it felt like coming home to something I have always known. Something that I always felt a bit weird about, because I don't see it out there, and to try to talk about it with other women; it could be interpreted in so many ways. I remember feeling like "Wow—here is a place where all this intense knowing can actually have a home and be seen and be respected and even make a difference. And where I can receive it as well." So that was a big experience and, of course, forming bonds and friendships with other women; I still have a friendship with one of the women from the first intensive who never came to another one. In this work you plunge into something that you might not plunge into in ten years of friendship in the outer world, because of the soul safety provided here. My body felt seen and loved and liked. It did not have to be any other than what it already was.

I think the most important part of the intensives for me has been the movement—no question about it. I loved all of it; the dream work has been profound, the voice work has been profound, but freeing my body to move and dance—to feel those energies at play—has been the most amazing gift of that work.

Now the second intensive was a lot harder.

Maja: You mentioned the healing of your body; can you describe what really took place— what that meant to you. What was it that gave you permission or what was it that re-freed something that was frozen or locked—would you like to speak to that?

Marlene: Well, there was Mary's deliciousness. I remember her saying, "Love of the body travels from body to body." I remember that every time my co-facilitator and I offer our workshop BodySoul Writing course. I start to hear that critical voice saying, "Who are you to think you can do the movement warm-up?" and then I hear Mary's voice saying, "Love of the body travels from body to body, so ladies if you are going to do this, you better be loving your own body!" It was the deliciousness of being invited to feel every part of the body, to be able to sing it, to be able to walk through the room and encounter other bodies, and feel the erotic element. We don't wear that lightly in the outer world, because we could get into big trouble there. But feeling invited to feel all that eros in the body and all that playfulness and erotic loveliness—that was home territory. I had never felt free to express it before, even though I felt it inside all the time. It was playful and serious at the same time. For example, Mary would say, "Can you move some part of the body that you have not moved before, and do it in such a way that nobody even knows you are doing it?"—the continual invitation to explore and not have any goal other than pure delight. The first intensive was very profound in many ways.

You know there are moments that are just so sacred, that you don't know if you should even put them into words.

I have to be honest and say that, like some other women, before every intensive I thought, "I don't have to do this—I could cancel." There was the simultaneous sense of

"I can't wait to get there and see what happens," and "Oh my God, what am I going to uncover this time." Sometimes there was a real feeling of dread and fear at what I might find hidden in my body that I had not known was there; some kind of terrible anguish or sorrow and I would be screaming so loud that everybody would flee the room! I felt great comfort when I heard other women say that even at the airport they felt, "I could still cancel the flight. I don't have to go to this." I always loved the check-in the first night of the intensives, because I always felt, "Half of the people seem to be glad to be here, a quarter seem to feel they don't want to be here at all, and the other quarter feel quite ambivalent, just like me." I mean, it is a chance to see an awful lot of shadow at play. Just to be observing my own process; to be observing my feelings, thoughts, judgements and opinions, and self-assessment of, "How is it going this week?" and at the same time being part of the whole process, noting where I would rather be off on the side, noting where I am feeling resentful because the same person has talked to Marion four times in two days and I've still not had a chance to do a dream. There were certainly times when I was frustrated because I thought the leaders could be doing a better job in making sure that there is fairness. That anybody who wants to see them gets a chance to see them. I think it is just human nature to say, "It is my turn now."

I understand now why they recommend that we only do one intensive a year and no more than two, because you go home and there is so much to work with. It is so much to try to live with, and see how it comes up in your dreams and see what happens. As Marion always says, "How do we take the treasure home?" How do we take something from the experience in the intensives home and make it real in our everyday life, not just for that week?

Maja: How did you do that?

Marlene: I did it through writing. Once I had a BodySoul Rhythms community in Vancouver we also began to meet, so that is an important way of keeping it alive now. For a while three of us were meeting to work on our dreams about once a month. Now there are five of us and we meet three or four times a year. We also have our Pacific Northwest group of twelve women, half Canadian and half American, who meet once a year for a long weekend and do our work together. On my own I have done a lot of writing and a lot of dancing, which is a different kind of dancing than I have ever done before. For me it is usually with music. How to describe that? It is an honoring of what my body wants to express. What music do I want? What music does my body want today and what are the impulses? What is the joy of the movement this time? I don't dance as much as I want to. Sometimes I am not even sure why not, but that has been a big gift of bringing it home. And of course, both in N.Y. but especially since coming to Vancouver, I have been bringing everything I have learned and experienced into my teaching. I don't consciously say, "What will I take from the intensives?" But I allow what I experienced during the intensive to be so alive in me that it spills into my teaching. And then sometimes I will think of it and just bring it in spontaneously or share an anecdote that seems fair to share. All of it re-animates me and it comes through in my teaching. There again I would say it is a validation and affirmation of something I have known always. I wrote an article that was published in 1998 and it has got all of this in it and that was before I ever did a single intensive. But I yearned to be able to realize it more fully. I would say that my teaching is more embodied, and now it is much more confidently a part of how I teach. It is how I teach. Once you do this work, it is a part of everything you are and everything you do. It's as if you have a new color in your life or an intensification of a color that you had before.

One of the things that struck me most forcefully about our team of three (Mary, Ann, and Marion) is the love and respect among them and how important it is. How hungry we are to see that people can work together and teach together and have that kind of love and respect for each other, so there is always that holding going on. And I think that plays a huge part in the way people are able to drop deeply in. If people did not feel it on a bodily level that the container is safe, the work would not go that deep. It really starts with the love that the leaders demonstrate towards each other. Without it, this type of work could not happen. You would not trust that the bowl was not going to break in the middle of your big experience. To see it embodied that way is really profound. I feel it happening in my work together with my co-facilitator. I felt it very strongly earlier this year when we did the Jung Workshop in Vancouver. As we build that trust and as we work together, more and more you can begin to play and experiment and improvise, knowing that the other person is there holding it and that say, "Oh we did not plan this," but they trust that you know what you are doing. I think it was the first time we both felt we did that with great confidence. Just to be able to say, "She has changed what we planned but it's great, let's just see where this goes."

From the time we started talking in the group about people forming teams, I felt very strongly that I don't want to rush into anything. I want to explore what kind of possibility might come up or what kind of energies my energy might want to play with. I know some people were feeling pressure about forming teams and my feeling was, "I don't want to get married before I have even dated!" I feel I want to be open and to explore whatever possibilities might come up. And at the same time I feel the strength and the solidarity of going through a number of intensives with a dear teaching partner, who is doing her best, as I am, for her own soul growth and discovery. And it's profound, the trust that builds over time and the chance to process some of the hard things. To see each other's shadow. To see, how do we work with that, and to have the shared kind of treasure chest of experience that we have. We had one moment in a workshop that was really very difficult to work with. We have seen what happens when there is a real crisis in a group and you only have each other to depend on. Nobody welcomes a crisis like that, but to feel that you can support each other and that there is not a moment of wavering in the solidarity of the team work, that is really a gift. After that, one feels that they have come through something. There is a kind of innocence that has gone, but there is a kind of trust in the strength that one does not really know until it is tested.

Maja: Would you like to share the development for you at the intensives?

Marlene: The second intensive was on the West Coast. I found it beautifully symbolic that my first workshop was on the East Coast and the next on the West Coast on Gabriola Island—that beautiful wild rocky Pacific coast and forest. That is my soul landscape. That is the nature I feel at home in. It was a very rough intensive. I made a mask I could not deal with. As I was making it, each of the three apprentices came over in the way they do, making sure everyone is fine with the mask-work. They were talking to me. One of them said, "I should just really leave you because I am distracting you," and I said, "No, this is really good, because when you talk to me I don't pay attention to what I am doing, so it is just happening. If you go away I am thinking about what I do." I made a mask that was very difficult to work with because there was a rigid perfection that froze me, and of course that was the 'Medusa-element'—the freezing gaze that turns you to stone. That was a big challenge that week and I did drop somewhere very deep and very dark. The dreams were saying so and I felt it. That was my dark night of the soul. Eventually I got the chance to work on it in analysis. I think I had been flooded by unconscious material… At the intensive, however, I made a couple of dear friends who were with me when I wanted to leave, feeling it was dark and that I couldn't seem to get anyone to notice that I was in this place. I did try to talk about it with one of the leaders and they did not understand why I was so upset and that made me angry. It was a rough week.

I don't think it's unusual when the first intensive is so glorious, that at the second one a lot of shadow is going to come up. But I never wavered about knowing that this was what I wanted to do. And I think it was at the second intensive that Marion asked me if I really wanted to join the leadership training program. The timing was perfect. I was very grateful that they allowed me to join after having missed the first seminar. I had had a miscarriage two years earlier and I knew it was unlikely that I was going to be pregnant again. I also knew that I had tremendous energy, and creativity and love that had to find another outlet, otherwise it would turn back on me and poison me. I loved everything I was doing, the teaching, the writing, the workshops, but I knew it would not be enough for the second half of my life. The timing was just beautiful because we had moved to the

West Coast and my husband was supportive so I was able to step into it with full heart and soul. It was also interesting because I am not actually a group person. I have never really been a part of groups. I have always been out on the fringe doing what I want to do. I think it is the gypsy energy. If I find kindred spirits, that's great and I am happy and if not, I just do what I want to do and move on. So this was really new territory for me too. How do I be true to myself and my own experience in the context of the group—wanting to speak my truth and not wanting to hurt anybody's feelings? How do I stay true to myself in an environment where that is the most important thing? If we cannot do it here, then where can we do it? The relationship between being there as an individual and also being part of a larger group was something I was always aware of. I have never had an experience that could honor both of those the way that BSR could. I can't imagine being part of a group with that kind of intensity without that loving container. I feel it is like eros-energy fields that come out from each person's body that go into the circle and create a field of common energy. I see it in colors and then one takes some of that color back into oneself. It is just a continual movement of flowing color throughout the whole week.

I did an intensive with Mary Hamilton and Paula Reeves in Georgia. It was the time that they worked together and it was great because there were only fourteen participants so it was very intimate and close. I remember the first time that I actually let myself go off. I think we had a deep relaxation and then they invited movement, and my body did not want to move. My head kept trying to talk my body into moving and my body just kept lying there. At some point, it might have been after half an hour, I said, "Okay, I give up. I am just going to lie here with this blanket and if I'm not doing what they want, well that's just the way it is." And as the exercise finished and they guided us towards the end, I suddenly knew with a flash, "this was exactly what I was supposed to do, so how could I have done anything else!" And it sounds idiotic but the light bulb went on and I thought, "All those times when I thought there was something I should be doing or I should be working harder to figure out what that impulse is." I had a very good chance during these intensives to see how hard I try! And Marion's voice always playing over and over in my mind saying, "It is so much easier to try to be better than we are, than to be who we are!"

Maja: Embodied reality of what the sacred feminine is?

Marlene: The whole temenos, the whole archetypal sacred space of all of the intensives is like modern Eleusinian mysteries and I could not talk about them. I would tell my husband some things because I knew he would hold them with the same kind of sacredness that I did. But I would be surprised sometimes, when I heard people talk about the exercises. Not that I wanted to keep it secret, I don't like people keeping unnecessary secrets, but to me there is a mystery in this work that you can't talk about it. You live a mystery and

LOVE MATTERS FOR PSYCHIC TRANSFORMATION

you hold it within you, but it is not something that can even be talked about. Over time I think it is more and more to me an embodied reality of what the sacred embodied feminine is. What it can be, what it is, what it is in us that we don't know about, what is in us when we feel safe enough to share that with other women, and hopefully with men at some point too, because I think certainly that is where we need to go. At the same time realising that someone can be a BodySoul sister and I can hold her with love and I may not even like her. If she needed something from me I would do my best to be there, but some personalities simply do not fit well together. And we will probably go on living out our complexes—it does not matter if we do thirty intensives, we will still be doing things that we would rather not be doing!

Maja: I am curious, Marlene, if you would speak to the transformation you feel in your body?

Marlene: I said earlier that I feel I live in a different body. There are so many ways in which I could talk about that, but the body does not speak in words and it is hard to describe. Maybe part of it was a real yearning that my body could be loved, just the way it is. My husband has always loved my body; I mean that it could be loved from the inside and not feel so judged by my brain, or by a culture that has certain ideas about how we should look, but just to feel itself glorious. My body knows what I can do and where I am pushing myself too hard. And it is always trying to tell me, which sounds funny, because it sounds like there is a split, but there is not. It is communicating in the best way she can about what I need and if I listen to it (it does not make sense to talk about it as if there is a split) but "she" loves me when I love her. Just feeling when I am pushing myself too hard and saying, "I am pushing myself too hard, I have got to stop, what do you want right now, what do you need? I don't have to push myself harder to meet another deadline. I need to just stop because this is so important." I don't think I did it that consciously before. Just that process of learning to be sensitive, to be open to it, to feel that unity—that my body and my soul and my mind are all one, and all need to love each other for me to do what I do, the way I want to do it. Otherwise some part of me is getting pushed aside and I'm feeling less and less like I can tolerate that.

There are so many ways to talk about this work. We talk about what we want to do with it, to take it into our own teaching and so on, and if all the BSR experience did was to revitalise my own teaching, that would be enormous to me. To bring the feminine—in a joyful, playful, erotic, embodied way—into everything I teach, I don't think it gets better than that! Another thing that brought me to the BSR work was that I had been leading workshops for about ten years and I loved doing it—it let me embody everything I love about the feminine, that I could not bring as explicitly into my university teaching, although I sure tried to bring a lot of it in! I know my students got it too. I knew it from the course evaluations, that they knew this was not about mastering content; they felt what the impulse was, and to the extent I felt I could express it there, they were picking it up. But after ten years of doing that in New York, I felt that I needed my well to be filled. I did not feel burned out. I felt very alive and I loved everything I was doing. But I also felt; "Now I need to draw from somewhere because I don't want to dry out and I need to be filled, so I can go on passing it on. I need to feed myself, really." That nourishment was also part of that first BSR intensive; of looking around the room and seeing everybody mirroring me, mirroring all of us in the group, and not to be the one doing all the mirroring. To feel it coming back to me in that way was just beautiful, so profound, and really such a feeling of being nurtured.

Maybe that is the most dramatic result of doing the BSR work—the feeling that I live in a different body. It has been a deepening of something I have known since I was born, and I have kept trying, sometimes at great cost, to embody, and then either gotten wounded or rejected, drawn back into myself and then tried in another way to express it. So doing the BSR work has been a deepening and like a stream that turns into a river. It has not been a turn in direction; it has been a profound affirmation of what my heart knows. And in some way I think we all could say that. It has been a profound recognition, and affirmation, and celebration of everything I have loved about the feminine. And it has been given another level of reality because it is now out there in the group and because I can talk about it a little bit differently.

Doing the BSR work has also brought me back to who I was as a little girl. I was a very energetic and imaginative little girl who got thumped down pretty consistently and thoroughly. But for me the world was full of magic—the books and the music. Nobody said to me, "Go ahead, you can do it," because it was so far from their field of reference they couldn't even imagine me doing it. So I did it! I wrote music, I wrote songs, I put on plays, and I wrote a novel when I was eleven years old, and I wrote poetry, and I designed clothes for all my dolls. I just lived in a world of magic—that was my world. And nobody said, "Who are you? You don't know anything composing!" So I wrote a song and when I was thirteen it was on the radio, and my parents were proud. Afterward I felt mortified because it was a Christian song but that was who I was at that time. I wrote a song and sent it in to the contest and then it was performed by the choir on the radio. I had all this energy. I look back and I don't even know how that girl survived and I am so grateful. To go into this work is another step in recuperating more of her. She never really died, she has just hidden well. That is the gypsy again. To keep recuperating her, and bringing her back, and saying, "Okay, you've got a little bit more room to play in now, honey, how about writing some music?" "What, I am not a composer!" "Yes, but what about writing some more music?" (That is the inner encouragement when the negative voice step in, gentle, just there.) I started writing, out of the blue fifteen years ago, a cantata for women's voices. I have been a singer and a pianist but I have never studied composing, but who cares. I started writing this cantata and last week I thought, "I think I need to get back to that cantata." It's there again. That to me is the feminine, the joy of creativity, but of course it is also the masculine. There is a voice inside saying, "I think I would like to do that," and then the critical voice says, "What are you talking about, you don't know anything about that," and then the first voice says, "Oh but I think I really want to do that," and then the masculine comes in and says, "Go for it, you can do it!" We will see if that cantata gets written.

Maja: You have mentioned the feminine. What is the feminine for you?

Marlene: For all the work that we have done with Marion, when I think about the feminine I go to Helen Luke's description of the feminine as receptive devotion and creative resonance. Marion would say "Being" but "creative resonance" and "receptive devotion" are such beautiful concepts. It's everything that holds with every fibre of its being, even though it may look to the outside as if nothing is going on.

Maja: It's like the uterus what you described there!

Marlene: It is trusting everything between the words. Trusting the silence. Trusting presence. Knowing that everything we can do or try to do is secondary to what we can call the rainmaker. To be right with ourselves and to be fully present, that is the most important thing. And I don't know if the story about the rainmaker is even about the feminine, but for me it is. It is the joy of life; it is eros as in the movie *Chocolate*.[80] That's what everyone was starved for that movie—the feminine. Vianne is the rainmaker[81] in the movie, she is right with herself, so everybody who comes into the chocolate shop, she is able to put in touch with their own unconscious. She certainly put them in touch with their own fantasy, and with each other. She is fully alive and so present. People who don't know Jungian concepts just love that movie and they feel that quality. I think that it is that joyful presence in every single moment that holds nothing back. It just delights in what is there. It's what Helen Luke talks about when she says she loves the word 'kindness' so much because it says we are living in kinship with everything—with every other being.

The feminine is also about darkness—everything that cannot be put into words, or is not seen or valued or recognized or given a place in our lives and in the culture. That is

---

80 Movie *Chocolate*. Dir. Lasse Hallström, Perfs. Juliette Binoche, Judi Dench, Alfred Molina, Carrie-Anne Moss, Aurelien Parent Koenig, Film. Miramax Lionsgate, 2011.
81 The story of the rainmaker was often told by Jung, see Appendix for the story.

partly why I love James Hillman so much. He does not talk about the feminine but about the realm of the underworld and the longing we have for shades and shadows. To me he is talking about the hunger for the dark feminine. The feminine is also very playful. I keep thinking of the image that Marion gave us of Sophia playing around the throne of God and being forever His delight. It is the same place that creativity comes from, that willingness to play.

Maja: You also mentioned the word 'authenticity.' Would you like to speak to that?

Marlene: I love etymology, so I always start with its roots. 'Author,' 'authority,' 'authoritative.' I don't know if I have that much to say about it except that for me external authority and inner authenticity are opposites.

The word that I have loved my whole life is 'integrity,' which is in some way very similar to authenticity. There is not really a verb for integrity, it is a noun. Integrity says the whole thing is woven of the same cloth, there is no false thread, all of it is of the same quality. It is very close to authenticity and, if you are authentic, you have integrity or you can say it the other way around. It goes back to Esther Harding's quote about the virgin:

> The woman who is virgin, one-in-herself, does what she does—not because of any desire to please, not to be liked, or to be approved, even by herself; not because of any desire to gain power over another… but because what she does is true.[82]

The virgin does not even aim to please herself, which is my favorite part. This means that she may do things she does not really want to do, but they are true so she does them. And that is also the core of the feminine. It takes us back to the recognition of what Being is, in the moment. It is not a kind of an idealized projection but that which is true for me right now this moment. I don't think it is easy. It's not even easy for me to talk about it. It's easy to get idealistic about it and then to say, "How do we do that in the world or in our relationships?" How do we walk through the battlefield of our own complexes and other people's complexes and keep trying to be true to ourselves when we can't always see when the complexes are at work?"

Maja: Do you feel that the BSR work has changed you in relation to integrity?

Marlene: I think that from the time I was tiny, I was a soul who could not live without integrity. But through the BSR work I got the support for honoring it and really seeing it as part of the feminine, and feeling again the validation that this is what life is. I cannot live in any other way than to hold that at the center in the best way I can. In our BSR work

---

82 Esther Harding, *Woman's Mysteries*, p. 125.

I think the real challenge has been to explore—what do authenticity and integrity mean in movement. What does that mean in how I am in the group? What does it mean to be following the impulses of the body?

The first year after the ending of the leadership training I spoke to Patty about a reunion in which we could come back and offer each other solidarity and encouragement, and share ideas. When Renewal came up it was more the shape of an intensive. It was clear to me that was not what I wanted. For me personally, finishing a certain arc of initiation and training meant that the leaders were now my sisters and I did not want to be taught in the same way anymore. I wanted to be in a sisterhood where we were all "feeding" each other. I could understand that others felt differently and were looking for something else, but that was my truth. I hope it can still happen.

Maja: Is there a danger in the BSR work that the closer we get to know each other, the less freedom there is to let out whatever wants to come out, and there is a kind of idealism that moves in to group? Not that this comes from the leaders, but from the group itself?

Marlene: Yes, I think that is part of the shadow. And I don't see how work that goes so profoundly into the positive pole of the feminine and the positive mother can help but constellate the opposite. I sometimes wonder if there would be a way for us to deal with that more consciously in the group. I think it is also at the root of the "team anxiety" that some people felt. I'm sure it can feel like being back in kindergarten where everybody is on a baseball team and you are the only one not chosen! I was fortunate not to feel that way because I had been teaching for so long and loved what I was doing already. I felt that if other opportunities come along, great, but I wasn't worried about it. I know there were some people who really suffered though. I think it's so important that we take our time.

Maja: We are coming to an end. Is there anything you would like to add or comment on, or that you have not voiced?

Marlene: The whole experience of BSR work was so profound, as you know. In trying to describe it, I hear a voice saying, "No that's not quite it, no, that's not quite it either." It would have to be more than spoken words that could convey what the experience was. I feel a kind of gratitude and puzzlement that I have been fortunate enough to be able to be part of this, and that it has been such a rich dimension in my life at a time when I was ready and able to receive it. I would have been scared shitless ten years earlier and might not have been able to do it. It is certainly the most powerful experience of unconditional love and of being held that I have ever had. I really feel we have been blessed to participate in a twenty-first century Eleusinian mystery rite, and I don't think many people have that opportunity. Maybe that's why I keep stumbling and repeating myself—because you cannot say it in words. It is a mystery, and such a gift. To Marion and Mary and Ann working together with us, to be working with that mystery with the three of them all the time. What courage, steadfastness, faithfulness, loyalty, and love on everyone's part. It has been one of the biggest gifts of my life. If my life was a treasure chest, this would probably be the ruby, because it certainly was important in that Rubedo! If I was going to try and say in a word or an image what the whole process has been for me, it would be "reclaiming the Rubedo!" Of course it was always there, but it really got stomped down. I don't want to take the alchemical metaphor too far, because I am going to trip over my own attempted profundity! All of that life and radiance that were always there needed a place to be safe. As more of that life energy is reclaimed, so is more and more of the grief. I never expected to go through the kind of grief I did at the intensives, feeling—where is this coming from? Feeling more and more of the life that was numbed coming alive again—I don't think it gets any better than that, Maja! Winning lotto—sure, why not, thank you! But I would not trade it! It does not get any better than to feel oneself alive in body and soul, does it? … No it does not!

> This is the point where love becomes possible. We see the other with the eye of the heart, an eye not clouded by fear manifesting as need, jealousy, possessiveness, or manipulation. With the unclouded eye of the heart, we can see the other as other. We can rejoice in the other, challenge the other, and embrace the other without losing our own center or taking anything away from the other. We are always other to each other—soul meeting soul, the body awakened with joy. To love unconditionally requires no contracts, bargains, or agreements. Love exists in the moment-to-moment flux of life.[83]

"Being Met with Unconditional Love, Over and Over and Over" Wendy Wilmot & Maja Reinau

> Beyond our ideas of right-doing and wrong-doing,
> there is a green field. I'll meet you there.
> When the soul lies down in that grass,
> the world is too full to talk about.
> Ideas, language, even the phrase 'each other'
> doesn't make sense any more.[84]

---

83 Marion Woodman, *Dancing in the Flames: The Dark Goddess in the Transformation of Consciousness*, co-authored with Elinor Dickson, p. 221.
84 Jelaluddin Rumi, (Coleman Barks, ed.) *The Essential Rumi*, p. 36.

Introduction

Wendy Wilmot is mother of two children, and grandmother of four. She holds two master's degrees: one in Environmental studies, one in Depth Psychology. She is passionate about ecology, BodySoul Rhythms work, Jungian psychology and thought and, when not home, she is to be found hiking in the "ever of green and the wonder of white."

Maja: Wendy, you have told me how much the BSR work means to you. What is so special about it?

Wendy: I feel emotion welling up as I think of this. I remember the very first night of my first intensive. We were sharing in the circle. I was already complexed about what to say, when Marion said: "You will have an experience this week of love." I was struck by this although I did not really know what she meant, and it has always stayed with me. I now know that Marion did not mean personal love but 'Sophia-love.' Marie-Louise von Franz writes about Sophia-love as the fourth stage in the development of eros. I had never before known Sophia-love in my life; I did not know what it does to the body to be in the presence of that kind of love, over and over and over. Once would not be enough. Once constellates the longing, the hunger. I could not express my feelings, nor could I approach Marion because I experienced my longing, I now realize, as nearly 'too much.' To be in the field of such intimate presence and love is to know the possibility of healing in those places that are felt as deep holes in the psyche. Sophia-love brings LIFE. It is like watering a desert, and they [Marion, Ann, and Mary] water the desert of the soul unfailingly, over and over and over again.

Maja: Such an apt metaphor, to water the desert of the soul. Could you say a little more about what this experience meant to you?

Wendy: I think that, quite literally, Sophia-love allows for something to be built up in the brain to balance or compensate other experiences, and so it has the power to heal old wounds. I have probably been melancholic, depressive for most of my life, always looking for a sense of belonging, never feeling I belonged because there was no mutuality in my family. Over time, through my BSR work, something happened to me which I can only describe as the birth in my body of a felt sense of belonging. I belong now. There is an "I." I really don't think I had an "I" before. Mostly I was awash in the power structures of my complexes. I was a bit like the salmon, always wanting to head somewhere but not quite knowing where. But I found my river with BSR. It gave me life.

Maja: How did you come to do this work?

Wendy: I was doing my graduate work at Pacifica Graduate Institute and Marion Woodman was sort of in the air. But my hunger was so great that I could not approach her, not even read her books. Then a friend of mine went to an intensive and she said: "Oh, you should do it." And I replied: "Oh, sure," but then I had a dream in which Marion Woodman was facilitating a residential program with a number of women. In the dream I approach her at this gathering and I ask her if she would be my mentor. And in the dream she said "Yes" immediately!

I took the dream to my analyst at that time (who was trained in both Freudian and Jungian psychoanalysis) and he said "I wonder if you would consider consulting with her [Marion Woodman]?" "Oh, for goodness sake, no" I replied, but then I did. I wrote to her and sent her the dream. She must have responded as soon as she received it. I was at home and my phone rang. The operator said: "Would you accept a long distance call from Marion Woodman." As I see it, something of the transcendent came into my temporal life at that moment. During our conversation I remember saying to Marion that, no matter how much therapy I had done, there was still such fear lodged in my body, fear that seemed to stand between me and my experience of life. She understood perfectly and said: "I would recommend you come to one of the intensives—it is difficult to go into that fear in the body in a fifty-minute hour, it needs more time." And I think that is one of the extraordinary things offered in the BSR intensives: time is not proscribed. One finds oneself in a timeless world for those seven or eight days. And this allows one to penetrate layer upon layer of the psyche, process upon process. The work is not intrusive or invasive. Anything constellated from the unconscious or through talking with the leaders is held and given a place to be worked through. The BSR process is deeply respectful of soul time. And so I did apply for my first intensive. It was already very late, just the day before it was due to start in California when the organizers called and said "Can you come?" and I said "Absolutely!"

That was the beginning. I had a special sense about these three Canadian women, I myself being Canadian. I remember saying to Mary, "I just have this feeling that you are going to help me come home." They have done that … [crying] literally and figuratively…

Maja: Your experience sounds extremely moving. Do you have any thoughts about anything specific in the BSR intensives that facilitated your journey to "come home?"

Wendy: I think there is something to be said about the structure of the BSR intensives. There are different ways of looking at it, but I have always experienced my soul being reflected in love over and over and over again or, as Mary Hamilton says, "molecule by molecule by molecule." So now, somewhere inside me, alongside the fear, is faith and a deep knowing of what matters most profoundly to me. I had never had my own values reflected back to me in love. I grew up with two brothers, an only daughter in a patriarchal family in which the feminine was devalued. My father told me: "Wendy, you are made for service." This meant service to the patriarchy which, as far as I can see, includes the whole of Western culture, a legacy of hundreds of years in which my family was firmly embedded. BSR work was to me the breath of life. It was possibility. It was seeing and sight. And it was time—time to allow something to take root in me that had never been rooted before.

Psychologically, I feel the BSR work has allowed me to experience that something operates deep within, separate from my ego. I have never before been religious but I am certainly spiritual. I feel I have been growing a sense of Faith with a capital "F." We talk about the Self, this sense that something within impels us on a gradient towards wholeness, those extraordinary moments when one experiences the transcendent crossing one's temporal path. What can one do except be on one's knees? One can never say 'thank you' often enough, and I feel the call to give back in some way—not out of guilt but out of love.

Maja: What would you say opened you to this faith? To this trust?

Wendy: In the afternoon, when we bring into awareness what is going on in our bodies, guided by Ann or Mary—a deeply personal, introverted time—my experience of myself was of always having been alone. There were times when my eyes would open and Marion was just sitting, or Mary would be right there with me. She might touch me or simply accompany me in the most respectful way so that this body [touches her body gently] had the experience of not being alone. Even in the mornings, when I would often be awash with feelings of aloneness, Mary would come up to me, look deeply into my eyes from that place of eternal wisdom in her, and just connect. We talk about being carried in the mind and heart of someone. I had that experience. Marion, Mary, and Ann held everybody in that way… so again and again, unfailingly, because my negativity would have taken one hint of failure and amplified it into a total lack of emphatic resonance. It never happened. So I think what opened me to faith and trust operated on all levels: speech, touch, gaze. Most important was consistency—there was no gap. This continuity of feeling in every expression is Sophia-love.

When I grew bold enough to ask for something, immediately they were there. Ann Skinner, in her special way, was there for me because I had such difficulty with anything creative. She helped me to bring in humor and I again felt met without judgment, not even a whisper. Being met in this way was the most remarkable experience I had ever had. Marion, Mary, and Ann seem to move beyond the personal in their capacity to love.

Maja: When you had those moments with Ann, what happened? What was her way of acting that made this difference?

Wendy: Oh, it was not so much what she said as her capacity to meet me where I was, unfailingly and without judgment, being with me in the place of not knowing. I would say, "Ann, you know this mask, I have no idea—I don't know what shape, how to cut it, what color to put on," and she would reply, "just go over and choose a color." And I would say, "I have no place inside of me that can choose color." Together we would try to get in touch with a color. In an empathic way, she would see if there was any place in the energy of the color that I could go. I said to her after a while, "Ann, these masks that I have made, they are all the same. They are like elements." "Wendy," she responded, "they are essence." In this way, she would reflect back to me something essential about myself. She met my critical side and my own diminishment and reflected back my own depth to me. There is so much energy now between us that at the last session we had such a good time: I said, "Ann, here we are!" We ended up in the bathroom and she said, "I am just going to get colors." I had my mask on and was painting it while looking in the mirror and somehow, when I was with her, I was able to be freer and I put red lipstick and red cheeks on the mask. She accompanied me, without taking over or diminishing me! Not solemnly but with life, so some place inside of me started to come to life. Ann would say that we go 'down' to do the work in order to move through to something else. She could help me move through, and if I could not, then I felt her acceptance of where I was. It happened all the time; I would say, "That's it! I can't do anything more."

I also think that seeing Ann's masks, seeing the improvisational work that she did with her own masks touched me deeply. Her masks are not beautiful masks—they are masks of some essence. They gave me permission because, you know, some of the people in BSR are very artistically gifted and make beautiful masks, and I had no relationship to any of my masks in that way.

Maja: It sounds as though this part of the work was challenging for you. Can you say more about how you met that challenge? And how Ann helped you meet it?

Wendy: I remember one intensive. I was working with Ann very intimately, with clay. It was difficult. I said, "There is nothing coming, there is just nothing coming," and Ann replied, "Just keep at it Wendy, just keep at it." She would ask me some questions and we would stay with it and then she would say, "That is it!" She could feel the process. I had no way of understanding it but she could feel it. It was like giving birth.

At one point I decided to do a course in expressive art so I asked Ann to write me a letter of recommendation. I was deeply moved by the reflection she gave me. She said rarely had she had a student who found this work as difficult as I did. She praised my capacity to stay with it. And I was blessed by Ann's, Mary's and Marion's unfailing support through repeated failures of my capacity for self-expression. Staying with, never giving up. Even though I despaired, I never gave up. And over time, simply by doing it over and over again, I moved beyond my shame of being needy, lacking, lost and not knowing, until finally I could just laugh. I would laugh and Ann would meet me there, "in that green field," of Rumi's poem, "beyond ideas of right doing and wrong doing." Perhaps that is the goal of our experience—to find a place of meeting beyond all opposites ... in that "green field."

It was difficult to stick with it! At my second intensive I made a mask that the leaders would not let me wear. It was a very destructive mask and they said "No, you ought not to wear it." So we decided that I could work with the mask but not wear it. Working with it was quite an experience in itself. I was doing the work of integrating it and was filled with the overwhelming feeling: "I have to get green, I have to find green. I have to!" I will never forget that intense feeling and so I went to get grass. My partner in the mask-work had heard my need for green. And so when we talk about the green fields in the poem by Rumi, I feel this huge opening in my chest and my heart. It was an opening of my whole body, my loins, everything. I became round. I just opened. It was at that moment that the defenses separating "I" and "Thou" dissolved. I do not mean dissolve in the sense of a symbiosis, as that would suggest psychosis. I mean a feeling of opening and dropping. I mainly feel it here [points to her heart] but I feel it in my whole body.

And instead of collapse, I had the sense, over time, of a spine growing. Vertebra by vertebra I grew a spine! In my very first intensive I had not been able to get off the floor during the bodywork. I could not stand up. But on the very last day I did stand up for a short while. I could not make contact with the mask or with anything else, and I remember Marion coming up to me to say something. I was amazed that she would make a connection, or that I had made any impression on her. She said something about how hard I had worked to get to the point where I could stand up. You cannot meet anybody if you don't have a spine or legs to stand on. I was growing those, you see.

So now I have little green boots as my standpoint as well as a spine. No standpoint without a spine!

Maja: That must have been a profoundly moving experience in your whole process…

Wendy: Yes! And in addition to the feeling of opening up and spreading out, I had a sense of orientation. It felt like a spinal process, as if both were happening at the same time: the opening of the heart and the growing of a spine. This was not an intellectual understanding; it grew out of my experience. Only years later could I find words to express a process that was essentially organic, an experience in my body. It all happened from the inside out, not from the outside in.

In the intensives, Marion would talk in the morning, and that would orient us to the direction that we would be going in, and provide some theory to support our understanding of the process. Eventually I could see the link, the integration between theory and experience, but not in the beginning. The process I experienced through BSR work involved a complete re-structuring in the body, a re-orientation. Everything was about "re": re-member, re-build, re-surrect, re-suscitate. In that way, it was about re-birth or a birthing of one's awareness, of one's body-soul. Over time something does get coagulated. Something is built inside. And I think that this healing happens due to the healing power of love. Love is not abstract. It is energy that … I don't know … I don't think 'build' is the right word. I have an image of my being stroked into being, a sense of body coming into being, into form which perhaps can only happen through love. One is too afraid to come into form without love. I can be here physically but not truly incarnate. I believe love incarnates, deep in the molecules of the body.

I want to stress that what I am describing is not regressive. Certainly not! There are times when we regress in BSR work but what I am talking about—coming into being through love—is not regression. This reminds me of my grandson and what happens to him when I gaze at him with love, deeply. Whether he is consciously aware of it or not, I can see what happens in his body and what happens in mine. I don't think my body really existed before I encountered the intimate gaze, energy, and way of being received unconditionally inherent to my experience of BSR. My body existed functionally but not in terms of the mystery and the exquisiteness of what a body is, what it carries. Now I know my body as a vessel receptive to the immanence of spirit, a little bit of Sophia incarnate. But I had no idea of that before, it was just a function.

Maja: Love for the body, could you say more about that? Have you been influenced by the way that Mary does her body guidance and relates to her own body when she is doing the floor work?

Wendy: In the beginning I could not relate to Mary's sense of the body—I rejected it because it was so far from my experience of my own body so I just went through the motions when doing the floor work. And then, over the years, that melted away and I could see how Mary related to her body, lived it with love. I was able to appreciate the truth of her experience, and hold it as some kind of possibility to which I might slowly move closer. I cannot say that I have what Mary has in terms of her love for the body, but I keep getting closer. I can now stroke my body and say "I do love this body." It is not the same as love for another person but more a quality of love that springs from a deep appreciation of what this particular body has gone through. I had a dream which I think reflects this idea. In the dream there was a large pool in an institution and, around it, a number of people ill with cancer. They are all crippled. I am there by the pool and then I am standing in this pool. There are all these salmon in the pool and then there is this old salmon. I can tell it is old because it is mottled in color and has a big scar along its spine where it has been wounded. I feel great compassion for this fish that has gone through so much yet is still here. That is the dream.

I feel grateful for my body, for its having kept on keeping on, enabling me to come to a deeper place of soul-understanding. Now I am exquisitely grateful for this body but did not always feel so. One of my earliest memories was when, as a little girl, I could not tolerate the strength of my feelings and wanted to rip them out of my body. I could not contain them, so my body was then a source of pain. But not now, and that is the healing. Now my body is a source of joy and I find such a capacity to love in this body. My body is more alive, for its own sake, than it has ever been.

I want to add something that has just come to mind: I remember when I took shamanic classes and the teacher said that most of us are walking around as the living dead. That was my experience—walking around as the living dead. And even though there is always so much more work to do, there is living life now. And I think that is the "before" and "after" of BodySoul Rhythms for me: Living life!

Pause …

Maja: Marion, Mary, and Ann each have a style, an appearance, a personal life, a personal story. What did that mean to you? And that the work was held by a triad, not by one person?

Wendy: I think they share their soul journeys. So it is deeply personal yet we can all share what they are saying. It is difficult to explain. They share their journeys of self-realization, their journeys of soul-realization, their journeys of coming to consciousness and their struggles with the opposites. But in the way they speak of their journeys, we see universal themes reflected in the particularity of each story. This gives us 'permission' to be human; it validates our own ordinary humanness, and the extraordinariness that is an indivisible part of human experience. I feel that their deepest values were discovered in their sharing. They shared their pain, not in a narcissistic way, but as an integral part of the healing power of storytelling. You know, in the shamanistic or native tradition, one of the healing powers is storytelling that comes from a place of deeply distilled essence and processed experience. When they shared their own lives with us, Marion's, Mary's, and Ann's stories became healing stories. They reflected something of our own stories and gave them value and meaning. And there is meaning. Things may seem random but, from a deeper perspective, there is meaning, pattern, coherence. You see, nothing really had any meaning for me before. The word 'meaning' has meaning now! The leaders' sharing of their stories also illustrated the shape and meaning of an individual life. And each told her story with a great sense of humor, the quality of humor that gives expression to the laughter at the heart of things. When one can see beyond conflict, beyond the opposites, one can appreciate life from that still point at the center and speak from that place.

As leaders, Marion, Mary, and Ann do not keep themselves out of the process. They teach from their own experience, which is deeply inspiring and moving. They are real. They don't set themselves above or apart from the participants; there is a powerful sense of "We," or "I and Thou," and no sense of "Us and You." There is a feeling that we are all in this together—this journey of coming to consciousness and moving towards wholeness. No separation; no hierarchy. Everything Marion, Mary, and Ann say is imbued with the deepest feminine values: relatedness and connection. And this supports each participant to deeper and deeper and deeper in her own process.

Maja: What do Marion's, Mary's, and Ann's stories give to you, personally?

Wendy: I feel they give me a new way in which to see myself. In their stories I see my own struggles and process mirrored, and that gives value and meaning to my life. Really, it is all about the human condition; their stories confirm the humanness of our stories. Respect is conferred on our struggles, my struggle, and I no longer feel myself the victim of my own life. Sharing stories honors our struggle to become more conscious and whole. This experience is anything but intellectual, it is so real. I can say that each time I go back to an intensive I am filled with hope and a renewed sense of possibility.

I would like to share an image that speaks to what we have been discussing. It is an image of standing stones. Earlier in my life I was isolated in my own experience, feeling that it was just me and that there was something wrong with me. But this image of standing stones gives a sense of being both encircled and a part of something deep and eternal. It gives the sense that what we are doing here in this lifetime is part of something larger than the individual's struggle but that the individual's struggle does matter. My analyst told me of a dream that Marie-Louise von Franz talks about. It was dreamt by a man who had not thought himself to be particularly successful personally but in his dream it became clear that his suffering had healed his family line seven generations in the past and several generations in the future, indicating that the personal struggle is integral to the unfolding of that larger something we cannot fully grasp. Such a dream confers nobility on human suffering and recognizes its healing potential. We each have to take up the cross of our own life. I don't think we can do this alone. I don't mean that in terms of dependency but in the sense of the standing stones, sharing in a circle, standing side by side. So when

Marion, Mary, and Ann share their stories and we listen, there is a feeling that we are on some level all here doing it together.

I would like to stress something else. Often when people tell their stories there is an implicit personal agenda motivated by power. With Marion, Mary, and Ann exactly the opposite is true. There is no sense of power in what they are saying or how they are saying it—not a hint! Jung said, "Where there is no love there is the will to power," and, conversely, where there is love there is no need for power. At BSR intensives it is as though you step into an archetypal field of love. A place where love is held instead of power. The leaders hold love in the field and, when it is not there, they know how to work with themselves to reconnect to the loving place. They do their personal work to re-center themselves in love and, if they cannot, they leave the room.

Maja: Could you say more about the "sharing of the human condition?"

Wendy: Yes, Ann, Mary, and Marion have all suffered a lot; otherwise they could not do this work. But their suffering is highly, consciously distilled; there is no wish for pity, for others to feel sorry for them, carry their pain or act in a particular way in response to their stories. They simply wish to share their experience from an authentic place—that is, share their experience of what it is to be human, an act which in itself confers a certain nobility on the human condition. This reminds me of my classes on clown work; in my experience of 'clown' I felt that 'clown' was about the alignment of the ego-self axis. 'Clowns' share stories told from a place of ego-self axis alignment as I understand it. I remember something my clown teacher said to me, when I was terrified and frustrated with him and we had to do a performance. I asked him "What does clown mean to you?" and he said that it is sharing something that you know about the human condition. And each of the three women facilitating BSR is able, from the conscious distillation of her own experience and process to share what she knows of the human condition. Each speaks comes from that place of clown, the integrity of the ego-self axis.

Maja: Does anything more come to mind that you would like to speak to—you look as if something is cooking?

Wendy: I would like to say something about the shadow. BSR offers a container into which shadow is welcomed, a place of possible healing and integration of shadow. During my BSR work I had to confront my projections onto other women in the group. Through the experience of working with them on the floor, I realized how my projections of shadow onto them dropped away as I began to see their humanness. The way we talk about shadow in BSR work, and how it is welcomed into our awareness, allowed me to bring more of my shadow to consciousness.

Marion, Mary, and Ann talk about what they do when they run into trouble themselves as a team, from the Japanese tea ceremony to lighting a candle and waiting for Sophia to come into this very human place, enabling us to see the light in the shadow. They invite the darkness in order that it may be seen, often through our mask-work or by becoming conscious of our projections onto others in the group. Occasions when I have been part of a team and seen how suddenly shadow comes up have been very important for me, too. And shadow must come up. Where there are humans there will always be shadow; and to learn not to be surprised by it but to create a space for it is essential. And in that space, the capacity to move beyond the personal and tap into love at an archetypal level promotes healing. I know Marion has said that some people have not wanted to continue in BSR because of the need for so much shadow work. But it is precisely in a secure container such as BSR that we can do our work on shadow. And that is a rare opportunity.

Another thing I take with me that is connected to shadow work is a different way to be in my relationships, especially with my children and grandchildren. I am aware how much more authentic I am in my life. I no longer push aside things that I think are negative. Marion's, Mary's, and Ann's stories helped us to look at ourselves, at our own shadow. Shadow—and its integration—was also an integral part of the readings for the Nietzsche seminars. Certainly the shadow comes out in mask-work. It is profound to experience the mask's energy, to give it a body through movement and to get to know what it says. In a way, BSR work is essentially about trying to give form to shadow, getting to know shadow, the unconscious trauma and previously unlived life so often lodged in the body.

As I mentioned, a huge piece of my shadow work concerned my projections onto other women in the BSR group and onto one woman in particular. My mother had been a 'star.' She had presence, a wicked sense of humor, and was extremely extraverted and gregarious. I projected that 'star' onto this other woman, and in so doing immediately diminished myself although, in a funny way, one can share a little bit of stardom just by being a friend! I remember a conversation I had with Mary. I said I had all these friends who are stars. And I remember Mary saying, "Yes, they are stars ... And you are a laser-beam. So one is not better than the other, it is a matter of a different quality, a different flower." Slowly, I have been able to take back the projection that those 'stars' had value and I didn't, just as my mother had value and I did not. Eventually I could allow them to be themselves, and I could stand in my own "laser-ness" and own its value.

A second piece of shadow work related to another woman also had to do with something around my mother. This woman always sat in the front row, right in front of Marion. She was beautiful, wealthy, knew what she wanted and how to get it. She always seemed to have her hand in the air. She just irritated the hell out of me [laughs]. Because there I was, always sitting at the back, hardly capable of raising my hand! Very strangely this woman and I ended up on a committee together. Conversations with her followed, then came her personal story, the projections began to slip and I could see what I had been projecting! Again, we are back to humanness and the human condition! Later, I had an experience working on a team with four other women, facilitating a workshop. A lot of shadow work needed to be done. And there was a need to "keep coming back, lighting Sophia's candle, keep coming back to that trust." The process worked like a meditation: it is not that shadow or conflict goes away but something else comes into the space so it is not only shadow, not only conflict. I find it profoundly humbling yet empowering that I am now much more able to "see" it, "feel" it and speak up when shadow manifests.

I had a really powerful experience of shadow with a friend and I don't know where it came from. I just said this: "Have I not given you enough?" I felt she wanted more from me. It came right out of the unconscious and for a whole week at the intensive I was brutal to her. I was aware I was brutal; I knew when it was coming up and all I could say was "Listen, I have no idea what this is. I am so sorry, if we can just hold on to this, I am sorry if this is hurting you. I don't know where it is coming from." And for six months we did not have contact but we are now back as friends, in even a deeper, more trusting way. But it came right up out of my unconscious and I just lashed out at her right at her most vulnerable place. I think I did not have so much control over myself and therefore it could come out. There was love between us and it is only in a relationship where there is this foundation that one can feel safe enough to let such unconscious material come up. These stories are such gifts.

Maja: What has it done for you, this shadow work?

Wendy: I find myself less defended against the darkness in myself. I have a different understanding now. I am not trying to be good. Of course, we always try to be good but I am not trying to be perfect. I really want to be authentic, and you cannot be authentic unless you acknowledge shadow. BSR work has given me the gift of integrating shadow into my most intimate relationships. Without that integration there is no authenticity, there is just striving towards some kind of perfection, which I certainly had tried to do most of my life—really as a defense. Now, when I have done something hurtful to someone close to me, for example, my daughter or even my grandson, I don't feel I must explain or try to undo what has been done. I can simply say, from a deep place, "You know, I am sorry, I too make mistakes." So, to answer your question, shadow work opens the field, it opens the work. There are no parameters to the field, there is only one thing: when one's psychotic corner manifests, it is imperative to observe it carefully and for that one has to have a healthy ego, another 'gift' of BSR work.

"Authenticity—Are You Going to be Real?"[85]
Daniela Sieff & Maja Reinau

This is the creature that has never been.
They never knew it, and yet, none the less.
They loved the way it moved, its suppleness,
Its neck, its very gaze, mild and serene.

Not there because they loved it, it behaved
as though it were. They always kept a space.
And in that clear unpeopled space they saved
It lightly reared its head, with scarce a trace

Of not being there. They fed it not with corn,
But only with the possibility
of being. And that was able to confer

Such strength, its brow put forth a horn. One horn.
Whitely it stole up to the maid, - to be
Within the silver mirror and in her.[86]

Introduction

Daniela F. Sieff, D.Phil. is writer with roots in evolutionary anthropology and an active interest in the dynamics of the psyche. The question that has engaged her is: 'What makes us who we are?' She has explored this question in relation to (1) the internal psychological and emotional world (2) the external physical, social and relational world, and (3) our species' evolutionary heritage. Her exploration has taken the form of both scholarship and personal experience. Daniela Sieff has a doctorate in biological anthropology from the University of Oxford. Her research took her to a wilderness region of Tanzania to live with a traditional cattle-herding people. She studied what families needed to survive, as well as how evolutionary processes contribute to shaping social behavior. For the last 15 years Daniela Sieff has focused on the dynamics of the wounded psyche. Her understanding has emerged through bringing together her own personal experience with knowledge that comes from psychotherapy,

---

85 ©Daniela F. Sieff and Maja Reinau.
86 R.M. Rilke, *Sonnets to Orpheus, Selected Poems*, p. 69.

neurobiology, anthropology and evolution. Her book, *Understanding and Healing Emotional Trauma: Conversations with Pioneering Clinicians and Researchers* was born out of this process, and was published by Routledge in 2015. For more information see www.danielasieff.com

Maja: When did you first do a BodySoul Rhythms intensive and why did you sign up for it?

Daniela: I did my first intensive in 2002. I had been exploring my inner world for a few years, but I was working with a man and we had talked about whether I needed to work with a woman as well. He encouraged me to explore that possibility and because Marion Woodman's books had spoken to me, I e-mailed her website to see what the possibilities might be. I received a reply saying that Marion was leading a workshop in the UK that autumn. I signed up! Since then I have done six intensives and a number of other seminars.

Maja: What did you experience at your first intensive?

Daniela: The first intensive was terrifying. I had no idea what was happening and whether I could trust it. I knew Marion's books, but I knew nothing about Marion as a person. I also knew nothing about the other two leaders, Mary Hamilton and Ann Skinner, and I did not know any of the apprentices or any of the participants. I had never done any of the exercises before, or indeed anything even vaguely similar. I had no idea where the week was going. That was both scary and exciting. That made the first intensive different to all the others. The element of danger felt very real during the first intensive because it was a journey into a totally unknown land. But despite my terror, the opportunity to enter into the unknown was incredibly valuable. During a healing journey we continually have to enter the unknown, and to have an opportunity to experience that in a safe and contained environment was incredibly precious.

Another advantage of it all being so unknown was that I had no preconceptions. The unknown creates a blank space into which something totally new can emerge. A Zen koan, that Marion loves, captures the potential of that edge:

> Ride your horse along the edge
> of the sword
> Hide yourself in the middle of the flames
> Blossoms of the fruit tree will
> Bloom in the fire
> The sun rises in the evening[87]

---

87 Quoted in Marion Woodman, *The Pregnant Virgin: A Process of Psychological Transformation*, p. 177.

During the first intensive, I felt myself riding along the edge of a sword in a way that was not repeated at later workshops. During the first intensive, the raw fear constellated by stepping into a completely unknown process created a sharp intensity that brought deep learning. Consequently, although later intensives have been hugely powerful — perhaps more powerful than the first — they lack the raw adventure that I experienced the first time, and I miss that. On the other hand, at later intensives, because I knew the format and trusted the process and the leaders, I could allow myself to surrender to the exercises, and so I dropped more deeply into what I carried in my unconscious. That brought different learning.

Maja: Can you talk more about that process of allowing yourself to drop to deeper levels and how that changed as you did more workshops?

Daniela: At my first workshop I was so guarded that I did not truly drop into a deeper space until the final night. Earlier in the week, when we were doing bodywork, it seemed to me that everybody else was genuinely into what was happening, whereas I felt that I was not getting it. I felt as if I was putting on an act. I was self-consciously deciding on something to do, and then doing it. It was only during the very last exercise that I finally allowed what was there to emerge more organically. However, at subsequent intensives I surrendered to the exercises more easily and dropped more deeply. I have not felt that I was acting since the first intensive. There were several reasons for that change—all of which centered on greater trust. First, I trusted the leaders. Second, I knew the exercises, had a sense of what was coming next and trusted the process. Third, I had got to know some of the participants and had a sense of whom I felt comfortable partnering and who I trusted. And fourth, as my ability to contain myself got better, I began to trust myself to hold the emerging energies.

Maja: I am interested in that deep drop you speak about—I can imagine the fear and feelings of danger at the first intensives when it was so totally unknown. Could you speak more about that?

Daniela: During the intensives we make masks out of plaster of Paris on our faces. We decorate the masks with whatever attracts us, and wear them during a series of improvisations. The idea is that the masks allow us to embody and recognize a previously hidden aspect of ourselves which is now ready to come into consciousness. At the end of the week, we do a final improvisation with our mask and at the end of the improvisation we organically find an 'I am statement' which encapsulates the energy held by our mask.

My partner did her work first. What emerged from her improvisation was 'I am joy!' and it was glorious to mirror that. It is with me to this day. Then it was my turn. I was frightened that nothing would emerge (and that I would be exposed as a fraud), so before the improvisation started, I asked myself, 'What shall I do to fill this space?' Marion had been talking about the 'sword of discretion' and I liked the sound of it, so I consciously decided to use that as the basis for my improvisation. I had a stone that I had picked up during a very significant run, and as I forcefully 'cut' through the carpet with my stone I said, 'I am a sword.' At the time I felt as though I was acting, although in retrospect I realized that my choice to act 'I am a sword' rather than, 'I am a pink elephant' came from somewhere real.

However, during that improvisation I also found myself saying, 'I am pain.' That took me by surprise, and so when the time came to settle on one statement I was unsure which to choose. As I was oscillating back and forth between the two statements, the woman who was mirroring me said that 'I am pain' had sounded more authentic than 'I am sword.' That hit something in me. I collapsed. Everyone else was emerging from the depths and preparing for the final night's ritual, and I was curled up in a heap on the floor in what felt like overwhelming pain.

Maja: What happened then?

Daniela: Somehow I got up, and prepared myself for the very final ritual, which involves articulating the essence of what we have discovered about ourselves during the intensive, and also deciding on a sacrifice which will create space into which the new energy can emerge. Then each of us comes to the center of a circle, and declares that, either out aloud or silently. The statement that captured the essence of my week was similar to the 'I am' statement of my mask, but it also included a consciousness of the shame that I carried. It was 'I am ashamed of my pain.' I came to the center of the circle and said that.

However one of the things that I had already learned in my therapeutic process, is that shame can only be healed if it is exposed to another who accepts us. More importantly, in order to heal shame we have to know that we are being seen whilst exposing our shame, and on sitting down I realized that although I had spoken my truth, I had been looking at the floor and had not made eye contact with anybody. That left me thinking I had missed an opportunity.

I had gone relatively early in the evening so when the others were taking their turn I contemplated returning to the circle. Did I need to go back and do more in order to make it real? Or had I done as much as I was capable of doing at that point in my journey, and should I leave it to next time, rather than forcing it? Was this an opportunity to accept my (current) limits and to learn a little about patience? Eventually, when everybody had had their turn, Marion asked, 'Is there anything else?' 'Yes!' I replied, 'Can I come back into the circle? I remember it to this day. In that moment I felt more vulnerable, frightened and connected to my pain than at any time previously.

Returning to the circle I talked about being ashamed of my pain. However, when I came to the end I realized that, yet again my eyes had been fixed to the floor. So I stood in silence and willed myself to look up. When I eventually managed to raise my gaze, I purposefully looked around the circle, making eye contact with everyone. And I was aware that Marion, Mary, and Ann, as well as some of the other women, were meeting my gaze with profound presence, acceptance and compassion. It was enormously healing, partly because I had found the courage within myself to return to the circle, and partly because of how I was received.

That said, I would have been in trouble had I not been engaged in an ongoing therapeutic process. I ended that intensive at the nadir of a descent rather than back in the light where I was 'supposed' to be, and I desperately needed a safe place in which I could continue to work with what had emerged.

Maja: You went back to your analyst, worked with it, and came back to the next intensive? Why?

Daniela: I came back because that first intensive had opened doors. It had touched something and had been a powerful and provocative week. Going back into the circle was what Daniel Stern calls a 'Now Moment'[88] - a moment when something shifts in our unconscious and we have an opportunity to take a step towards a new world. Also I am an explorer, and I wanted to return to the environment in which I had been able to explore. In addition, I had made a connection with Mary and that left an imprint. The intensive was held on the edge of Dartmoor National Park and in the early mornings I had gone running on the moors. Most mornings I had bumped into Mary, who was also out running, and our silent early morning nods of acknowledgment forged a bond.

Maja: And your next intensive? How was that?

Daniela: My next intensive was held at Landegg in Switzerland, and I was disappointed. I did not like the place. It was on the edge of a town and I missed being able to get out into nature. The food was not great—it was rather like bad school food, and felt unhealthy rather than nourishing. Outside the room in which we worked was a large television that was permanently switched on and which was loud and distracting. And Marion could not make it because she had been ill.

---

88 Stern, *The Present Moment in Psychotherapy and Everyday Life.*

Maja: What does Marion add to the workshop?

Daniela: A huge amount. For me journeying into the unconscious depends not on the form of the exercises, but on the person who is facilitating the process. If I am going to that edge, then I need to work with somebody who has actually lived it. Marion has lived it in a way that few people have. She has faced her darkness head-on. That gives me permission to do the same. It helps me build the trust needed to risk change. During the intensives knowing that Marion, Mary, and Ann have been there, and that they have come through, offers me the freedom to let go because I trust that they can pull me through if I am in too deep.

I believe that when we do this kind of work we intuitively sense how deep it is safe to go, depending on who is facilitating the process. For example, I recently went to a Jungian workshop where two separate speakers each led different active imaginations, as part of their respective sessions. One of them had clearly been to the edge—and the work that I did with that person was profound. However, with the other analyst I thought, 'I am not doing this exercise with you. I do not trust this. It doesn't feel safe.' When I started doing BodySoul Rhythms intensives, I intuitively trusted Marion, Mary, and Ann.

Marion also offers a lived example of what it means to be well, despite having suffered childhood trauma. Marion's energy implicitly says that there is a way through our wounds. Growing up in a less than healthy emotional environment we bury parts of ourselves, devise a set of erroneous internal beliefs, develop a shame-based identity, and construct a set of fear-driven implicit rules. At some barely conscious level we know this is causing us suffering, and we have a desperate need to change. However these beliefs and behaviors are all we have ever known. They are hard-wired into our psyche, and we cannot actually imagine any other way of being. Thus to have any chance of changing, we need a model of somebody who has lived through trauma and who has found a new way to be. Marion has been one of my models. She has incredible vibrancy and passion, and what became clear to me was that her aliveness was rooted in her acceptance of her pain and suffering. She has shown me that there is a way through and that has been inspirational. Marion says that the poet, Emily Dickinson, gave her hope that life could be different. Marion is one of the people who have given me similar hope.

Another inspiring thing about Marion is how she shares her own experiences so generously and vulnerably. For example, I remember her telling us of an occasion when she had to leave Canada for Zurich, to continue her studies at The Jung Institute. Marion was unsure about leaving Canada because her mother was ill, but her mother encouraged her to go, saying, 'Marion, if you can be free, then go! When Marion shared that story, she followed it by saying, 'And I will say the same to all of you ladies; if you can be free, then go!' That was a Now! Moment and opened a door to healing. It hit me at a visceral level and created sparks of possibility. And it had that power because it was being said by a woman who had actually lived it and who was vulnerable enough to let others into what she had lived.

In Rilke's poem, 'Sonnets to Orpheus,' there is a line about how they feed the unicorn not with corn, but with 'the possibility of being.' When I encounter somebody as authentic as Marion, I feel that I am being fed by the possibility of being.

Maja: You say that the intensives have provided you with a space in which what you hold in your unconscious can come into the light of consciousness, grow and unfold. Would you be willing to talk about what has unfolded during the workshops? Can you see a thread? Do you see something working itself through?

Daniela: I do see an unfolding thread, and that is most easily described through my masks. The first mask that I made, which I now call The Devon Mask, was a split mask. On the left there was a gash in the jaw line, and when I was in the energy of this side of the mask I would crouch low, feel as though I was cowering at the back of a cage, and move like a wary, hesitant, frightened martial artist. I called this side 'The Injured Cub.' However, if anybody approached me I would switch into the other side of the mask, whereupon I would stand up tall, bow to them, but then turn away. I called this side 'The Marble Figure.'

When I created that mask I was not converse with Jungian theory, but I now understand that split as a classic manifestation of the archetypal self-care system that Donald Kalsched has described.[89] Kalsched argues that following trauma a self-care survival system is constellated and at the core of this system is a split. On the one hand there is the wounded, threatened, child-like part of us, which retreats into the dark in order to remain safely hidden (The Injured Cub). On the other hand, there is part of us which grows up prematurely and becomes a rigid defense system whose attempts at self-protection often swing into self-persecution (The Marble Figure).[90] In retrospect, the fit between my first mask and the dynamic that Kalsched describes was astounding.

Actually, that is one of the things that I find most precious about the BodySoul Rythms mask-work—it gives me the space in which I can live aspects of my psyche in an

---

89 Kalsched, *The Inner World of Trauma.*
90 Donald Kalsched and D.F. Sieff, "Uncovering the Secrets of the Traumatized Psyche: The Life-saving Inner Protector who is also a Prosecutor. In, D.F. Sieff, *Understanding and Healing Emotional Trauma: Conversations with Pioneering Clinicians and Researchers*, pp. 11-24.

unfettered and intense way, and so develop an embodied, experiential consciousness of what I carry.

I have now done a lot of work with that mask and it has been amazing to witness how it has changed, and how those changes reflect what is happening in my actual life. I have repainted it several times. I have cut away sections of it. I have added new textures to its surface. In other words, The Devon Mask has unfolded and grown and now exists in a different incarnation.

Every time I have altered the mask I have felt afraid. I have been scared that I would not like the new version as much as the old. But of course that fear simply reflects what is happening deep in my psyche. Altering a mask highlights the fact that I am in a process of psychological change, and that invariably terrifies me. However, I photograph each incarnation, and, unsurprisingly, I always find that I prefer the new version to the old one. In fact, when I look back over the images of the four or five different incarnations of The Devon Mask, it documents quite a journey.

Maja: Could you speak a little more about your journey with that mask?

Daniela: One aspect of that journey has centered on what that gash means to me. Over the course of the intensives I discovered that the gash is fuel for my curiosity and for my desire to become more conscious.

That became clear towards the end of my third intensive. I had been working with The Devon Mask, and when it came time to articulate the 'I am' statement I found myself saying, 'Curiosity did not kill the cub! I am free to be curious. I AM free to be curious.' The exercise which opened the door to that statement happened earlier in the week. We were doing improvisations to draw out the energy of our masks, when Ann produced a large ball of string. I (or rather the half-hidden part of me that was being expressed through that mask) saw this densely wound ball and gleefully thought, 'This is mask-work and I can do whatever I want!' With that I proceeded to unravel the entire ball of string. I had no sense of the meaning of what I was doing at the time, and I did not particularly care. All I knew was that I was full of delight and joy. I could make as much mess as I wanted, knowing that because this was mask-work nobody would stop me.

It was only after the exercise, when reflecting on the experience in my journal, that I became conscious of its deeper meaning. Something in me is driven to unravel the tangled ball of beliefs that is written into my unconscious. Something in me delights in releasing a psychological knot, and discovering an underlying pattern. And when The Wounded Cub saw that ball of string, it provided a hook which enabled that part of myself to be lived in a playful, exaggerated and embodied way. Through that I learned something important about myself. I already knew that I would always carry an injury and that there would always be a bloody gash. I believe that the pain of our deepest wounds does not ever go away. However, through that exercise I became more conscious of how my wounds fuelled the explorer in me and, as a consequence, I began to give myself permission to live my curiosity more fully and generously.

Maja: You said The Devon Mask is a split mask. Will you talk about the other side of the mask?

Daniela: The Marble Figure also transformed during the intensives. It began as a hard, rigid, stony defense system, and over time it changed into a much more alive, flexible and healthy protective energy. That change became manifest during my fourth or fifth intensive. The alternative 'I am' statement from my first intensive of 'I am a sword' had stayed with me, and feeling ready to explore that energy, I had brought a wooden sword to the intensive and had worked with it throughout the week. However, at the start of the final improvisation I found that I was very ambivalent about picking up the sword. I knew where my ambivalence was coming from: picking up the sword symbolized the letting go of a layer of my victim-identity and owning more of my power. That felt very frightening. I stood quietly with my fears, and only after some minutes could I muster enough courage to pick it up. Once I had picked up the sword, my cautiousness and ambivalence faded, and I spent the rest of the exercise cutting dead branches off trees whilst leaping around the garden. It was great fun. It was immensely satisfying and it gave me an embodied taste of a new way to defend myself.

The animal response to a perceived threat is to freeze, flee, fight or collapse. Whenever I felt threatened my habitual response was to freeze, whereupon I became panic-stricken, disconnected and rigid. The energy embodied by the original Marble Figure epitomized that dynamic. But it was something that I needed to change because it was limiting me and causing me pain. Yet at the same time I was terrified of change, because I had no idea if I could protect myself without The Marble Statue. During that exercise, when I felt myself using a weapon in a fluid and discriminating manner, I got a taste of the way forward. The experience of selectively cutting away the dead wood gave me a glimpse of how my life might be if I could cut out the obsolete parts of my defense system, and develop new ways to protect myself which were more fluid, responsive and discriminating.

On reflection, it is not only Marion, Ann, and Mary who offer me a model of a different way to be, but my own masks also give me precious models. Marion often quotes Meister Eckhart who said, 'When the soul wishes to experience something, she throws an image of the experience out before her, and enters into her own image.' Although the primary impetus for change and growth is my day-to-day reality rather than images and dreams, my masks have provided me with embodied images of new ways of being.[91] Moreover, when I then try to actually transform my lived reality, I can turn to the visceral experience of working with my masks for encouragement and inspiration.

Maja: Whilst you were telling the story of your mask-work with The Injured Cub, I was taken by the fact that neither you nor Ann could know what a ball of string might mean to you. However, when you followed the impulse to pick up the ball of string, and to unravel it on the floor, it opened up a new way of being for you. It allowed you to live the joy of your inner explorer in a more meaningful and conscious way. I am fascinated that you didn't know what was happening when you were going with it. I also wonder how that is different from sitting down and saying, "Yes, I will unravel this string and then I will do this and that."

Daniela: Sometimes I have a sense of what is going on whilst I am living the mask energy, such as when I was ambivalent about picking up the sword. Other times I do not. Both experiences can be valuable. For me it is not about knowing or not knowing the meaning of what is happing as it happens, rather it is about being in an environment that fosters the capacity for us to be surprised by ourselves. The intensives create a safe, yet spirited atmosphere in which anything is possible. I had never experienced anything like it before. During intensives I often feel the painful turmoil of journeying into darkness, but at the same time I feel the childlike delight and wonder of being free to try on different energies, and to be surprised by what comes through from my deeper self.

That element of surprise is not there if we sit down beforehand and think 'I will do this and I will do that.' When we think our way into what we are going to do before doing it we remain in the land of the known. That feels safe, but it means we shut down the opportunity for hitherto unlived parts of ourselves to become animated, embodied and enlivened. We have to be able to surprise ourselves if we are to grow and change.

Maja: What do you think happens when you have an experience like that? What happens when it unfolds organically, and you live it through your body? Are there any other experiences with your masks that speak of this?

Daniela: It seems to me that when experiences unfold organically, and we live them through our body, the memory of that experience is written into our being in a way that can change us. It is one thing to think or imagine 'X' or 'Y,' and quite another to know it in

---

91 Maja note on mask: yes and with mask-work you create the image, the form, and you become it, you move like it, you are in the world like it and relate from it—like practicing a new role, a new not before lived (at least consciously) way of being in the world). You get a lived experience.

our nervous system, muscles and bones because we have lived it. For example, Marion talks about an archetypal energy that she calls Death Mother. For Marion, when Death Mother energy comes at us, we feel that we have been hit in our bodies as well as in our psyches, and we collapse.[92] We feel that we have been caught by Medusa's stare and we turn to stone. We retreat into what Marion calls 'possum-psychology,' whereupon we make ourselves as small as possible in an attempt to disappear. Marion describes how, in the face of Death Mother, our life-energy drains from us and end up yearning for the oblivion of death. She says that if we spend long enough in this state, that yearning permeates our physical bodies as well as our psyches, and we may become ill. During one piece of mask-work I got a visceral sense of what Marion was talking about. It was pouring with rain, and horribly windy, but my mask 'led' me outside to begin the exercise lying in a flower bed. Then I buried myself under leaves and earth. At that point my actions seemed to symbolize the healthy acceptance of a journey into the darkness of the underworld, and being covered in moist, rich soil felt organic, nourishing and grounding. I felt earthed and rooted in a wholesome way. But suddenly my sense of what was happening changed and I felt suffocated by the earth that I had piled on top of me. I found myself thinking, 'Is this a tomb? Am I trying to bury myself alive? In short, I experienced the sudden shift of a positive energy flipping over to its dark side, and in this case it was very dark because it was an experience of Death Mother.

However, despite being freaked out by my awareness that Death Mother had been constellated, I stayed with the energy and eventually it changed again. Then I found myself in a place where I was as alive as I had ever been. At the conclusion of the exercise my 'I am' statement was: 'I am alive and at home in the earth and the water, and what others call dirt... and I am VERY, VERY alive!'

So that exercise gave me an embodied sense of several of the dynamics that Marion has talked about. First, how archetypal energy can swing from one pole to its opposite. Second, how the Death Mother energy constellates the desire to sink into the oblivion of death. And third, how the Death Mother energy can catapult us back into a vibrant life, if we can bring it to consciousness. Moreover, I now have some understanding of those dynamics not just because I have heard Marion speaking about them, but also because I have experienced them, albeit in a safe and contained way.

It seems to me that at times people can use their intellect to escape from experience, and their imaginative dream-world to escape from reality. BodySoul Rhythms bodywork takes us out of our intellect and at the same time it provides us with an opportunity to

---

92 See D.F. Sieff, *Confronting Death Mother: An Interview with Marion Woodman* in Spring 81, *The Psychology of Violence*, pp. 177-199.

ground our imagination in embodied reality. Certainly, the experiences of the intensives can be left at the intensives, rather than brought back into daily life — it is far easier to live something in the safety of an intensive than to live it for real. All the same, BodySoul Rhythms intensives offer an opportunity to bring what we learn through active imagination one step closer towards reality.

Maja: Earlier, you mentioned that mask-work has helped you to 'build the trust needed to risk change.' Can you talk a little more about that?

Daniela: The wounded part of me wants the safety of knowing what I am doing when I am doing it, but staying in the known precludes change. Through mask-work I began to learn how to trust what is happening in the moment, and to go with it, even when I do not understand it. Unravelling the ball of string was a classic example of that.

One reason why I have been so scared of opening to the unknown is that I have been scared of what might emerge from my unconscious. Maybe it would be a part of me that would bring disapproval. Maybe it would be a toxic energy that would sabotage what I cared about. Mask-work has helped me to combat those fears, because it has shown me that most often it is creative, wholesome and life-enhancing energies which are waiting to emerge, rather than destructive energies.

Mask-work has also helped me to learn how to trust the quiet and apparently empty space that is integral to change. During the process of change we have to let go of the old and wander around in no-man's land before the new can emerge. I used to feel hopelessly lost when I was in the no-man's land. It seemed to me that I was in a black void, and I was terrified that I would never find my way out. To escape my terror I would turn to my intellect and try to think my way out as quickly as possible. In so doing, I would block the process of change from unfolding in an organic and fluid way. However, during body-work Ann and Mary encourage us to trust the lulls, rather than force it. They emphasize that there is no right and no wrong. They urge us to wait quietly, whilst listening for the next impulse. Through that I have learned to trust that something more authentic will emerge, if I can only wait and listen. As a consequence, I am now more patient with the apparently empty space that is part of the process of change (even though I still do not like it!).

Additionally, when I am in no-man's land, I can now hear Marion reciting some of her favorite lines from T.S. Eliot's 'Four Quartets.' These lines—infused with Marion's voice and experience—also help to sustain me whilst I wait:

I said to my soul, be still, and wait without hope
For hope would be hope for the wrong thing; wait without love,

For love would be love of the wrong thing; there is yet faith
But the faith and the love and the hope are all in the waiting.
Wait without thought, for you are not ready for thought:
So the darkness shall be the light, and the stillness the dancing.[93]

Maja: I am interested in what happens when we give ourselves room to explore, and when we follow whatever wants to come through. With your masks, was there some kind of bigger unfolding line in what came through? Was there a basic issue that was working itself out?

Daniela: When I first wore The Devon mask, I experienced an Injured Cub hiding at the back of a dark cage. The cage had been built for defense but it had become a prison which was guarded by a rigid, marble, protective-persecutor. Each time I worked with that mask, a little more of the cub's energy dared to emerge from its cage, and much to my surprise, that energy was received with acceptance and love, rather than fear and hostility. As a result, The Marble Figure did not have to be so rigid in its defense, and I could begin to dismantle the protective prison that my psyche constructed to secure my survival. So, yes, there was a basic issue that was working itself out, and that issue centered on transforming the self-care system that Donald Kalsched talks about.

Mind you, I have to say that most of that work of transforming my self-care system has happened in my ongoing therapeutic process. What is more, in that process I focus on what is happening in my daily life, rather than on dreams and active imagination. So to return to your question, it is primarily my ongoing work with 'ordinary' reality which has enabled me to work with my basic issues. However, because mask-work has helped to make my psychological dynamics more visible and tangible—and because it has allowed me to experience those dynamics in an embodied, exaggerated and playful way — it has augmented and enriched the work that I do at a more prosaic level.

Maja: Were there other parts of the intensives that were significant for you? Were there other 'now moments?'

Daniela: Absolutely, and some of the most significant moments happened outside the formal structure of the intensives. For example, one of my most profound experiences centered on a run during my first intensive.

Marion, Ann, and Mary, together with the apprentice facilitators, had acted out the myth of Kore going into the underworld. They portrayed Kore's transformation in the underworld, showing how the woman who returned was no longer Kore, but Persephone.

---

93 T.S. Eliot, *Complete Poems and Plays: 1909–1950*, pp. 126-127.

LOVE MATTERS FOR PSYCHIC TRANSFORMATION

Following that we did an exercise called 'The Dance of Three,' in which one person is the dancer, a second person mirrors the movements of the dancer, and a third person contains both the dancer and the mirror. The dancer was encouraged to imagine herself as Persephone returning from the darkness of the underworld, and to let her 'movement' be inspired by that image.

After each member of the triad had taken on each role, we were encouraged to take the emerging energy of the dancer onto paper or clay. However, art has never been a powerful medium for me, and on this occasion the energy that had emerged during the exercise wanted to go running on the moors. So I asked Mary if I could go for a run and she said that was fine.

I had run every morning during the intensive but had had to turn round when I came to a stream, because there had not been enough time to go any further. However, during that intensive Marion had been talking about 'crossings' and when I headed out after the Dance of Three, the energy was pushing me to cross into a new land. Thus, when I got to the stream, I silently asked myself, 'Am I going to go on? Am I going to cross this stream?' I was not sure. There were only a few small rocks that I could use as stepping stones, so it would mean getting my feet and trainers wet, and I was nervous that running with wet feet and trainers might create blisters. Also, it was getting late and I was concerned that if I continued, I might not make it back for dinner. However, overriding those doubts was an inner voice which said, 'I AM going to cross the stream. I AM going to go on to explore new lands.' Also, a little way beyond the stream I could see a tor—a rocky hill that is typical of Cornwall and Devon—and I wanted to get to the top of it. So crossing the stream became a hugely symbolic private ritual, and with some nervousness and much elation, I went for it.

The journey continued. Although I was pretty fit, jogging up the tor was hard work and I had to push myself to continue. As I got closer to the top, I was struck by the immense granite boulders that formed a circle around the 'summit.' They were weathered into fantastic shapes, and what I saw in them were terrifying mythological creatures, such as gigantic vultures and razor-beaked griffins. The creatures appeared to be looking down on me. To get to the summit I had to walk between these boulders, and it seemed to me that they were the guardians of the summit. Being in an altered and imaginal world I thought 'Can I walk through this, or not?' In the mythological creatures I saw my fears and I knew that I had to walk through them to get to the top—but did I have it in me?[94]

---

94 Maja's note: Initiation Ritual.

Something drew me on and, filled with awe and fear; I bowed to the granite guardians, to my fears, and reverently walked between the boulders. Arriving at the summit, I was greeted by a small, shallow, grassy hollow—a natural bowl. From that bowl the boulders were far less threatening. That side of the boulders was much rounder, and because I was at the summit they did not tower above me. In fact, once in that grassy bowl, the boulders felt like they were protecting me rather than threatening me.

There had been a lot of talk in the intensive about containers, containment and bowls, so the image was very present, but that run turned the image into an embodied experience. That run gave me a bodily sense of what it was to walk through my fears and to come to a safe container. As I stood there in wonder, I bowed to the four directions and let the experience sink in.

Returning across the stream I picked up two stones as tangible links to the experience—one of which I used in the mask exercise that brought me to 'I am a sword.' But that was not the end of the experience. Up to that point there had been clouds in the sky and the light had been dull, but just after I crossed the stream the sun came out and so my shadow appeared, running next to me. I smiled and thought, 'That is appropriate: I may have just walked through my fears, but my shadow is still by my side!'

Maja: Were there any other aspects of intensives that were meaningful to you?

Daniela: As I have already mentioned there were things that Marion said which made a big impact. There were occasions when a sentence resonated in a profound way, and I suddenly understood a little more about some aspect of my psychological makeup. There were things that she shared of her own story that helped me realize that change really was possible.

Also, I really enjoyed working with Jung's seminars on Nietzsche's *Thus Spake Zarathustra*, during the BodySoul Rhythms leadership seminars. Although I do not remember any 'now moments' as such, huge portions of that text resonated, helping me to define my values and sharpen my understanding.

I am grateful for the poetry that Marion has introduced me to. I have never really been drawn to poetry, but with Marion infusing the words with her energy, many of her favorite poems have stayed with me and they have helped me to remain connected during times of transition, joy and darkness.

I am also grateful for the way that Marion has introduced me to mythology. I grew up with a scant knowledge of classical mythology, and I had no experience of looking at myths from the perspective of depth psychology. The way that Marion taught both the

Psyche and Eros myth, and the myth of Medusa, gave me a deeper and more vibrant understanding of psychological processes.

Similarly, Marion gave me a feel for elements of Christian mythology and symbolism. I grew up in a secular Jewish home, and I did not have similar images from my Jewish heritage. However, thanks to Marion, images like The Crucifixion, The Divine Child, The Virgin, and The Resurrection do now contribute to my world.

Maja: To conclude, I am wondering if you could articulate the essence of what BodySoul Rhythms intensives have given you.

Daniela: During the last decade my challenge has been to change how I relate to my trauma, transform my psychological self-care system, and confront the unconscious beliefs that limit me and bring me new layers of suffering. BodySoul Rhythms intensives have provided me with a safe, healing and vibrant environment in which I could do some of that work.

> But there come times—perhaps this is one of them -
> when we have to take ourselves more seriously or die;
> when we have to pull back from the incantations,
> rhythms we've moved to thoughtlessly,
> and disenthrall ourselves, bestow
> ourselves to silence, or a severer listening, cleansed
> of oratory, formulas, choruses, laments, static
> crowding the wires. We cut the wires,
> find ourselves in free-fall, as if
> our true home were the undimensional
> solitudes, the rift
> in the Great Nebula.
> No one who survives to speak
> new language, has avoided this:
> the cutting-away of an old force that held her
> rooted to an old ground
> the pitch of utter loneliness
> where she herself and all creation
> seem equally dispersed, weightless, her being a cry
> to which no echo comes or can ever come.[95]

---

95 Adrienne Rich, *The Dream of a Common Language: Poems 1974–1977*, pp. 74-75.

"Finding My Feminine Voice"
Wendy Bratherton & Maja Reinau

The Song of Amergin

I am a stag: of seven tines,
I am a flood: across a plain,
I am a wind: on a deep lake,
I am a tear: the Sun lets fall,
I am a hawk: above the cliff,
I am a thorn: beneath the nail,
I am a wonder: among flowers…[96]

Introduction

Wendy Bratherton is a Jungian analyst (analytical psychologist) in private practice. She is a professional member of her society and a supervisor in a variety of settings; she runs an infant observation seminar for therapists and trainees. Wendy has also trained in bio-dynamic cranio-sacral therapy. She has practised Tai Chi for 30 years and is a gifted potter and painter.

Maja: Wendy, what brought you into the BodySoul Rhythms work?

Wendy: There is a long history. I became a mother in the early 1970s and realized there still existed an enormous conflict between motherhood and having a career: the expectation was that young women would either pursue careers or raise children. Then I discovered other young mothers who had worked but not developed the careers they had anticipated. We loved looking after our children but also wanted meaningful work. Out of our frustration, we became involved in the women's movement and formed "consciousness raising" groups. These groups enabled us to explore our feelings, identify personal problems, and share concerns of a collective nature.

This was an extremely difficult period in my life and, encouraged by my mother, I entered Jungian analysis. I had a strong inner sense that I would get better if I continued to work with my analyst. And I did. Then, after years of analysis (1979-1989), I decided to train with the Society of Analytical Psychology in London (SAP) to become a Jungian analyst myself. I continued to be interested in women's issues and the "feminine" aspects of the psyche, and in 1996, three years after I had completed my training, I was asked

---

96 Robert Graves, *The White Goddess: A Historical Grammar of Poetic Myth,* p. 13.

to write a chapter for a book on the "feminine," with a focus on feminism in relation to analysis.[97] This proved to be a turning point for me. I took a week by the sea and thought: 'How am I going to write what I want to write?' 'How can I pull together what I have learned through my analytical experience and my earlier interests in women's issues?' I went to a local bookshop and Marion Woodman's books literally fell off the shelves into my hands! I realized: 'This is what I am trying to say!' I did not want to write in the traditional academic style; I wanted my article to stir the deeper feelings of the reader.

A colleague had agreed to edit my work but reneged because he found it was not sufficiently academic. It was then that I knew I was up against the sexism and biases inherent in the world of academic publishing—and that was what I was writing about! I was witness to the silencing of a feminine voice—this time my voice—by the collective power of the patriarchy. I sought guidance from the *Tarot* and the *I Ching*. The *Tarot* reading suggested: "justice will be done." I wrote to every member of the committee overseeing the papers being written for the book, explained the history of what had happened and how I felt that my work had not been assessed fairly. Two committee members came forward and said the article needed only a little editing. I was later gratified to learn that, when the manuscript was sent to America to be read, mine was the only chapter that did not need to be altered.

After this experience, I thought I would love to meet Marion Woodman. I talked to a colleague who happened to be going off to attend one of Marion's intensives. At the Intensive, she asked Marion to come to England and Marion agreed. So we ran a weekend workshop, and many of the women who attended that weekend later went on to train in Marion's work.[98] After meeting Marion at the weekend workshop, I was inspired to attend an Intensive. I felt that Marion spoke to my own experience and to the way in which the feminine was currently viewed in the collective.

Maja: What is it in Marion's way of describing the feminine that resonates with you?

Wendy: That is a difficult question to answer. I think what happened was this: I was having great difficulty expressing what I wanted to say in a "feminine" or soulful way—and had discovered that my way was certainly not the way of the editorial committee! Marion

---

97 Ian Alister and Christopher Hauke, (Eds). *Contemporary Jungian Analysis: Post-Jungian Perspectives from the Society of Analytical Psychology*, pp. 181-198.

98 Leadership Training requires the completion of a number of Intensives plus three seminars on Jung's Seminars on *Nietzsche's Zarathustra*, James L. Jarret (Ed.), *Nietzsche's Zarathustra: Notes of the Seminar Given in 1934-1939 by C.G. Jung*. Information on the Leadership Training Program in Marion Woodman's work may be found on the Marion Woodman Foundation website: www.mwoodmanfoundation.org

talks to the soul level. She allows the feminine to come through in her writing. This is what resonated with me. When Marion writes about "addiction to perfection," the animus as demon lover, and so on, she does so without being too academic. Her writing reflected what was going on in me; it put into words what on many levels I already knew and had been struggling with.

Maja: As you speak, you gesture with your hands as though you are gathering something from the ground, as though you have a sense of gathering or feeding something into your writing?

Wendy: Yes. I think that was what I felt in Marion's writings—there was something more fluid, more moist, more poetic coming through. I felt I knew the process Marion was talking about and it echoed my own. She gave voice to my experience.

Maja: When did you next work with Marion?

Wendy: As I said, Marion gave a weekend workshop in the area where I live. She talked to an audience of 80 people on the Friday evening. In the morning she talked a little more; then we did some relaxation, some movement and worked in triads. Marion conducted it all on her own, which I found pretty amazing. It was a wonderful experience for me, as I chaired the event and had the pleasure of introducing Marion.

Maja: Do you remember how you felt doing the Dance of Three, the triad work, for the first time?

Wendy: In that first Dance of Three, I worked with my own analyst and an analyst I knew from infant observation seminars—both were members of the society through which I trained. I remember how everything came very easily through my body, and the wonderfully liberating feeling of being able to let my body move as it wanted ... of finding the freedom to move.

Maja: And what was in that sense of freedom? Do you have an idea of what about the experience was so liberating and how that was felt in the group? Does anything come to mind about what you saw in the other bodies or what it was that seemed to welcome—allow—that liberating feeling?

Wendy: It is actually quite difficult to think back to that first experience of BSR work—so much has happened since then! Marion created an extremely supportive atmosphere that welcomed the body. With the Dance of Three, you have the mirroring and support of your two partners. That made it safe for me, so the tension I had held in my body most of my life could be released; I could let go of my self-consciousness. We were in that huge group of 80 people, and I was amazed how it could feel so safe in our own little group of three.

Maja: Do you think anything else contributed to this—why it felt so safe?

Wendy: Having my analyst there was important to me. And also I knew and trusted the third person. I think it also helped that my partners were analysts and knew how to give attention. I remember the mirroring was very good—and the holding. The body feels the security of a containing triangle. And Marion's role was crucial in helping me silence the inner voices that were saying: 'You must not move like that' and 'I wonder what the others think?' She led us in a few fun exercises before we did the Dance of Three and that helped everybody to loosen up and work through quite a lot of embarrassment. Marion told us: "It does not matter how it looks," "Don't listen to those negative voices," "Just let the body move in the way it wants to love." That was so helpful.

Maja: Do you remember your body's response to meeting Marion?

Wendy: My body response was simply that I liked her. I liked her energy, the way she spoke and also that her vulnerability was apparent. I respected that she asked for the quiet time she needed. I experienced Marion's energy as quite nervous and excitable but it felt alive and fine. My body felt: "This will be alright."

Maja: I imagine you then went to an Intensive. What moved you, what touched you—do you recall?

Wendy: Everything we did absolutely terrified me. I had terrible headaches and it was a struggle to be present. I enjoyed making the mask, that was not a problem, but wearing the mask was very difficult: my mask could not speak. I was frozen, petrified inside, and working with a part of myself that could not speak, that had never really spoken. When we went to the "Evening Mask Ball," I remember Mary Hamilton came over to me. She tried to get me to speak, asking "Who are you?" "Where is your home or land?" because she was responsible for introducing us as each 'mask' entered the room. Nothing! I had little bells hanging from the mask and I could tinkle the bells but I could not speak. I liked the mask—it is red—but it just could not speak. So it was very difficult being in the mask and being with others. On that last night of the Intensive, when you have to stand up in front of everyone and do something, I really just wanted to run away! I dreaded it but I knew I had to do it. I cannot remember what I said but I stood up and said something.

Maja: This part of you, this woman in you that could not speak, do you have any idea where she came from?

Wendy: I know I was very angry about what happened to me at my birth. I was a breach baby and my mother was in labour for a long time. She nearly died, so I also nearly died. Then, when I first went into analysis and was not in a good place, I heard this inner voice saying: "If you get through what you have to go through with this woman (that is, with my analyst), you will be alright." It was a good voice, as if a wise woman were guiding me. My analysis focused on my birth trauma, on connecting with my anger, finding motivation and my ground, and learning to protect myself. Now I feel that an inner wise woman had been guiding me silently all along; it was her "voice" that guided me into analysis. But her voice retreated during the analysis while we worked on early reconstruction. When that work was completed, I knew that I needed something more, and I think that 'something more' started to emerge at the Intensive. By that time, my ego was strong enough to find that real voice, to allow "my voice" through. And there was an actual feeling of 'something' coming through—almost like a birth—as though, this time, I was being born the 'right-way up.'

Maja: Can you say more about what that 'something more' was for you? And do you have a sense of what it was in the Intensives that enabled you to find it?

Wendy: Since my twenties I felt there was something to do with the "feminine" that I needed. Certainly the women's movement had not provided it—that movement was too much about annihilating men, as far as I could see. But the BSR Intensives enabled me to connect with other women. It was very important to me when I started to feel and to be in and around that feminine energy. My experience of that first Intensive was excruciating but the way we were supported to do the work—'going down' into the body, the unconscious, and coming up again over the course of a week—was very holding and very valuable.

Maja: I am touched by your feeling, at that first intensive, that you were "being born the right-way up." Can you say more about that experience?

Wendy: Yes. It felt as though something was ready to be born. Something was saying, "You are the right way up now." In other words, "You don't have to be turning cart-wheels for other people." "You can stand and be who you are." This happened through my work with that first mask. But something else also happened that was really important. It was one afternoon after the deep relaxation. I was working on the floor, going into a terrible screaming place in my body, and then I felt as though a spring began to uncoil inside me and the energy came shouting through. Mary was there and I ended up in her lap. That is the moment when I felt I had been "born the right way round." It felt good but it was difficult, too, when the woman 'caring' for me took me up to my room and put me to bed. She brought me my supper, as really I was in a state of shock. Then she left me to be quiet in my room alone. It was very healing and powerful. I was able to let myself settle in, rest and enjoy the experience. But the next day it felt less safe.

Maja: Do you know why that was?

Wendy: I saw the woman who had taken care of me the previous evening in the dining room. She talked to me about Mother Teresa's capacity to love everybody, however poor and whatever the state in which she found them. I am sure she did not mean to send me a negative message but I suddenly had the awful feeling that what I had done was bad, wrong, and this meant I was unlovable. Fortunately, I had a strong enough ego to be able to hold myself and tell myself everything was okay, that *I* was okay. But this turned out to be an invaluable experience because it taught just how vulnerable we often are during an Intensive, and how each one of us needs to be so very careful when others are as vulnerable and 'opened up' as I was. It is so easy to create what I call a 'doubting edge.' I found that the doubt stirred in me and undid some of the good of that profound experience of the previous day, when I felt I had been 'born the right way round.' It was difficult to hold the edge, the tension but, in the end, it was fine.

Maja: What was your experience at the next Intensive that you attended?

Wendy: It was a Phase 1 Intensive, so I made another mask—a more masculine mask. It was very powerful and full of energy. I had to speak in this mask. It made me speak, find some kind of voice. This bit [pointing to her jaw] was free.

Maja: The mask-work seems to have been profoundly transformative for you. Would you like to tell me about this more masculine mask?

Wendy: Yes. It was particularly interesting because the first mask I made in the BSR work picked up where I had left off with a series of masks I had made in clay during my analysis. That early series expressed a wide range of images, some very radiant and it ended with two masks: one masculine, one feminine. The feminine mask without a voice that I made in my first Intensive followed from the clay masks—I realized this later. Then the voice I still had to find came through the masculine mask of the second Intensive. This mask carried huge pure energy—not driven energy—it was Qi. The mask had a dark side, too, and at times was too powerful to wear. Later, when I attended a Phase 2 Intensive [where you work with a previous mask to integrate it more fully—MR], I had to wear both masks. When I could make myself speak, the voice came from my more masculine side, from 'will.' I made myself speak but the feminine voice was really not there. Wearing the two masks together was about getting them to work together, so that each would allow the other to have a voice, and they could dialogue together. That was what it felt like. Also, the feminine calmed the masculine energy.

Maja: Something was ready to be birthed?

Wendy: Yes, I think so.

Maja: Was there something in the room, in the setting of the Intensive that was important to the unfolding of your process? Or could it have happened anywhere?

Wendy: There was already a process at work—coming through the clay work I did in analysis, in particular. The Intensives gave me a space in which I could deepen the process. An Intensive also gives you time—it lasts a whole week—I did not have to pack up and leave after an hour! I had sensed that there was a place I could not go in my analysis but my analytical work had built up my ego so that I could come to this place of the Intensive and use it for whatever I needed to do. Something in me felt: "This is safe enough." And although I could not say: "This is what I am going to do," it simply came forth.

Maja: Your body movements as you speak ... moving slowly up and forward...

Wendy: Yes ... and this kind of movement seemed to come after that experience of feeling a spring uncoiling from the base of my spine. As I said before, it felt like a birth. Something new. A new potential being released and I did not know what it was because I still could not speak.

Maja: You mentioned that there was 'space' in the Intensive. What qualities did that space hold?

Wendy: It was contained—the room, the people—felt safe and contained. And I knew what I needed to do to keep myself in a reasonably good place. There was silence in the morning, too, and that was very good for me. Every day, for years, I have 'put myself together' when I wake up in the morning. Here, I could do whatever I needed to help me, such as Tai Chi, and have it accepted by the others. At the BSR Intensives, I find there is always an opportunity to say what you need, individually, and have it acknowledged. I felt safe in all stages of the Intensive except for one. I found I had to learn to take time during and after each Intensive in order to integrate the work, so I did not find the ceremony of making the sacrifice at the end of the week very helpful for me.

I did write to the leaders about how I felt. They did not say anything but introduced the possibility of voicing an intention if any of us did not feel able to make a sacrifice. So I knew I had been heard. I knew someone had read my letter, taken it seriously, and understood. It did not have to be talked about. Those little things were signs to me that this was a safe place in which to continue to do the work. But there were a few times when I did not feel that way and then I missed a year or two … After a while, however, I would feel the need to go back.

Maja: Do you remember why that was … and when?

Wendy: I remember it was after the second Intensive. It was nothing to do with the leaders but more an inner feeling that I was discovering something and did not want others near me. My process had reached a point that was proving difficult and painful; I felt angry and unheard, and thought that I just could not continue with this work. Then, after a year, I had a dream and felt I needed to go back. A Phase 2 Intensive was being offered and I thought it could be useful to work more deeply with an old mask—so I went, and had a much better experience. I also remember a couple of workshops after that Phase 2 Intensive, where there was talk about a possible Leadership Training program. I found it frustrating and a bit of a waste of time because no one seemed to know what they were talking about. But, again, I went back! And when next there was discussion about Leadership Training, I realized that the leaders had clearly 'done their work.' It was as if they had said: "We try to know and if we don't know we will work on it until we do know." So it felt safe to me once again. We started the Leadership Training and I did some Intensives back to back—both the seminar and the Intensive. I found that was better—a longer experience, and I was also becoming more confident in working with my own process. Again, I heard that feminine voice in me saying, "You need to go for that [the Leadership Training]. You need to do the seminars …" This voice grew stronger—stronger than another voice that was saying: "Oh, I don't want to do that." I completed the training in 2006.

Maja: What do you feel there is in the BodySoul Rhythms way of working that allows one's process to unfold and come through?

Wendy: I think the relaxation in the body, the bodywork, is central. I don't remember a great number of dreams; so much of my analysis did not proceed through dream work. I worked with clay, never knowing what form might emerge. I also practiced Tai Chi and Qi Gong. Again, that inner feminine voice had said: "You have to do it. You need something you can do for a few minutes every day." Even with a family to take care of, I found that I could go out into the garden and do my exercises every day. I am sure that the bodywork I did every day enabled my body to support my analytical work without becoming sick. Through the clay work, I became practiced in letting things emerge, and I saw the bodywork as helping the body contain what was going on psychically. I knew that bodywork was essential to my life—physically and psychically—but had no way of talking about it until I found the BSR Intensives.

I found that the bodywork we did at the Intensives was freer than the form of Tai Chi I practice. Qi Gong bodywork contains repetitive movements and helped me gather myself together so that I could function well during the day. The BSR bodywork allowed me to sink deeper and deeper into the body, and to access more and more energy. I could do this because years of Tai Chi and Qi Gong had taught me I was not going to disintegrate and that I could 'come back.' I was often amazed by what came through [laughter] with the deep relaxation but I was not scared or freaked out by it. Because I could not speak at the first Intensive, it was really important for me when we linked sound, the voice, with the bodywork and deep relaxation. Then I think of the mask-work and the BSR way of working pulls it all together, drawing all the different threads together into a whole. It was just what my body and soul needed.

Maja: We each have our experience of what BSR work is. But what is it for you? What made you come back?

Wendy: So many times I tried not to go back! But always that feminine voice came through with the message that I needed to continue. Marion made it possible for me to work with the masculine and the feminine. My analysis had helped me repair from my birth trauma and from a childhood in which there was precious little modelling of the positive feminine. My mother had no help and was sick, depressed. She survived through sheer will-power. And her mother, my maternal grandmother, was a tough lady who preferred her sons to her daughter. My father dominated the home, and I tried to emulate him because he was the more 'alive' of my parents. So, you see, in my family of origin, the feminine was not valued, which is why I found the women in the BSR group both nourishing and informative. They modelled aspects of the feminine my mother could not model for me, aspects that were not 'just' or 'animus-driven.'

It was important for me to work in a group, too, especially one like the BSR group that models love, compassion and the capacity to care in a nurturing way. When I left analysis, I was able to fight my case and establish boundaries around me but I had not yet discovered a way of being that embraced the woman in me who was meditative, who could see what was going on, and was more intuitive. I found this new way of being through my work with Marion and developed the ability to speak as a woman—in an embodied voice that takes the speechless, traumatized infant into account.

LOVE MATTERS FOR PSYCHIC TRANSFORMATION

Maja: Did the body- and voice-work in the BSR group—and the new way of being that you discovered—lead you in any new directions?

Wendy: Well, yes. I explored sensation in my analysis but it was not quite integrated. I would have this energy in my hands. My hands would even hurt by the time I had done my Tai Chi, and I would go and put them into the clay and something would emerge—but the clay was always cold and hard and wet. Then this idea suddenly came to me: "I need to do something with the body as well." In my analytical work with patients, I often had the sense that they wanted me to use touch. I knew it was taboo but I also knew it was needed. I had read an article in the *Journal of Analytical Psychology* many years earlier, written by a woman training to be a Jungian analyst who did bodywork at the same time. Then I read Donald Kalsched's book[99] in which he talks about the need to use touch sometimes arising in the work. If I felt it was needed, I would say to my patients: "We can agree that you may hold my hand in the session." I was careful with boundaries but wanted to explore the use of touch in therapy. The BSR Intensives had given me a voice which could value what was happening on the inner level, so I listened to that voice and enrolled in a cranio-sacral training program. Of course, there was another side of me saying: "What are you going? Why are you making life more difficult for yourself? Why are you spending a week sitting in a dark basement learning this stuff when you could be out in the sunshine?" But, again, it was like being catapulted by the Self into something I needed to do.

Maja: Could you say more about your experience of the cranio-sacral training. Was it a difficult shift for you, and did the BSR work help in way?

Wendy: It was a bumpy ride! I had to suspend a lot of my judgment and criticism in the cranio-sacral training, but I wanted to stay open to this new experience, and to broaden my spectrum. I really enjoyed being able to engage with the energy the therapy releases, and for that I have to thank the BSR Intensives in which we talked about and worked with energies in the body and psyche. I came to appreciate the importance of touch from my own experience with the therapy, and to find a way to integrate it and use it in my work. I realized how cranio-sacral therapy works to free energies that are blocked in the body-psyche system, and so enables someone to get through her day without the need to 'shut down' [i.e., dissociate—MR].

Maja: I would like to return to the feminine voice that emerged in the Intensives. Who is that feminine in you?

---

99 Kalsched, *The Inner World of Trauma.*

Wendy: Who is she? I call her "my wise woman," and she actually has a bit of a history. She has been guiding me for a long time, and the BSR work has allowed me to engage with her more and more. I first met her in analysis when I made a lot of female figures in clay. Now I have found ways of talking to her but for a long time there were no words. I remember going to a workshop in the 1980s, which was not a BSR workshop, and in which we had to talk to each other in a kind of nonsense language. I could not do it. Everyone thought that I was being difficult but I was mute because I had met "Mute Wise Woman"—that was what I called her in the beginning. She could not speak, I now realize, because she was non-verbal, sensate, and at that time I had no way of translating what she was sensing into words.

Other figures followed in clay: a woman with big shoulders, big hands and big feet, but with a small face, closed eyes and not much of a mouth, as if she cannot express what her body senses. Then, later, a similar figure but this time she is holding transformative animals, like the frog, in her lap. A little earlier, though, there was a forerunner to these female figures in the form of a sphinx. It has the same kind of expressionless face and a bull's head on her back looking over wings that are holding a frog, birds and snakes. The wings are on the back of a lion with a long tail and big feet; in front are large breasts; and there is a large penis underneath. I think the front feet are paws and the back feet cloven hooves. Now I see that this figure of the sphinx combines the masculine, feminine and instinctual but hidden behind, or turned away from, the massive front. In the female figures I made after the sphinx, the instinctual elements came more and more into the foreground. I feel the female figures represent the 'good voice' that pushed me into analysis, and also the 'good mother' that began to take form through the analysis, although I was not yet ready to embody either.

Maja: Your sphinx presents a profound image ... the whole process of the gradual emergence of your "wise woman" is interesting. What happened next?

Wendy: Well, I found myself responding to an urge to make masks in clay and worked on a series of faces—clay reliefs about 30 x 40 cm. The early reliefs were very frightening and violent, especially the mask I call Medusa because she is this terrifying Gorgon, the one keeping me held in fear. Then the masks began to change into the Green Man or they had leaves around them. Most of the masks were male—I made a Sun God as well as the Green Man—or they carried a masculine energy in some way. But the last in this series was the mask of a passive feminine figure. I call her the Moon Goddess. The masks seemed to erupt out of the clay, and that was when I began to understand that the archetypes are in us—and when the time is right the images will emerge. So by the time I started the BSR work and made the mask of the red woman, a long, slow transformative process had already taken place.

Maja: After such intense work on your series of clay reliefs, how did you find the BSR mask-work?

Wendy: The masks in BSR work are made of plaster and worn on your face. This is such a different experience. The mask of the mute red woman was on my face, no longer a clay mask to look at! The energy was not 'out there' in the clay, it was actually me, and I needed to find its voice. And then the next mask I made at the BSR Intensive was masculine again and had a voice, a rather loud voice. But after that, in my next series of masks, I met a feminine which I did not like. I really struggled with her. She had a mouth like an 'O,' and felt very isolated. I hated her colors: she seemed dark and deathly, like autumn. But then Marion called me to one side and said, "Go and look up Robert Graves' book on the White Goddess and look up 'O.'" I discovered that 'O' in the old Tree Alphabet stood for the gorse. It was March at the time and, on the moors at Grimstone in Devon where the Intensive was held, the only thing in flower was the gorse. I learned that gorse can survive the harsh winter and was important in the past because it blossoms very early in the year, before the grass has grown. Gorse was grown to feed the animals and keep them alive; they could eat the young shoots even though the gorse is prickly. So gorse became a complex, wonderfully meaningful image, and the mask began to hold those same qualities. My next mask, interestingly enough, was "The Old Man of the Sea."

Maja: First a feminine, then a masculine mask. Can you comment on this?

Wendy: I feel that masculine and feminine energies have been active in my psyche over the past sixteen years of my work in analysis and BSR Intensives. I—my conscious mind—could never have foreseen what emerged. It has all made me profoundly respectful of the unconscious process. That was what I said in the talk yesterday.[100] Despite all our new theories and ideas, I realize the importance of Jung's claim that there is an unconscious process which will unfold in its own way, given the space. I believe this is profoundly true, and that we need to allow that process to unfold. Yes, you can perhaps repair the mother-baby relationship but underneath that, at the deepest level, the river of archetypal energy is flowing. When it turns negative because there has not been 'good-enough' mothering, it is terrifying and can drive you into difficulties. But if you can transform that energy with 'good-enough' mothering, it becomes a resource that is creative and positive, and that one can drop into, however difficult that might be at times. It is a wonderful re-

---

100 Wendy Bratherton chaired a talk on the topic of healing trauma—MR.

source, not something to shy away from. But to turn it around, from negative to positive, is often a long, hard process.

This is what I wrote about in my article—what happens if the infant who has not had enough good mothering is exposed to the archetypal bad or negative mother. It is terrifying. Analysis, like a good-enough parent, can mediate this archetypal negative mother. I wrote about a patient of mine, a young boy who was terrified of going to school. A teacher could, in a split second, say something which would set off the bad mother in him and then he would become so petrified he could not learn. He could not stay in the classroom; he just wanted to run home. We worked with that problem until it changed. When I wrote the article, I brought my knowledge of infant research to my understanding of this case. The 'bad' can be experienced as an overwhelming force, a 'whoosh' of powerful archetypal energies from the unconscious. In my own process, I, too, felt the power of a force breaking through from the unconscious but in a good, flowing, solid way. One has to be careful—an archetypal energy can overwhelm the ego and drive one to do terrible things.

We learn a lot about the mother-infant relationship from the Freudians but my experience has taught me that we have to take on board the autonomous power of the archetypes. And we can use mythology to speak to that level of the psyche. I feel that was what Jung did when he emphasized the importance of mythology—it was as though he spoke directly to the child in the adult, saying, "I understand where you are ... I understood the full force of what you are experiencing as humanity has understood it for millennia. And here is a myth that may give you hope of transformation." Yesterday, Jean Knox talked about ways in which to help a person re-establish a sense of self-agency, and this, I believe, is what Jung achieved through his use of myth.

Maja: Yes, the telling of a myth can give one hope that there is a way forward, so one does not feel victimized or paralyzed by a particular situation. Now, to back-track a little, you mentioned earlier the importance of the BSR Intensive lasting a whole week. Would you like to say more about that?

Wendy: I feel that time and space is essential for one's process to unfold. My experience of infant observation taught me that simply my being there, watching and interested but not intrusive, allowed the child to 'use' the space and then I found that things happened. I certainly felt the importance of the space when I did my own work through clay. Although creating 'space' in this way is not part of the analytical tradition in which I was trained, my own analyst did allow me space to work with my hands. We would sit at a little table; I would bring my clay and she would just sit and watch. I would be terrified but I would start to work and an image, some form would emerge. I worked in silence;

my analyst said little. Sometimes I talked about what I had made. She kept everything I made in a cupboard in her room until, eventually, I was able to take them back, take them home. The process was physical and spontaneous. It all started when one day I thought: "I want clay" and I bought some and started to fiddle with it. The process of working with clay, and the things I made, gave me insight into what was going on in my mind in a way that nothing else did apart from dreams. It was difficult to value the process and the objects that emerged from the clay—perhaps because it happened within an analytical session I felt "this is all crazy stuff." Being with the women on the Intensives helped me to begin to value what came out of my work with clay...

Maja: Because?

Wendy: Because everyone else was struggling with some of the same—or similar—things. I could see that some of the women's pictures were images of the places I had been.[101] I did not feel quite so isolated and that "this was all my madness." My clay images were validated as psychic expressions, not as madness. The BSR work has had so many spin-offs for me at so many levels—this is just one.

Maja: What was another spin-off?

Wendy: Well, another spin-off was certainly the way in which I came to value the feminine and how that affected my work with patients. Recently I worked with a woman who had ended a previous analysis. We worked through her grief at the loss of her analysis and then she started to speak about a part of her that had never been allowed to realize its own voice. What she told me felt like an echo of my own experience. The focus of our work was to allow that true voice to come through. I don't think I could have seen what was needed and supported the process had I not done the BSR work. She needed to work in a different way—not solely in a traditional analytical way. I had done 'different' work in the Intensives and was able to work differently with her in the analytical setting.

Another spin-off from the BSR work was that it enabled me to leave the critical voices behind. This allowed me to follow through with the cranio-sacral training, despite the scepticism of my analytical colleagues. The BSR and cranio-sacral work both validate the

---

101 Note: at the Intensives participants are encouraged to hang their paintings on the walls of the work room. These paintings are treated with respect, as expressions from the soul and therefore not commented on with any evaluating words. If the painter wants to share and speak to a painting, she is free to do so. Slowly, over the week, the room is wallpapered with these paintings, expressing the process and the images that contain the themes worked with. It is a way of silent sharing and expansion of the reflector. The pictures are taken down at midday of the last full day of an Intensive as a way of beginning the process of gathering the energy in again—MR.

sensate and the intuitive. The same, of course, is true of clay work. These three ways of working—BSR, cranio-sacral and clay—complement each other and I have been able to integrate them professionally. The cranio-work, in particular, tied in with my energy work in Tai Chi and Qi Gong. I find that when I do 'hands-on' cranio-sacral work with my patients, I am less exhausted and more creative than when I work only verbally. I know from my own experience how cranio-sacral therapy can clear the vestiges of a trauma as no talking therapy seems able to do. Talking therapy is a powerful vehicle for healing relational and emotional wounds but I do not think it can clear what trauma has locked into the body. BSR work gave me courage: it freed me to do bodywork and train as a cranio-sacral therapist. I am reminded of Mary Starks Whitehouse's words: "The body is the physical aspect of the personality and movement is the personality made visible."[102] I must add that when I met my husband, he also validated the intuitive and sensate functions, and taught me some hands-on work!

Maja: The combination of analytical training, BSR work, cranio-sacral therapy, creative and energy work sounds powerful and allows you a great deal of flexibility. Can you say more about this?

Wendy: I find that the different experiences and ways of working enhance each other. I had worked on my birth trauma in my analysis and then I worked through it again in the cranio-work. This gave me another perspective on the BSR work: when I attended an Intensive after the cranio-work, I realized that in the Dance of Three my movements were the movements of my birth! That was a very profound experience. And later, as an apprentice at an Intensive, holding and watching the room, I saw birth traumas coming through in the authentic movement of some of the women. Cranio-sacral work gave me another eye with which to see what was happening in the body. BSR work and cranio-sacral therapy together have helped me to understand more about trauma and to appreciate how precise, how specific, the body is in recording trauma.

Another thing I have gained is a deep understanding of the distance you need to allow a person who has suffered trauma. This became very apparent in my last Intensive when I

---

102 Mary Whitehouse "Physical Movement and Personality" in P. Pallaro (Ed.), *Authentic Movement: Essays by Mary Starks Whitehouse, Janet Adler, and Joan Chodorow*, p. 39. Mary Starks Whitehouse (1911-1979) was a student of Martha Graham. Interested in Jungian thought, she trained as a psychotherapist and integrated dance and Jungian theory into an experimental psychotherapeutic practice. Whitehouse created individual, dyadic and group experiences to allow people to explore psychological processes kinesthetically, through expressive movement and sound. She originated the 'dance of three,' and much of her work later became known, and further developed, as Authentic Movement.

worked in the positive mothering exercise with someone who could not come anywhere near me. It was important to give her enough space, allow her to come an inch closer, then move away, an inch closer and back, dealing with her fear little by little. That is an example of how trauma work feeds back into the BodySoul work.

Maja: Did your knowledge of trauma work come through the cranio-sacral training?

Wendy: A lot of it did, and from working with Babette Rothschild,[103] although I do not agree with her views on early trauma. That is where analysis is so helpful.[104] My realisation of the importance of touch, and how a therapist using touch needs to know what she is doing and why, grew out of my own analysis. The BSR work gave me the bodywork experience and the confidence to do the cranio-work and that work heightened my understanding of trauma and trauma work. Bessel van der Kolk writes that "[Trauma] therapy needs to consist of helping people to be in their bodies and to understand their bodily sensations. And this is certainly not something that any of the traditional psychotherapies, that we have all been taught, help people to do very well."[105]

Maja: I would like to shift to a different topic for a moment. Witnessing is important in BSR work. Would you talk about your experience of witnessing, and your thoughts on witnessing?

Wendy: Witnessing in BSR work is part of what I call the encouragement. The power of this kind of witnessing and containment is huge, as it is totally accepting and non-critical. But it has to be done with presence—by this I mean that the person doing the witnessing must not let her issues get in the way. If that happens, she cannot be present. In fact, it is important that no other person's issues contaminate the experience. This is why we have to do our own work all the time in this profession. Then you can be who you are and allow whatever needs to emerge to come through and find expression through movement and words—otherwise there is no way, really, of knowing what it is.

---

103 Babette Rothschild is a psychotherapist and body-psychotherapist, member of the International and European Societies for Traumatic Stress Studies, the Association of Traumatic Stress specialists and the National Association of Social Workers.

104 Wendy is referring to analysis in the form practiced by her training society, where analysis takes place four to five times a week and the couch is included; this allows for deep regression and holding, and hence to working through early material—MR.

105 Bessel van der Kolk, MD, (November, 1998) "Neurobiology, Attachment and Trauma." Presentation at the annual meeting of the International Society for Traumatic Stress Studies, Washington, DC, quoted in Babette Rothschild, *The Body Remembers,* p. 3.

Maja: You suggested that being witnessed with love is encouraging. Can you say more about that?

Wendy: Yes, to be witnessed with love is like the early gaze of the mother and the baby. To be witnessed in that way—to receive the "wow" of that early experience we probably did not have enough of as a baby—that is encouraging.

Maja: Can you say something about what that gaze and the witnessing does to your body?

Wendy: That depends. When it is good witnessing and the person doing it is truly present and attuned, I would describe the effect on the body as a kind of warm flow—an expansion. It gives confidence and allows you to move and expand, a little like the experience in cranio-work when somebody's body is just beginning to 'flow.' The tissues begin to fill out, become more moist and fluid. Good witnessing allows this to happen, even if one's partner is not touching but simply following the body in her witnessing.

When the witness is attuned, she follows the mover's energy and the mover can let her energy flow as it needs to. But the opposite can happen. If you are mirrored or witnessed by someone who is 'fired up' and exaggerates your movements, even in the kindest possible way, it can all go terribly wrong. If this happens—Daniel Stern calls it mis-attunement—roles may switch. For example, when I start to think "Oh, is this what I am like?" then I am mirroring her and I may well work up my energy to a point that is dangerous for me.

Maja: Are you saying that witnessing is a great deal more difficult than it might appear?

Wendy: Oh, yes. Witnessing is a very difficult area and it is so precise. If it feels the slightest bit 'wrong' to the person being witnessed, it can take her out of the authentic movement that is perhaps just beginning to come through. This is especially true if the person being witnessed was not mirrored adequately enough as an infant and child; if, for example, the caregiver used the child as a self-object or could not attune to the child in a 'good-enough' way. Of course, you are not always going to get it right! And I know from my own experience that sometimes I have needed to step out of the exercise because I felt the energy was not being allowed to flow as it needed to. But good witnessing can really bring something through—it's a bit like the mother-baby interaction: If you watch a mother who can regulate her baby's affect well, she is able to exaggerate the baby's movements and sounds, and this will energise the baby, but equally she knows when it is too much and then will 'down-regulate' the baby's energy again.

So the witnessing links the BSR way of working with mother-baby interaction. But it is difficult because you are working with an adult, although you have also got "a baby in the adult" in front of you and that baby probably needs you to attune to it and engage with it. The inner infant develops in the interaction but we must remember that it has had early experiences of possibly traumatic interactions with its mother. This is why it matters precisely whether the witness or mirror is adequately attuned or not. I do think it is a very complicated issue. There are times when it is good to exaggerate the movements to bring them out, as the mother does with the baby, but you also have to be able to down-regulate. Certainly, the person trying to be attuned is bound to make mistakes. All of this ties in with the theory of agency. If you are witnessing a person who needs to engage her agency, it is important to witness and mirror the impulses that come from her own agency. You need to ask the question, "Am I mirroring the other person or does she have to turn around and mirror me?" We have to be very careful about that.

Maja: I became very aware of this through the work of apprenticing. As a witness, I sometimes found I needed to exaggerate something a bit more to feel the emerging confidence in the one being witnessed—and then I could mirror her expansion of movement, and equally the contraction of movement when that occurred. But it is so important to try not to impose on the other person's experience. I agree that it is difficult to get the tempo right. Sometimes you 'down-regulate' to enable the other person to reconnect back into herself again—a sort of quiet movement—and you can see how that allows a new impulse to be born. It is the same in the verbal dance, really—the need to attune to the background rhythm of a person's energy or vitality. And, as you emphasize in the mirroring of the body movements, it is important to remain sensitive to the process of repair. Yes, I agree there will be mis-attunements but how we handle them is key—how we observe them, become aware and readjust ourselves so that re-attunement is experienced in the other.

Wendy: Yes!

Maja: Can we go back for a moment to your experience of somehow 'meeting' your feminine voice in the Intensives? Would you have the words to describe that feminine?

Wendy: Yes, at one Intensive I had a quite remarkable dream the night after the positive mothering exercises. In the dream there was this big, square room that was completely dark and, hanging over it like curtains in a theatre, was flesh—big loops of flesh. I realized that the dream image was like a box, a part of me that had never been 'fleshed out.' I had never been able to take in and receive genuinely warm and positive mothering; it was a really new and positive experience to be able to take in that energy in the Intensive. This was also one of the experiences that led me into the cranio-work, which is very much about positive mothering in a safe environment. It can be dangerous, of course, because it can set up too much desire but the quiet 'ongoing-ness' of that holding touch has powerful healing potential. In the cranio-work we don't talk about it. The body feels the positive mothering environment, the support underneath the back and, little by little, is able to take it in. It is transformative to realize, "Oh, this is what it feels like for a child to have a really aligned, interested, good-enough mother." When defences are established very early in life, one is often too 'shut down' or dissociated to be able to receive any positive mothering. And then, if one should have a mother who is also depressed or angry or sick in any way, the early trauma is re-enforced.

Maja: Can you go back into your body and recall the experience of the good mothering exercise, that feeling of "Oh, this is how it feels to have good mothering?"

Wendy: Yes, I can remember it. There was real attention and holding, and there was warmth. I felt strong, too, and I could engage and take in the positive mothering. I could also say if something did not feel right. The dream came right after the exercise, so I feel it was a really deep experience. My body could interact with another body and receive a whole new experience from that other body. It was an experience of the body being freed up through the holding.

The focus of much of the analytical work in my tradition is on working with the negative. And, yes, sometimes you need to do this, but a shift in perspective from what a person did not have to a lived experience of positive mothering can be more important. Focusing on the negative may also increase defences, although, of course, it is essential to appreciate the need to mourn what one did not have. But I am not going to be prescriptive! We can't be positive mothers all the time as analysts but I think that we can often provide enough positive mothering to make a difference.

Maja: Earlier you said that as an apprentice you saw bodies in the Dance of Three 'dancing' their birth trauma. I found that very interesting. Why do you think the body goes into that movement?

Wendy: I felt it in myself and I saw it—in the Dance of Three and also in some other types of work that we were doing. I think the body goes into that kind of movement because that is where it needs to be healed. I don't think my body would necessarily go into that movement now that it has all come together in consciousness ... but it might. I don't know. I would need to do more BSR work to explore whether the body always goes to where it has most needed to heal. It is an interesting question. Of course, in the cranio-work, you sense how the body communicates: "I need to go here; this is what I've got to do." Or perhaps you have not been going to a place and the body keeps taking you there until you become conscious of the need. Maybe then it changes. I do remember feeling, "Oh, this is like the experience I had at my birth trauma," and then a sense of "Oh, I could do something else; this does not have to be repeated." We tend to repeat certain movements automatically and there is an excitement when we realize, "Oh, there are lots of ways I can move."

Maja: You have already said a little about the way in which the BSR work influences your practice as an analyst and cranio-worker but would you like to say more?

Wendy: I have been doing BSR work for a long time—since Marion first came to England in 1998. So I feel its influence has been integrated gradually and in different ways. I said earlier that it gave me the confidence to pursue my interest in touch therapy. Really, it's like having a much bigger toolbox. It's like having the confidence to say, "Let's take this in another direction," or "Can we work in a different way?" It gives me a range of options. For instance, I have paints and clay, and I have a sand tray. This enables me to say, "If you want to work with poetry, music, movement, paints, clay or sand tray—these things are all open to you—I am happy to follow your way." Sometimes I might say, "I think it could be very helpful if we just paint this image." The other day, a patient made an image from a dream. She had not brought it into the session. She knew there was a lot of grief, but she could not feel it; and she knew she wanted to cry but could not. I suggested that she take up the pose—the image—from her dream. And, when she did, the grief and tears were released. So my expanded toolbox allows me to say, "Yes, you can get off the couch; you don't have to stay in the chair; you can use the space. We can find ways of working." This reminds me of what Winnicott says:

> Psychotherapy takes place in the overlap of two areas of playing, that of the patient and that of the therapist. Psychotherapy has to do with two people playing together. The corollary of this is that where playing is not possible, then the work done by the therapist is directed towards bringing the patient from a state of not being able to play into a state of being able to play.[106]

I have had experiences when, for example, I have introduced a patient to sand tray. Now that I understand more about neuroscience, I realize that often when the traditional way of working is 'stuck,' it is helpful to introduce a modality that engages the right brain. My own process was very 'right brain.' It is a powerful moment when you engage the right brain and later process through the left brain what the right brain has produced. Then you can integrate into consciousness what has been released through right brain activity. We get far too fixed on words! My experience with clay and bodywork has taught me that it is often helpful when we are working with an image, for instance, to handle something, touch it, get a sense of it, to make it a bit more real. To work in this way

---

106 D.W. Winnicott, *Playing and Reality*, p. 44.

enables the patient to connect to her sense of self-agency and her capacity to control, especially if, as an infant, she did not have sufficient opportunity to play or felt she had to do what mother wanted. To realize "It can come from me" and "It is my sand tray and it is my painting" is powerfully healing. [The experience of agency—having the space to make, create and produce something—is very much encouraged in the BSR Intensives, inviting in the impulses through various modalities: dance, poetry, paintings created with everything from crayons to finger paints, clay and mask-work. Again, how our creations are received by the 'significant other' is essential to our feeling of validation both of the product per se and its source—the person who created it— MR].

> The potential space between baby and mother, between child and family, between individual and society or the world, depends on experience which leads to trust. It can be looked upon as sacred to the individual in that it is here that the individual experiences creative living.[107]

Maja: It is interesting how you started out by speaking about space and now you are coming back to analytical space and how that space has changed for you.

Wendy: Yes, it has changed. However, I had to face a kind of "row of elders" from my training society who told me, "You are doing it wrong." But the BSR work, my inner intuitive feminine voice, and the 'authoritative voice' of neuroscience told me, "Yes, you can do it in this way."

Maja: Is there anything you would like to add—anything else that comes to mind?

Wendy: I would like to thank you very much for creating the space for me to 'unfold' my experience to you. We don't need too much interference if the process is to unfold! And this reminds me of an experience I had when I worked in a psychiatric department. I was asked to lead a group of very ill people. I asked myself, "Well, what can I do that I really enjoy?" And the answer came, "We will work with clay." I had to be careful not to step on the art therapist's toes, so I was not allowed to make any interpretations. I showed the little group a couple of techniques on how to work the clay. They just sat and chatted and started to make things—and these were precious things! I guarded them with my life and did not say anything about them. This was another way of witnessing, watching and sensing. I was moved by the process that unfolded. Some could not touch the clay at first, or they just made a big mess or whatever—and then the next week, when I brought clay and their pieces back into the group, they said, "Oh, you've got it again." Their precious

---

107 D.W. Winnicott, "The Location of Cultural Experience," 1967 Published in the *International Journal of Psycho-Analysis*, Vol. 48, Part 3 (1967).

things were still there and they had been guarded, and this realization enabled the participants to make something else. The things they made began to change and take form and, as they changed, you could feel something change in the person—a little confidence came back. I had to hold and just allow something to come through—and it did. That was an important learning experience—just witnessing, shutting up, not having an opinion or interpretation but holding 'clear' space in which the psychic process could unfold.

I would also like to add a comment on dreams. In my analytical training, we never shared dreams in groups. There were no dream workshops in which someone would work with a dream in front of a group. So, for me, one of the most valuable learning experiences in the BSR work was the dream work Marion did in the group. It was enriching to learn more about symbols, to see how she valued the symbols. It was enlightening to see how she worked with dreams, especially on the collective level, as my own training focused on the personal level of dream interpretation. My use of dream work was broadened by Marion's teaching. And I am aware that I work more readily with the dramatic movement of a dream, as well as with the personified parts of a patient's psyche.

Last but not least, my spiritual practice and my diet were accepted by the BSR community, included as part of the whole BSR experience. So I felt that no part of myself had to be excluded.

Maja: You spoke earlier of the reaction of your training society to the changes in the way in which you work as an analyst. What is the reaction from your clients?

Wendy: That depends on what mood they are in! I still get beaten up—it is not all good! But at times I have been able to introduce something new which is good, and I have been able to be more authentic in myself. The training society can constellate the judgmental father, so it is often quite difficult to hear the grounded, authentic voice that says, "It does not matter what they say, it has been my experience, and I will stick with that. And if it helps somebody, fine." The BSR and cranio-work has taught me that I can work with patients in many different modalities. That does not mean clients do not struggle with me! I am not going to be the 'good mother' all the time. But I hope, with the support of the toolbox I now have, that I will be *good-enough*. It just depends on where you are from day to day, really.

Maja: When you tell your story, courage stands out. Your courage to follow whatever "she is," how you listened to that voice and how your process has slowly woven all the threads together. I am reminded of the Irish song of the weaver:

Weaver, Weaver

Weaver, weaver, weave our thread,
Whole and strong into your web
Healer, healer heal our pain
In love may we come strong again.

We are dark and we are bright
We are formed of earth and light
From joy and pain our lives are spun
But all too soon the spinning's done

[Weaver chorus]

No one knows why we are born
A web is made, a web is torn
Like wand 'ring sea birds we alight
To rest one moment, then take flight

 [Weaver chorus]

May we find the hidden way?
Beyond the gates of night and day
To that sweet land where apples grow
And endless healing waters flow

[Weaver chorus]

At that spring may we drink deep
And wake to dream, and die to sleep
And dreaming spin another for
A shining threat of life reborn.[108]

---

108 From an old folksong adapted by Starhawk, author, global justice activist and a respected voice in modern earth-based spirituality who generously has allowed me to quote it. For more information please see www.starhawk.org.

"Living Metaphor"
Marian Dunlea & Maja Reinau

The Root of the Root of Your Self

Don't go away, come near.
Don't be faithless, be faithful.
Find the antidote in the venom.
Come to the root of the root of yourself.

Molded of clay, yet kneaded
from the substance of certainty,
a guard at the Treasury of Holy Light –
come, return to the root of the root of your Self.

Once you get hold of selflessness,
You'll be dragged from your ego
and freed from many traps.
Come, return to the root of the root of your Self.

You are born from the children of God's creation,
but you have fixed your sight too low.
How can you be happy?
Come, return to the root of the root of your Self.

Although you are a talisman protecting a treasure,
you are also mine.
Open your hidden eyes
and come to the root of the root of your Self.
You were born from a ray of God's majesty
and have the blessings of a good star.
Why suffer at the hands of things that don't exist?
Come, return to the root of the root of your Self.

You are a ruby embedded in granite.
How long will you pretend it's not true?

We can see it in your eyes.
Come to the root of the root of your Self.

You came here from the presence of that fine Friend,
a little drunk, but gentle, stealing our hearts
with that look so full of fire; so,
come, return to the root of the root of your Self.
Our master and host, Shamsi Tabrizi,
has put the eternal cup before you.
Glory be to God, what a rare wine!
So come, return to the root of the root of your Self.[109]

Introduction

Marian Dunlea holds a M.Sc. degree in psychoanalytic psychotherapy. She is a Jungian analyst working in private practice. Her trainings include Psychoanalytic Psychotherapy, Psychosynthesis, Psychotherapy and Somatic Experience. She has taught in psychotherapy training institutes and in university programs. She is a core faculty member of the Marion Woodman Foundation and facilitates BodySoul Intensives, both nationally and internationally. Her particular focus lies in working with the dream and its resonance in the body.

Maja: I am gathering tapestries from women about their experience of BodySoul Rhythms work, and this is what I would like to ask you about. Going back to the beginning, what brought you into this work?

Marian: My first connection with Marion's work was in the mid '80s on the Victoria line of the London underground. I have no recall of any other book that had such an impact on me at that time, when I was training in Psychosynthesis. Marion Woodman was not discussed in the course but her writings excited me. As I read, the lights were going on in me: Marion's knowledge and love of theatre and english literature and her capacity in her writing to bring together imagination, body and passion fired my own imagination. That was my first connection with Marion Woodman.

The Psychosynthesis training in which I was engaged was innovative, creative and stimulating. It included body, mind and spirit in its map and I found a number of parallels with Jungian psychology, especially the focus on the transpersonal will (the Self in terms of analytical psychology). Yet, I think I was still "talking *about* the body" as opposed to "being *in* the body." In our training, we worked with ideas such as: "I have a body"; "I

---

109 Rumi, "The Root of the Root is Your Self," in *Love is a Stranger,* pp. 16-17.

am my body," and "I am more than my body." But when I read *Addiction to Perfection*,[110] I discovered a whole new dimension: the body is not only a *place* where we access an image or feeling; the body has its own reality, its own living wisdom. The body is not to be transcended but listened to as the locus of immanence, where spirit meets matter *in me*. I learned from Marion that my body is my own sacred temple, containing shadow and light. Suddenly the approach to the body of Psychosynthesis ("I have a body, I am my body," and "I am more than my body") felt like a room which I had been able to name and feel into but in which I had not yet dwelt.

Maja: It sounds as though your introduction to Marion's writings was profound. Was it also transformative?

Marian: I was captivated by Marion's work. Joyce McDougall's 1989 book, *Theatre of the Body*,[111] now comes to mind, perhaps because I suddenly felt Marion was opening up the theatre of the body *in me*, as a three-dimensional lived experience. But at the time I just 'parked' the idea—it had fired my imagination but I did not have anywhere to go with it.

Maja: I have a sense that's not the end of your story. What happened next?

Marian: We left London and went back to live in Ireland as a family in 1989. I began a Jungian analysis, and embarked on a psychoanalytical training which included studies of the work of Freud, Jung, Klein, and Lacan. My favorite part of this course was infant observation: it was such privileges to witness the mother/infant relationship evolve over a period of two years. During my training, I attended a few weekend workshops that Marion Woodman facilitated in London: I kept her alive in me and attended her seminars whenever she presented on this side of the Atlantic. So, by the time I finished my training, I knew that I wanted to pursue an archetypal approach to the psyche and to study with Marion Woodman. Then Marion came to Dublin to launch *Dancing in the Flames*.[112]

I encouraged some friends to attend the one-day workshop that was to mark the launch of Marion's book. Three of us went. Marion spoke in the morning, and Ann Skinner and Mary Hamilton led the afternoon work. I was thrilled to be with Marion in Dublin, and meeting Ann and Mary for the first time was a treat. I found myself chatting with Ann and Mary at the coffee break as if we were old friends, totally uninhibited. I told them about the mythical Irish landscape and the places they should visit. I also said

---

110 Marion Woodman, *Addiction to Perfection*.
111 Joyce McDougall, *Theaters Of The Body: A Psychoanalytic Approach to Psychosomatic Illness*.
112 Woodman and Dickson, *Dancing in the Flames*.

that they must come to do an Intensive in Ireland! I was on fire with the work that they brought and felt "this is it."

In the afternoon, Ann spoke and invited me to "come and attend a week-long Intensive in America." I became aware that an Intensive in Pajaro Dunes, California was soon approaching and on the way home in the car I remember telling my friends of my dream of participating in that Intensive. Back then, in 1996, travelling to the USA was a 'big deal.' It was huge to say, "I am going to California to do an Intensive," and to go home and say to my husband and family that I *needed* to do this work, at the same time wondering how and where I would get the money to support my dream. Yet I felt that I must follow that dream, and this was confirmed by a friend in the car as we drove home from Marion's workshop: "This is your path," she said. "You are going to be doing this work. I see you teaching this work ..." And, when I went home, things fell into place financially. I received a gift of money that would support me to go, and my family was all on board; I set off for my first intensive in California.

Maja: It seems that something was coming together for you. What was your experience of the Intensive at Pajaro Dunes?

Marian: Well! On the first night, Marion said: "Those who want to do meditation, please gather and I will talk to you about the format we use ... Tomorrow will be the first of February and Day One of our Intensive, so I will lead the first morning. Then you will have an idea of what we are doing." Marion spoke for a while; then I found myself telling her, and the group, that the first of February is Brigid's Day[113] and I asked if I might share a Brigid ritual. In her inimical way, Marion took a moment, her blue eyes taking me in. Then she said, "Tell me what you want to do." After I had explained the ritual, she said, in total faith, "Good—okay. You do it!" Today I have had the experience of running many workshops and I am still stunned when I remember her reply. Think of it! Who was this woman who had just shown up from Ireland? I could have been a jet-lagged madwoman but Marion said: "Good—okay. You do it!

Looking back now, I can see how Marion's entrusting me with the group was a threshold moment, a crossing over, for me, into a new quality of life experience. Marion's expression of trust helped dissolve self-doubts and criticisms that I had carried into adulthood from a childhood in which it was dangerous to show oneself or step forward (as the Irish poet, Seamus Heaney, writes: "Whatever you say, say *nothing*."[114]) I experienced

---

113 Brigid is an Irish goddess; patroness of poetry, medicine, arts and crafts, cattle and other livestock, and spring. Her feast day is Imbolc, celebrated around February 1.

114 Seamus Heaney, *North*, from the Poem: 'Whatever You Say, Say Nothing.'

Marion's trust and recognition as enabling, inviting me to walk free of the collective bind or complex which had always inhibited me.

Maja: I am interested to hear about the Brigid ritual and how it was received by the group.

Marian: I had brought with me a beautiful big golden shawl from India. I asked my house-mates to help me: "Can you come and help me spread this cloth outside on the grass, be-cause then Brigid's energy will bless the cloth. Blessed with her dew, we will bring it back into the circle in the morning." A few helped me lay out the beautiful saffron cloth ... but, of course, the rain came! I woke up the next morning at six and there was a massive down-pour. The shawl was soaked through, dripping with Brigid's dew. We squeezed it and the cloth was still soaking wet, so somebody said, "Put it in the dryer." So this magnificent golden shawl went into the dryer and shrank! We took it out when it was still damp and brought it to the gathering room, where Mary and Ann each took an end of the cloth. We all learned and then sang together the Gaelic song of Brigid's blessing—*Faoi bhrat Bhride sinn*—while we walked beneath the cloth: "*beneath the cloak of Brigid we are held.*"

Maja: I can appreciate how important a moment the Brigid ritual was for you. Were there any other memorable experiences at that first Intensive?

Marian: The whole Intensive was in many ways extraordinary. The unexpected happened more than once! During the first few days of the Intensive, the El Niño Pacific storm raged wildly, sweeping massive cedar and pine trees into the ocean and tossing them like matchsticks onto the beach nearby. A flood warning was issued and residents started to evacuate the area. We were in danger of being cut off on an isthmus but there was also a sense of excitement about being on an island together. It seemed a mythic space.

We chose, as a group, to stay put and it all felt apocalyptic, although that is a huge word to use. Yet it was quite something, choosing to stay on the island which, like the island in Shakespeare's *The Tempest*, seemed "full of voices."[115] Each one of us had to work with our fear of being stranded, of rising water, of cold. As much as we were in the land of actual and imminent danger, we were also in the land of the symbolic. With Marion, you are always working on the metaphorical level: in making the decision to remain on the island, we were entering into a commitment with a deeper layer of the psyche. I found it an extremely powerful experience to discover that I was *living metaphor* consciously with this community of women. Inner and outer, feeling and intuition, body and soul, were coming together. And we were reflecting on the experience, making meaning together.

---

115 William Shakespeare, *The Oxford Shakespeare: The Complete Works 2nd Edition*, pp. 1221-1245.

In this community, living metaphor was everything: metaphor was the tuning fork, its resonance the body—which is why we voted to stay on the island in the first place.

Maja: What happened then?

Marian: In the early hours of the third or fourth morning, when it was still very dark, there was a knock on the door. "Evacuation!" In a trice, we were up, packed and out. We gathered in our work-room and waited. Marion was consciously holding the tension for us all. We were living this crisis so graphically—it was as if *The Tempest* had come alive!

Then we heard the sound of running feet, like a drum beat. The National Guard had arrived to lead us through the flood waters and off the island. It was as though the masculine, the *animus*, had arrived to rescue us, and this resonated deeply in both body and psyche. We made the crossing, driving through the flood waters at a snail's pace, following close behind the men in the lorry ahead, not knowing if we would be swept off the road: a convoy of cars, driven by women, led in the front and held at the back by the National Guard. There was an archetypal quality to the experience, as though we were moving into a new country which reminds me of a line by André Gide, "One doesn't discover new lands without consenting to lose sight of the shore for a very long time."[116] That's what it felt like. Highly symbolic and we were living it. You are *in* the play—you are *in* your life at such a moment—vitally alive.

Maja: It certainly sounds as though you were living the archetypal core of an epic or medieval romance, perhaps a myth. Would you like to say more?

Marian: There is a fabulous photograph of Marion taken on that morning. She is wearing a bright yellow jacket with a red beret, holding the bouquet of flowers from the altar and looking radiant among the troops! And they came with such warmth and a sense of fun, despite the seriousness of the situation. Marion tells the story that I offered them Irish whisky and we had a great laugh before we left the island! But we arrived safely in Santa Cruze where Patty, our administrator, had managed miraculously to set us up in a hotel at short notice. Arnold Mindell was running a workshop there with a group of about 300 participants, and here we were a little group of bedraggled women, with Marion and Ross Woodman, tossed up on the shore, like the huge cedars and pines that were being thrown against the wharf by the storm. The wind was so strong that they had to fasten the balcony doors of my bedroom with a chain; it felt and sounded like the howling gale was in my room. Yet I feel that the poignant sense of vulnerability experienced by us all deepened the work for the remainder of the week. Sharing, reflecting on, and making

---

116 André Gide *The Counterfeiters: A Novel*, p. 326.

meaning of what had happened proved a profound experience for all of us. The container, so lovingly nurtured by Marion, Ann, and Mary, held fast.

Maja: Taking a deep breath after such an experience, I would like to ask you, what part of the Intensive was the most meaningful for you?

Marian: The mask-work really touched my soul. We worked in pairs. The woman I part-nered ... the energy of the mask she made was extremely shy and introverted. The mask retreated into a "cave," hiding behind some chairs draped in cloth. To me it looked as if the skin of the mask was baked dry from the sun: dry earth, dry boned. I remember the moment when I met the mask and fed it a piece of orange. As I fed it, the mask received. It was as though we were sharing bread together, a communion or *coniunctio* of souls. I think something about "wholeness" became conscious in me at that moment and, in hindsight, I can see that while I was feeding my partner's mask, I was also feeding my own introverted, shy, baked-dry soul, and not just as a projection. Now I know, from neuroscience, that my actual cells would have been resonating with her mask and being fed, opening neural pathways and creating new synapses in my brain. That might sound like an extraordinary statement, but we are only beginning to know the wonder of the plasticity of the brain from neuroscience.

Maja: I feel your excitement about the neuroscience. Could you say more?

Marian: Yes, I find the advances in neuroscience exhilarating. We are only now exploring the role of mirror neurons and how they help us to develop and grow in relationship. Mirror neurons get their name from the way in which they act like mirrors in our brain. They register an action we see being carried out by someone and it is as though we are carrying out that same action. My brain responds as if I, too, have performed that action. And not only does the brain mirror the action or *motion* but also the *e-motion* that accompanies the action. We can actually *feel* the emotion that is behind the intention of the action or gesture. We take in the whole action: the form, the facial expression, the tone of voice, the emotion. If a mother, for instance, gives a smile to a baby, this will elicit a smile from the baby in return, and a feeling of well-being. Mother and baby are sharing the action and the emotion involved. There is reciprocity: the baby's synapses fire and, when the mother receives the baby's smile, her synapses fire in return. Such *mutuality* grows each brain—'what is wired together fires together.' In this way our brain's capacity is enlarged and our ability to tolerate new behaviors and emotions increases. When an experience of mutuality is pleasurable it increases the production of endorphins and this whets the appetite for more such experiences. We integrate these new experiences and become more the person we have the potential to be. In Jungian terms, we would say we start to live the unlived life, to reclaim what was in the shadow and make it our own. This is central to the mirroring work we do with partners and in triads.

Maja: Let me take you back to the mask-work for a moment. Can you say more about why it was so profound for you?

Marian: What was so surprising to me was that I had a stronger relationship to the work of mirroring my partner in her mask than I had to my own mask at that workshop. But maybe that is the extravert in me! I can still see her mask and feel what it constellated in me. It was as though this particular mask broke open or awakened something in me at the level of soul. I was so deeply affected that, at my next workshop, I made a mask which clearly grew out of that first experience of mirroring my partner's mask. There was recognition in my psyche of something I saw as I mirrored my partner, which seems to me to be what Bion captures in his concept of the 'unthought known.' This recognition (or previously unconscious 'known') grew in me and came to consciousness as it became integrated, at the level of both body and psyche, through the experience of mirroring. And so, at the next workshop, I made a mask which was in a way inspired by that earlier experience of mirroring my partner. I made an Egyptian mask, emerging from a tomb.

Maja: Can you say more about mirroring? How important is it?

Marian: An understanding of the phenomena of mirroring and witnessing is really important in BodySoul work. The safe container of the relationship allows for deep transformation at a psychic and biological level, and this deep work can evolve through our partnering another. Seeing something in another really influences us. I saw that happen one night when teaching my own weekly group. One woman, witnessing another walk across the floor, was profoundly affected as the witness. The mover's posture, attitude and energy stirred something in her and this shifted her in her own work: her partner embodied just what she needed to make conscious. What I found so remarkable was that the feedback the 'witness' or 'mirror' gave to her partner (the woman who had walked across the room) proved equally essential to the 'mover.' It brought something to consciousness in her, too. The mover had not been able to recall her own movement as she walked: she remained unaware of the quality of her energy, her attitude or the words she had spoken at the time. Back to neuroscience! We now know that an experience such as being witnessed by a partner who has felt in her body the 'mover's' gesture, with its intention, emotion and action, stimulates a connection between the two hemispheres of the brain. The findings of neuroscience suggest that when the 'mover' was witnessed, seen, a link-up occurs between right hemisphere processing and left hemisphere processing; this is reflected in the 'mover's' experience of becoming conscious of what had emerged through her gesture as she walked across the floor. The right hemisphere is the store-house of the right-brain *implicit memory field*. The 'mover' had the *experience* but only when she received feedback from a witness who had a 'felt-sense' connection with her movement, could she make that experience conscious and integrate it. The connection between right- and left-brain is essential for the making of meaning, which in turn stimulates the creation of new neural pathways. It is so exciting to realize that our work with such experiences confirms the research being conducted in neuroscience on mirror neurons, as well as in quantum physics and field theory—but I will say something about field theory later.

In the Newtonian model, things remain separate, which leads to the notion: "I am essentially alone in the world, isolated from other people." Quantum theory describes how, when two systems meet, they overlap and combine to form a new identity or entity. The patterns of dynamic energy within systems change dramatically when in relation to other systems, leading to the emergence of a whole new thing that is greater than the sum of its parts. Human systems are also patterns of dynamic energy. Our bodies do not have hard and fast boundaries. What or who we interact with changes us, even at the psychological level. From this perspective, it is no longer about "me and you" but about "us." It's not about separation; it's about integration. It's not isolation; it's an understanding that we are all part of one great big interwoven system.

Maja: The connection between BodySoul work and research in neuroscience is exciting. But I would like to backtrack a little. Tell me about the first mask you made at Pajaro Dunes— and later I would like to hear about the mask you made at your second workshop—the Egyptian mask emerging from a tomb.

Marian: That first mask was of a cat. It grew into itself, as masks do, and has its own story to tell. I remember one night in particular. A few of us sat up late, putting the finishing touches to our masks, telling the funniest stories and laughing hilariously. That night freed me from the negative complexes, the voices that paralyze me and say "you are not an artist" or "who do you think you are." Instead of hearing those voices, I found myself surrounded by playmates. These women knew how to play and I wanted to join in. I was like a child "let out." The recognition and witnessing of the group allowed me to move through the negative feelings, be outrageously bold, and have great fun. I soon discovered that my 'cat' mask was becoming tiger-like in form and I was deeply touched when one of the women, who had brought with her a beautiful collection of stones, offered me a tiger's eye. Later, working into the *essence* of the mask was for me a non-verbal process. I did not know what might come out of the mask. Then Marion came and watched the work—you know how she just sits and watches—and I think her presence allowed me to be more deeply present to my experience and so to "come to the *gold*." ["To come to the gold" is a phrase originating from the alchemical process through which the alchemist 'makes gold' out of the 'lead' or *prima materia;* Jung saw and explored parallels between the alchemical process and the process of individuation—MR.]

Growing up in Ireland, I was one of seven siblings at home, and at school there were thirty or forty children to one teacher. There was no mirroring to reflect back to us the value of our own "gold," our individuality. Collective winds warned us all not to put our heads above the parapet; there was fierce envy and we knew it was dangerous to be different. Consequently, I was not able to realize and value my own gifts, so the mirroring I received at this first Intensive affected me profoundly. It allowed me to 'drop' into the work to discover the 'essence' of the mask, the cat energy in me. I am even shy to say it aloud now, but what the mask communicated was really simple and clear. I recognized my cat at home and how her body carried the same energy as the mask, and I found I was able to 'be' with that animal presence of cat in my own body. Despite all the negative inner voices, I was able to claim the experience. Whoever I was at that time, I hadn't really come into my fullness. The mask-work allowed me to embody something more of my potential fullness; it gave me the incomparable gift of my first "I am" moment. I think I made a covenant with the work at that time; it felt as though the work was feeding someone who was hungry. In those days, Marion, Mary, and Ann demonstrated the mask-work. I absolutely adored—that is the word, adored—their work. They became like inner figures alive in me, like friends I had known for years. There was such recognition and I had the profound feeling that "these are my people." I am thinking of the Bible, the Book of Ruth:

Your people shall be my people and your god, my god.[117]

Maja: You have given a strong sense of how deeply significant this first mask-making workshop for you. Would you like to tell me what moved you in your next workshop?

Marian: Yes, my next workshop was at Abraxas, in the deep countryside north of Toronto. This is where I first met Paula Reeves. A very striking thing happened on the first morning: somebody shared a dream and in it there was the image of a peg. Paula talked about the image of Inanna hanging on a peg in the Underworld, and it was decided that, at the end of the day, anyone who wished might sit and hear Paula tell the myth of Inanna. Paula told the story in her inimitable fashion and I felt as though everything inside me had been lit up. By the time the story was finished, I was screaming and yahooing in delight—delights at hearing the story, and also delight that I was recognizing Paula, the

---

117 *Ruth,* 3:13:16, *Holy Bible,* Standard English Version.

storyteller. My exuberance and spontaneity, so often put down, was suddenly the vehicle for my recognition of another human being. A strong bond formed between Paula and me in that moment. We have worked together ever since, creating sacred space in which Paula inter-weaves her story-telling wisdom with the ancient lore and landscape of Ireland, enabling participants to feel, bodily, the age-old container of the land that is still alive and accessible, and providing secure ground for BodySoul work.

Maja: You are describing profound transformative moments at BodySoul Intensives.

Marian: Oh, yes. I remember a special moment in the first Leadership Training. Marion had asked us to gather in her sitting room. "I have been awake early this morning, thinking and shaking with fear," she told us. She looked around at everybody, one by one, eyeing us, and said, "What we are doing is huge. Each of you has to choose for herself to say 'yes' to this. Everybody has to be free to choose to stay or to leave, if it is too much, if you feel you cannot do it; because I cannot say that for you. Only you know what is right for you." Then she quoted T.S. Eliot, from his poem, "Four Quartets":

> Quick now, here, now, always—
> A condition of complete simplicity
> (Costing not less than everything)…[118]

It was as if Marion were articulating that place again—the threshold or the crossroads where you have to let go. You have to cross the waters, though they are deep and you may be swept away, as in the journey we made in Pajaro Dunes. And, if you cannot cross the threshold, then honoring that you cannot is equally important. But I knew that this was where my life was leading me. At times I felt I had no choice, that destiny intervened. My only choice lay in how I would respond to what life presented—I am still working with that. At this point in my life, I was in the process of moving to the west of Ireland to live. I saw the move west as affording me a place that would nourish me, an introverted place which would enable me to deepen my connection to myself and to the land; I felt it would enhance my sense of being in my body, present to the here-and-now, in a very particular landscape.

Maja: Could you say more about the deepening of your connection to the land?

Marian: I want to live and teach from a more spacious and grounded place. The land holds me at a very physical level. My heart rate and breath are changed by my contact with the land—I feel more regulated, physically and psychically. I am nourished by being close to

---

118 T.S. Eliot, *Complete Poems and Plays: 1909–1950,* Little Gidding, p. 145.

nature and her rhythms. My connectedness to the energy, or 'spirit in matter,' the *anima mundi*, is a powerful resource for me. So it is important to me to honor consciously the times and rhythms of the cycle of nature, marked in the Celtic calendar by the Four Quarters: Imbolc, Bealtaine, Lunasa and Samhain. Indigenous wisdom—the stories, myths, legends and traditions of the people connected to the land—is also extremely important. The pulse of nature speaks to us through such wisdom, putting us in touch with the collective unconscious. The Irish poet, W.B. Yeats, speaks of the collective memory of a people, which holds things together in the culture.

I will arise and go now,
For always night and day
I hear lake water lapping
With low sounds by the shore;
While I stand on the roadway
Or on the pavements gray,
I hear it in the deep heart's core.[119]

So, through BodySoul work, I started to revisit my old connection to the land but in a new way, this time through my body—now I feel that my connection to the land and my connection to my body are inseparable, and that both are essential to this work. This is why I appreciate so much what Jung writes in the Nietzsche Seminars.[120] He emphasizes the importance of "going-down," descending into the depths and bowels of the body, as necessary to the path of individuation. The place where I have chosen to live, the Burren in the west of Ireland, holds me at the interface between outer and inner landscapes, between land and body. With the living matter of our bodies resonating with the living matter of nature all around us, we experience ourselves as part of that great whole, as part of an interconnected field. If I am able to offer anything to the BodySoul Rhythms work, it is a reminder that we meet the animating force of nature in the cells of both inner and outer landscape—in the body and in the changing seasons—and this is where we experience being held by the "Great Mother." John O'Donohue is an Irish author and poet from the Burren; this is what he writes about the land and its power to fuse with, and infuse, the Celtic soul:

With complete attention, landscape celebrates that liturgy of the seasons, giving itself unreservedly to the passion of the goddess.[121]

---

119 W.B. Yeats, "The Lake Isle of Innisfree" in *The Countess Kathleen and Various Legends and Lyrics.*
120 Jung, *Nietzsche's Zarathustra: Notes of the Seminar Given in 1934-1939 by C.G. Jung.*
121 John O'Donohue, *Anam Cara: A Book of Celtic Wisdom*, p. 85.

And Jung speaks of *Anima Mundi*, the World Soul, as the unifying force, as "a natural force which is responsible for all the phenomena of life and the psyche."[122] It is alive in matter all around us, inner and outer; it is the aliveness in matter all around us.

Maja: Would this be a good time to keep your earlier promise to say something about field theory?

Marian: Oh, yes, thank you for that reminder! We talk about "Field Theory" in the New Physics, and about the body's participation in the wider, inter-connected field. A strong connection to nature can be so important in supporting a strong connection to the larger inter-connected field in our work. It enables one to experience the immanence of the Great Feminine, ever-present in the moisture of the land, the dew on the grass, the soft air we breathe; in the horses, donkeys, cows, foxes or birds we may meet on our morning walk; in the huge trees that line the avenue, linking earth and heaven; in the deep well that reflects the light; and in the soft moss that grows in the shade. A vital connection to the resonance of this Great Feminine presence in the landscape grounds us in the inner landscape of bone and soft tissue, muscle and internal fluids. Each reflects the other, inner and outer.

This is the field of nature, the Great Feminine that we partake in. And there is also the inter-connected field that develops through our creative work in the intimacy of a BodySoul group—the group itself becomes an inter-connecting field. When I reflect on how deeply I was affected by my partner's mask in that first workshop, I realize now that it was the 'field' with which I resonated. Marion talks of this phenomenon in the BodySoul Rhythms work when we influence each other through our witnessing of the other. She speaks of the importance of building the container, the archetypal container and the physical container of our particular body to hold our work, to enable the spirit to infuse matter and matter to receive spirit. I think the container is the field and the field an actualization of the Self, the totality, the circumference and the center. And I see Jung addressing this concept of "field as container" when he tells us that a dream or an image is only alive when it is experienced in the body. He says that anything not experienced in the body is not alive and, because it is not alive, it is not in the *here-and-now*. Bringing the image alive in the here-and-now is the focus of my work: body and psyche, inner and outer landscapes, constellated and honored in the "field" of the physical and psychical present.

---

122 Jung, *The Structure and Dynamics of the Psyche, CW 8,* ¶ 393.

Maja: You emphasize the importance of being in the here-and-now. Can you elaborate on this idea?

Marian: There are two things: *here* [pointing to her body] and *now* [pointing to the space around her]. Being in the here-and-now is at once temporal and personal *and* collective and transpersonal, or timeless and impersonal. Experience in the here-and-now involves a physical resonance with the body and the ground right down there [makes a gesture of showing her body roots]. When you go down into the ground—of the body and the ground on which you are standing—you are immediately in a field. That feels like the 'edge' in the work for me. That is my focus.

When I teach, I like to bring the dreamer into the here-and-now by focusing on where the *dream image is resonating in her body*. This focus opens the field which allows me to track the energy of the image in the body. I work with the concept of *lysis*: where does the energy want to go at the end of the dream; what new impulse or possibility is stirring?

Often in the dream there will be two opposing energies. Jung describes psychic conflict as the tension between two opposites—or opposing poles—for example, consciousness and the unconscious. If one is able to 'hold the tension' between the two, something new arises which Jung terms the "new third" because it transcends the original conflict. This dynamic Jung calls the "transcendent function of the psyche" and he argues that it is the dynamic underlying and promoting all psychic growth.

When working with the dream I am trying to track the 'felt-sense' of the opposing energies, watching for a "new third" to emerge as the energy of the dream moves in the body. There is often an observable opening and shifting of the energetic flow in the body. This, I believe, activates and then metabolizes the "transcendent function" to the point where, on the physiological level, new synapses are forming in the brain, creating new neural pathways. The formation of new neural pathways seems to me to be a neurological manifestation of what Jung describes as the "transcendent function of the psyche." The original conflict or tension is transcended both psychically and physiologically through the emergence of a "new third." The development of a neurological "new third," or a new neural pathway, may well describe how the brain "grows," just as Jung argued that the conscious personality "grows" with the emergence of a "new third" in the form of a metaphor, symbol, idea, insight or attitude. Tracking the energy in the dream as its imagery impacts upon the body is key because it allows the metaphor to 'light up' the brain, creating new pathways and metabolizing the 'transcendent function.'

Maja: Could you perhaps talk in more detail about how you work to promote the flow of energy in the body?

Marian: In BodySoul Rhythms workshops, we encourage the energetic flow, and our awareness of it, through different exercises. The exercises link symbol in the body and symptom in the body. We do this through relaxation, and through breath-, voice-, art- and maskwork. Ann Skinner always reminds us to 'hover,' to wait for that next inhalation, to wait for the new impulse. I listen to individual dreams in a similar way. I try to attune the dreamer so she may realize that, in this moment of the *here-and-now,* what is heard in the body is a resonance of the dream.[123] Often, when we listen to a dream, we are aware of the opposites, the conflict presented, but not of the site of the conflict in the body.

The first thing we need to establish when working with the body and the dream is a place of *resource* in the body. This term has been coined by Peter Levine.[124] He defines *resource* as "anything that helps a person maintain a sense of self and inner integrity in the face of disruption: Internal or external anchors that help a client feel calmer, less activated."[125] This might be an image, a memory, a person, animal or place. It is important to remember that the Great Feminine or nature-around-us supports the body to be resourced. So I like to begin the dream work by recognizing where we feel *resourced* in the body. When we are sufficiently *resourced* or grounded in an effective body-connection, we become aware of a sense of over-all calm and ease. The nervous system is regulated; heart rate, blood pressure, breath are all in homeostasis. We can then explore the images in the dreams and whatever activation, tensions and symptoms they trigger in the body as we are speaking. We are watching out for any change, or *activation*, in the body—tightness, tingling, changes in breathing, temperature, etc. We explore the 'felt-sense' of the experience—the sensations, movements, sounds, gestures that resonate with the dream image in the part of the body where the change, or activation, has occurred. We then begin a dialogue between the *place of resource* in the body and the *place of activation.* All the time we are tracking the physical sensations, emotions and images, behaviors and meanings that emerge, moving our attention between the two sites in the body, the *place of resource* and the *place of activation* or symptom. Returning frequently to the *resource* in the body builds the capacity for self-regulation in the face of an overwhelming *activation* that might threaten the system. In terms of neuroscience, this dialogue describes the exchange that occurs between a highly activated *limbic system* and *Vagus nerve,* and the *neo-cortex,* the executive part of the brain that makes the decision to move back to the somatic experience of the *resource.* An effective dialogue between these two 'places' in the body enables

---

123 The interviewee has developed a way of working with individual dreams in the body which she calls Body Dreaming—MR.

124 Peter Levine, *Waking the Tiger* and *In an Unspoken Voice: How the Body Releases Trauma and Restores Goodness.*

125 Peter Levine, *Somatic Experiencing Manual,* 2007.

a release of blocked energy to take place—slowly. The once trapped energy begins to flow through different pathways in the body and with it a new impulse arises—perhaps in the form of a tiny movement or an image. With the release of previously blocked energy, new neural pathways open and the system moves towards integration. Such integration takes time. It is a process that goes hand-in-hand with the gradual emergence of new images, movements and gestures. It mirrors Jung's description of the Transcendent Function, where a new third is born out of the tension of the opposites; it opens the whole system, and the dreamer's sense of standing in her center, connected to her own ground, becomes palpable.

It was really exciting when I discovered in my own work that the tension of opposites is not only a mental force. That tension resides in the 'pathways' of the body, which are resonant with one's complexes. Jung stresses the centrality of emotion and argues that it is the key factor when one is working with the unconscious. How significant that neuro-scientist Candace Pert[126] uses the term 'molecules of emotion' to describe the transmitters—the neuropeptides and the receptors—in the 'mind-body' that we are! She also talks about how different circuits and patterns are stimulated alongside each other in the body. The emotional response informs who we are and, as Jung said, the critical task is to come into relationship with the emotion, with the emotional response in the body.

Marion addresses the same crucial point in her focus on metaphor—the *living* metaphor—when she uses metaphor to open new connections in the mind-body, or the body-soul, as we call it. So on Day One of an Intensive, Marion asks us to meditate on what is the "still point" for us, asking each of us to establish her "still point" before moving into the work. And the image of the "still point" comes, of course, from one of Marion's best-loved poets, T.S. Eliot:

> Except for the point, the still point,
> There would be no dance, and there is only the dance.[127]

Maja: What do you mean by finding the still point in the body?

---

126 Candace B. Pert, *Molecules of Emotion: The Science Behind Mind-Body Medicine* 1st Edition, New York, NY: Touchstone, 1997. Pert explains her theory that neuropeptides and their receptors are the bio-chemicals of emotions carrying information in a vast network linking the material world of molecules with the non-material world of the psyche. Her views on mind-body cellular communication support concepts of energy espoused by many alternative therapies.

127 T.S. Eliot, *Complete Poems and Plays, 1909-1950*, From the Poem 'Burnt Norton,' p. 119.

Marian: For me, it is aligned with Peter Levine's use of the term *resource*, as I described earlier. He focuses on finding the *resource* in the body so that we can come back to it as an anchor when working with disregulation, activation of any kind. In a similar way, in the first morning's meditation, Marion asks us, "What is your still point? See an image for it." She works with us to help us see the image as a 'living metaphor' and to feel it in our bodies and psyches. Already in that first hour she is opening us to the power of symbol. And sharing these images in the group creates a *field* of images, of shared resources, bonding us together in the wider, inter-connected 'Field.'

Working with these different concepts or metaphors, I see how they meet and converge. So I try to locate and work from that "place" where the BodySoul Rhythms work of Marion, Ann, and Mary converges with research in the Neurosciences, the New Physics, Trauma work and Attachment Theory. Awareness of this convergence of different fields of study, theories and practices, deepens the BodySoul Rhythms work and gives my own work validity, affirmation and more 'ground.'

Maja: Could you say more about the development of your work—Body Dreaming?

Marian: It was when I decided to gather a weekly group for dream work, bodywork and voice work that I really began to explore the connection between the dream and the body dreaming. I would begin each session by listening to the dreams—as we do each morning at the BodySoul Rhythms Intensives. This would be followed by body warm-up, movement and voice work; and, finally, I would bring in the art materials. Developing this work was a wonderful experience for me, a time of deepening and growth.

Then I began to work with my colleague, Candace Loubert. Her specialty was in bodywork and art, while mine, after 20 years as a psychotherapist, was in working with the psyche. So Candace became a mentor to me in bodywork. In Candace I discovered someone who had a relationship to the body in a way that I had a relationship to the psyche. The body had been her territory for all her professional life. Candace was a dancer with Les Grands Ballets in Montreal and then studied massage and creative arts therapy. She had worked with her body and lived the connection with it very deeply. So, as we worked together, I started to see a new 'field'—*body-psyche*—taking shape and form on the floor. Body and psyche were informing each other, each taking turns, one sometimes leading the other, sometimes responding to the other. It was no longer body and psyche, psyche and body—their *inter-connectedness* became truly alive for me.

Working with Candace helped me to slow down in order to meet the entry point into the body. It was about pacing and giving space—and being able to be in and hold that space. I found that working at the pace of the body added enormous depth to the dream work. The image field of the dream was taken into a whole new dimension. The dream became a 3-D alive-in-the-body experience—no longer something I was simply listening to and attending to with the inner eye or inner ear. Candace and I suddenly found ourselves in a new 'field,' together with the women in the group. We saw dreams and images come alive; watched bodies speak the dream and live the dream; watched the images cover the walls in the women's art. We saw how the amazing creativity of the women embodied a "new third," born out of the fluid interplay of body and psyche.

Maja: You and Candace come from very different professional backgrounds. I am curious to hear how you devised a way to work together so effectively.

Marian: When Candace and I led the group-work together, we talked through the session beforehand. We developed a plan that also left some openness for whatever might emerge spontaneously and unexpectedly. Candace would guide the floor work and open the field of the body. At some point she would look at me. It was as if a note had been struck in the field between us and I knew I could move in to take the group into sound and breathe work. Candace might come back in again and take the group into movement or art. For example, she might put a ball of clay into the women's hands to enhance the somatic experience in the body through engagement with the clay. The field opens wider and wider, bringing psyche and body into creative expression. Such rich compost for learning about inter-connectedness!

There is one other important point I would like to make. I feel that the inner landscape, the outer landscape and the *here-and-now* are all paramount to the space—or field—in which we *speak* the dream. One change we made to the program was to work first thing each day with a body warm-up in a group session. This was at Candace's insistence and soon I adopted the practice in my own groups that I ran solo. By working first with the body, we were shifting focus from left-brain analytical, logical, linear thinking to a right-brain space where implicit memory is stored, buried in the somatic unconscious, and accessed through symbolic language, in other words, through art, image, music, body-movement, dance and dreams.

The body is then less rigid, more fluid and open to receive the dream. The bodywork also creates an 'attunement' so that, when the dream is spoken, there is an immediate resonance with the dream in the *body-psyche*. The body hears the dream differently, and receives it differently, from the Ego that is speaking the dream. We track the energy of the dream in the body, and ask all the women to track their own resonance with the dream, which means that everyone in the room becomes 'attuned.' This process creates a very strong 'container,' as Marion would say, and develops a powerful capacity to shift the energy through into the *lysis* of the dream—the field becomes alive with possibilities.

There is not just a single body sitting down to speak her dream but a 'group body' that moves and takes the shape and form of the dream energy. This is extraordinarily powerful! The group has enormous potential to amplify the energy of the dream. Sometimes I may ask a group member—another body—to hold different aspects of the dream for the dreamer. That person will stand in for the dreamer and amplify the energy of a complex, for example, by resonating with and holding the energy in her body. She holds up a mirror to the different aspects of the dreamer's psyche reflected in the dream; and this allows the inner world of the dreamer to become embodied in matter and externalised in the landscape. So the inner dramas and conflicts take on life, breath and voice, right in front of us in the here-and-now.

Of course, the dreamer paints the picture and describes the energy of the dream to the other bodies. But the resonance within the field—felt by each person who steps into the field—is what seems to "click" with the dreamer. This may sound like psychodrama but it is different from psychodrama because the focus is on the energy of the dream. The energy may simply be expressed in a *tableau* or 'still-life,' enabling the dreamer to see how it is held in the bodies around her. The group situates the energy in the room, sculpting it in response to how it is felt in the body, presenting positions and gestures that embody different aspects of the dream.

Maja: I was struck by a phrase you used a little while ago—"the pace of the body"—could you speak more about that?

Marian: Yes. The "pace of the body" always makes me think of Mary Hamilton. She has this mantra: "The body's pace is slow." We know that it takes seven years for the body to renew itself, for each cell to go through a life cycle of renewal. We can have a new idea or thought in a flash but, as Peter Levine claims, it takes longer for the body to "get" something. After a "connection to a resource," to use Levine's term, it takes time for the body to re-establish its strength and integrity so that it can integrate energies, emotions and symptoms that have been constricted in the body and repressed in the psyche. New cells can grow and new plasma form, but for something to take root in us, for new pathways to establish themselves, we need time and a safe holding environment. The body must feel safe, contained, connected to its own ground. We may think we have finished our work but then, as Ann Skinner would say, "You know, there is always another impulse ... just wait!" It takes seven minutes for the new synapses—the new linking networks—to be formed in the brain. But there is no instant "Oh, great—got that," on the part of the body. The body may still need time to realign itself with the new energy, the new imagery, the "new third."

Maja: I have seen you work with the dreams in the body—the timing of it—it is like slowing time down—being aware—listening—to how the energy moves in the body—and following that movement. But you yourself need to slow down and to be so aware.

Marian: Yes, I have to be attuned to my own body: making sure I am not constricted, uncomfortable in my position on the chair, not leaning too far forward, making good eye contact, adjusting my voice to the speaker, making sure I am in a 'resourced' body. I often begin by asking each member of the group to connect to her own 'resource' and that is a reminder for me to connect to mine. Then we are, as a group, in a shared field, with an established container. As I listen to the dream, I try to stay attentive to the shifts and changes in myself in response to what is happening as we are working together. My body will often give me clues. For instance, I might be prompted to ask the dreamer where in the body the energy feels stuck because I may be picking up that feeling in my own body, in a tightening, rigidity or numbing of one body part. I am continually working with my body while I am working with another person's dream. And I may shift attention away from the dreamer toward the group to reflect on what is happening. This also helps keep everyone involved and helps regulate the nervous system of the dreamer and of the group. It gives the dreamer's body a chance to integrate, recuperate, and restore equilibrium. And it brings in the thinking brain, the neo-cortex, which helps the dreamer make conscious and integrate the experience. We are relating to body-psyche as a living organism by engaging with the dream in this way and the body responds. It responds to the affection; it responds to the attention, in what is for the most part a right-brain to right-brain communication, body to body. The mirror neurons, of which I spoke earlier, respond to the empathy and permission is given for possibility and play. The imagination is stimulated. The dream becomes *alive* in the room. Body and psyche merge in a common field—*the dancer becomes the dance.*

LOVE MATTERS FOR PSYCHIC TRANSFORMATION

Part III

Weaving the Tapestry

Having given the reader a broad account of the BSR work and presented six interviews of the subjective lived experience of it, I would like to weave together the essence from each interview and put it in perspective with the Jungian theory, as well as neuroscience and developmental psychology. This will be done in two parts. First I will look at the interviews individually and then I will look more generally at the BSR approach as such, including the neuroscientific and developmental perspective.

These perspectives will be the foundation for the discussion—around the question of where the BSR approach and the Jungian understanding of the psyche meet with the new neuroscientific and developmental theories as referred to in the introduction, and where do they add something in areas not yet included in the recent scientific and developmental theories?

The discussion will be followed by the conclusion: why love matters for psychic transformation—receiving the soul.

Perspective: The Essence of each Interview

It is my aim to try to distil what seems to matter for psychic transformation and what seems to foster transformation as perceived by the subject in the lived experience in the context of the BSR work.

I will try to condense the essence into something tangible by filtering the material of the interviews through two questions: Firstly, what did the BSR approach give the six women interviewed? In essence, what did it enable them to do or feel, and what mattered for psychic transformation from the subjective lived experience of the BSR work? And secondly, what were the qualities of the container that enabled that, the attitudes and approach of the leaders who 'midwifed'[128] this transformation? In essence what were the described qualities of the container?

I will go through each interview, drawing out themes that reflects the answers to these questions and finally make a remark on the overall theme that seems to be indicated in all the interviews.

It is my hypothesis that the essence of each women's story such as being held in the mist of despair, receiving space and encouragement to reclaim the Rubedo, being met with unconditional love, finding and expressing one's authenticity and having one's authenticity reflected back to oneself, having space to be real, finding one's feminine voice, perceiving life as living

---

128 I deliberately use the word midwife to stress the nature of psychic transformation—the transformation is 'born' the 'mother' and the 'midwife' co-create the facilitating support. As facilitator, you assist something ready to be born—and do your best not to hinder the process or damage the new life.

metaphor, and finding relations of kinship and a sense of belonging all reflects aspect of the experience of the BSR approach on a general level too.[129]

In addition, it is my suggestion that what matters in the context of the BSR work has a general validity for what matters in the one-to-one therapeutic relationship,[130] and that the BSR approach can enrich our way of working in the therapeutic relationship as can knowledge of neuroscience and developmental psychology. The metaphors the interviewee used to describe their experiences seem to reflect this back: being held in the mist of despair, reclaiming the Rubedo, being met with love over and over again, being authentic and being real, finding one's feminine voice, and living metaphor.

THE ESSENCE OF INTERVIEW 1: "BEING HELD IN THE MIST OF DESPAIR"

The Essence of the Subjective Lived Experience:

Looking at the essence of the subjective lived experience of this interview the following points are extracted and discussed:

- Being held in the mist of despair.

Being held in the mist of despair is a sublime metaphor for the experience of holding created by the attuned therapist. Whether the analysand feels the despair to arrive from the inner world or the outer world, the containing relation is perceived as holding. The containment and the receiving of soul gives the analysand the feeling of being held, of feeling safe, despite the despair (often the emotional chaos created by overwhelming affects)—and thus to be able not to be overwhelmed by it, but find the still point: a holding center connected with consciousness within oneself. As described, the lived experience of being held by an outer caring other enables a growing sense of feeling held by a nourishing inner source thus strengthening the ego-self axis.

- Receiving validation of who one is as being, and the quality of that in relation to the whole.

---

129 I take the liberty to draw some generalizations from the six individual women's experiences. I am aware that this can only indicate, not validate, the general experience of the work.

130 In the text the words analysand/ analyst, participant, container is used interchangeably for ease of the reading of the text. Although the BSR intensives are not advertised as therapeutic, much healing takes place and the healing relation is constellated. It is this healing constellation as such, that is referred to when the words analysand/ analyst/ container/ participant are used.

In terms of validation by the collective, the extraverted thinking type seems to be the main typology validated in modern Western cultures. The consciousness of that collective bias in group work on a Jungian basis can facilitate the validation of the whole spectrum of psychological types. This can potentially lead to a more balanced appreciation which, for the individual, can be the validation of one's own being often longed for in a collective setting. Beyond typology, reflecting more on the unique individual, the validation of who one is, the sense of being 'seen' and having that validated, is the reflection that can open the individual to live that, to validate it herself and thus to come "home" to herself. Essentially this is the acorn for the process of individuation.[131]

- Being part of a community that is open to reflect on deeper values of life.

The profound sharing that takes place in the BSR setting, both within the structured context and in the space between, are in themselves of great importance. As Jung pointed out, the collective religious symbols have been losing their meaning and there is a fading away of the collective contributors of meaning that formerly gave symbols and life-values to live by. According to Marion Woodman, the collective is increasingly moved by materialistic values. This lack of deeper meaning, of a spiritual, ethical and philosophical ground to be rooted in, is perceived as a deep longing manifested with different intensity in many Western people. The answers to that longing—no longer given by the collective—become the individual's quest for her[132] own answers.[133] Among female friends, colleagues and analysands, there is an experience of a deep longing for talking about their reflections, as mentioned in the interviews, and it seems that the longing is answered to a great extent in the community of the BSR work. To have a community where one's deeper reflections about life can be shared, where one's spiritual life and one's feminine being can be expressed in a more differentiated way than immediately apparent in the collective mainstream, is felt as a deep validation of all the shapes a woman's life can take. (I am convinced that modern men feel equally narrowed by the conscious collective and feel a longing to explore the different aspects of the masculine in its multiplicity).

- A growing capacity to contain.

The interviewee describes a widening of her own inner container through the experienced lived containment by the other, who is mirroring back to her a reflection of herself. She describes the non-verbal dialogue that takes place in the dyad during this encounter where the

---

131 One cannot individuate if one tries to be something which one is not in order to be accepted.

132 This is of course absolutely equally valid for modern men too. The comments here, due to the context of the BSR work, refer to women. In order not to write 'men and women,' 'his and her' etc. and make the text difficult to read, I only mention the female perspective here.

133 Woodman, *Addiction to Perfection*.

experience is: *I feel that you feel what I feel* and where the container radiates: *I feel what you feel and I can contain that—I can contain you.*

In that sense, regarding the issue being contained, the interviewee's own "window of tolerance" is widened and the emotional field is experienced as sharable and contained. It depicts the growth-facilitating experience of feeling held and contained by a caring and present other—holding with her gaze, her body, her face, her voice, her whole being as known from developmental psychology.[134]

WHAT WAS IMPORTANT—THE ESSENCE OF THE DESCRIBED QUALITIES OF THE CONTAINER

Looking at the essence of the described qualities of the container in this interview the following points are extracted and discussed:

- Giving validation of the participant's way of being and of her uniqueness, without judgement.

Genuine mirroring is a skill of great art and is often underestimated both in its difficulty and its effect. What one expresses as therapist, both implicit and explicit, is often perceived through the filter the person usually sees the world through, and if that is a criticising complex the meaning of what one is saying and what is perceived by the person can be quite different.

What seems to be very prominent in the BSR leaders is the feeling quality of validation. It is never shaped as a framing definition of what the person is as such but, rather, it is voiced like a mirror, simply reflecting back what is seen. Reflections that resonate are perceived as deep validations by the person; reflections that do not resonate are not perceived "as me." The key seems to be the lack of wish to define the other person and, rather, to focus on validating the expression.

If the parents could not mirror the child but instead used the child to mirror them, the "you are…" has been used as a continuous misattunement to shape the child in the image of the parent, demanding a certain shape from the child for it to feel loved. The "you are…" might constellate the same in the later analytical work robbing "the child" of its self-reflection. Giving back the self-reflection by deep validation of what is actually there, allows for the individual's own image to come forth, facilitating the slow process of seeing oneself as one is and reflecting that to the world.

- Providing community with openness to discuss life values and approaches to the spiritual dimension of life.

---

134 See Gerhardt, *Why Love Matters.*

The BSR intensives offer a community for women. The group consists of women from several generations as well as several nationalities. This context creates an atmosphere that opens for the women to share their life stories and ways of being in the world, expanding the individuals' ideas and perceptions of the possible shapes a woman's life can take. The trans-generational, trans-national context becomes an enriching place to receive support, form deep friendships with other women interested in the inner life, and deepen aspects and reflections on women's lives today. Sharing deep aspects of life in a group that continues at least over three years leaves a profound imprint.

It would be equally profound; no doubt, if it was a mixed group, but being a group of women gives naturally a possibility to tend more to what Helen Luke would phrase, 'The Way of Women.'[135]

The atmosphere in the group is influenced by the leaders and their style. They set a note of depth and honesty that influences the general atmosphere. I would like to illustrate this aspect with a story. Often, when groups start up, people would introduce themselves from the persona level with occupation, marriage status etc. It was not until I set out to do the interviews that I became aware of this level of life in the interviewee. The opening round of presentations at the intensives will be taken to the feeling level or reflections on soul-matters. Equally the valuation of what is 'profound' to say and other kinds of small dynamics that can get going in a group is quite clear—with a good deal of humor, balanced with a pinch of salt—brought to the level of what is really going on. I recall an introduction round where the participants became 'deeper and deeper' in their reflections on 'why they were there.' When it was Ann Skinner's turn she simply said, "I am so excited I can't think, but I am so glad to be here"—that is the crone archetype bringing the floor into its own authenticity.

- Embodying being the self-regulating other.

As expressed by the interviewee in her words: "My body learned to hold the image," Marion Woodman, sharing with the interviewee, seeing her, committed to be in it with her, and holding an attitude of love became the self-regulating other in Stern's words. Winnicott would name it the good-enough mother. In the Jungian frame, this level of meeting reflects the therapist holding the archetypal image of the conscious mother resulting in what Allan Schore would say is an experience of widening of the window of tolerance, which in Jungian terminology, would be strengthening of the vessel or the inner container. What I would like to emphasize is the effect on the body of the interviewee and her felt capacity to hold her own images through the experienced embodied holding from the other. (The theoretical aspect of the self-regulating other will be elaborated in the section on the neuroscientific and developmental perspective).

---

135 Helen Luke, *The Way of Women, Ancient and Modern*.

- Reflecting the person's essence back to her.

In the interview, the interviewee describes a meeting where she felt she saw herself reflected in the eye of the other. Now this experience described as seeing oneself in the eye of the other is known form developmental psychology as described by Winnicott (The gleam in the eye of the mother[136]). But somehow this situation has another feeling quality that captures something only described within the Jungian model of the psyche. The situation described does not seem to be the reflecting eye of the mother but more the reflecting eye of the crone that Marion Woodman is embodying. That is, the analyst, or here Marion Woodman, is not (in this encounter) holding a projection of the mother but rather a projection of an aspect of the Self that is embodied in the crone archetype. The gaze and its reflection makes the interviewee see herself in the eye of the other, seeing a reflection of the essence of herself—a reflection of her soul. Marie-Louise von Franz says that the hard work with complexes and ego-desires in analysis is done to clear the dust from the mirror so than one can see oneself reflected through the Self. The crone has done this laborious work and can therefore reflect that level of the person back to herself. (The mother's reflection is addressed more to the level of the child, whereas the crone's reflection addresses more to the level of the female-soul.)

THE ESSENCE OF INTERVIEW 2: "RECLAIMING THE RUBEDO"

The Essence of the Subjective Lived Experience:

- A freedom to dance—an invitation to embody one's passion.

Dancing is embodied life energy expressed with delight. The dance can be perceived both literally and metaphorically as an expression of how one's soul loves to move and express itself. The dance is an ancient expression used in rituals, healing ceremonies, storytelling with the body, marking initiations, flirting, love-making to name a few aspects. The trauma researcher Bessel van der Kolk describes that he went to South African to study non-white Westerners' ways of overcoming trauma. He explains how he observed women who had been raped, sitting in a group all silent until one would start to hum and move. Like ripples in the water, the other women gradually joined in until they all were on their feet dancing, singing and telling their stories in the dance. He describes it as a shared dance that freed their bodies and helped them to process what had happened both physically, emotionally and socially. He adapted

---

136 See for example Davis & Wallbridge, *Boundary and Space: An Introduction to the Work of D. W. Winnicott.*

what he had seen and now uses dance and storytelling through dance in his trauma healing programs at the Trauma Center in Brookline.[137]

In the interview 'Reclaiming the Rubedo,'[138] the dancer literally and metaphorically is reclaiming areas of life that have been repressed by family or cultural values being introjected by the individual. The form of the "Thou shall not" that prevents the lifeblood from flowing and expressing itself, seemed to be danced off and, through the dance, the passion is reclaimed and lived. Rubedo is the life force itself—the pulsating passion. The movement with passion becomes "dancing life."

- A love for the body.

The interviewee describes an evoked love for one's own matter or a love for oneself grounded in ones feminine tissue. Why is it stressed that it is a love for ones feminine body? Ninety-eight percent of all women in the Western world dislike their own body.[139] It is interesting to imagine what that does to the body to be related to in this way and how that is perceived by the cells, living with constantly being told they are "too this" or "too that." And it is equally moving to imagine what it does to move to a state where you, your cells, are loved and appreciated for being part of a magnificent living body that is cared for, nourished and listened to. The bodywork and the attitude with which the body is met and talked about in the BSR work, fosters this process. A process where the body often moves from being perceived as an object to being evaluated according to certain concepts (a stereotype only two per cent of the women seem to fit), to being perceived as an actually living organism welcomed and freed to express itself in its own being including moving, being loved and cherished. Reflecting further on the way we receive our bodies, connecting this to the fact that the body-soul are one, raises the question of whether the perceiving of the body's reality mirrors the perceiving of the soul's reality. If this is the case it would mean that only two percent welcome their souls, cherish it and nourish it.

---

137 The Trauma Center is a program of Justice Resource Institute. The Executive Director of the Trauma Center is Joseph Spinazzola, PhD, and the Medical Director and Founder of the Trauma Center is Bessel van der Kolk, MD, who is an internationally recognized leader in the field of psychological trauma. The Trauma Center provides comprehensive services to traumatized children and adults and their families at the main office in Brookline.

138 C.G. Jung, *Mysterium Coniunctionis, CW 14,* ¶ 308. Rubedo is the stage of becoming red. It is the third stage in the transformation process of matter in alchemy (in the Jungian context, a metaphor for the individuation process and the psychic work). It follows Nigredo and Albedo. Rubedo denotes an increase of warmth and light coming from the sun (consciousness). This corresponds to the increasing participation of consciousness which now begins to react emotionally to the content produced by the unconscious (the marriage between "Sol et Luna."

139 According to a study referred to by Mary Hamilton.

Thus, parallel to receiving the body's reality, is receiving the soul's reality. To value, cherish, and welcome the soul in whatever form it comes and in whatever form it expresses itself is a permeating value in the BSR approach. There seems to be a created feeling tone of love for soul and its own subjective beauty.

Mary Hamilton's words, "love for the body travels from one body to another body,"[140] appear equally true for the soul. Love for the soul travels from one soul to another soul. It is picked up in the field. And this love for the body-soul and the commitment to be there for it in all its expressions, cherishing and nourishing, it might be the essence of the powerful field formed in the BSR approach.

As for the body, the manifestations of soul are often met with an equally narrow ideal form in our culture. We are living in a culture that to a great extent focuses not on inner depth—the beauty of the personality—but on the immediate external appearance. This focus and the value given to the outer appearance dispels cultivation of the inner life, leading to what Jung named, "the atrophy of the personality."[141] The longing for acceptance, our need for others, and our strong motivation for belonging, shapes our development. It emphasizes the importance of the human mirror and of what is mirrored back to us.

- The instinctive act, "seeing the loneliness"—archetypal movements in the group—bringing healing into the collective field.

In the interview, the interviewee describes an experience in the group that she refers to as an *archetypal moment.* A moment loaded with intensity, and embracing a dimension that feels more than individual. In his study of psychic change, Daniel Stern says that change happens in two ways: in a steady continuation of *moments of meeting* and in quantum leaps described as *now moments.*[142] What the interviewee describes in the episode of the masks in the circle could be perceived as such a *now moment.* According to Stern, the *now moment* is an inter-subjective moment, highly charged, calling for a spontaneous human response to the psychic conflict in the other, and where the spontaneous act results in a deep psychic transformation moving both.[143] The moment described in the interview was such a moment of profound

---

140 As quoted in the interview "Reclaiming the Rubedo" and as heard by the author (MR) from Mary Hamilton several times during the training in the BSR leadership program, Europe 2001–2005, Grimstone, UK.

141 DVD: Face to Face: Professor Jung, An informal BBC interview with Carl Gustav Jung by John Freeman in Switzerland at Jung's lakeside home near Zurich, B&W, 1959.

142 Stern, *The Present Moment in Psychotherapy and Everyday Life.*

143 Stern, *The Present Moment in Psychotherapy and Everyday Life.* The central idea about the moment of change is that a real experience emerges somewhat unexpectedly. The experience happens between two or more people and it is about relationship. It happens in a short "now." The "now" is a present moment in which a micro-drama, an emotionally told story, about their relationship unfolds. The

importance, where something transformed and was healed—not only in an individual but reaching the group level as well as the archetypal dimension.

The interviewee describes how she saw the grief in the other, recognized that level of grief in herself, and spontaneously stepped into the circle and reached out to the other to comfort and to share the suffering, which initiated the same reaction from the rest of the group. The woman who initially was standing alone in the circle was received by the group through the individual's capacity to embrace her own grief and resonate with a shared compassion.

This genuine act in this moment impacted the rest of the group, shifted the field and resulted in a shared compassion, relatedness and capacity to enact 'holding' on a group level. The interviewee describes what could be named as a shared feeling voyage on a tribal level, which broke the isolation on the individual level and brought both the pain and the compassion into the shared field of the group. A "shared feeling voyage" is a term used by Daniel Stern to describe the sharing of a sequence of feelings experienced. A shared feeling voyage is different from just listening to a narrative of a life story, because in a shared feeling voyage the experience is shared as it originally unfolds. It is direct; it is co-created by the partners involved and lived in an original way, unfolding in the now.[144]

This act not only brings healing to the individual but also to the group, whose capacity to hold and process pain together creates a bond of healing. The experience that this can happen in a group gives hope for the individual, not only through the small conflicts in our personal lives, but also in conflicts in our cultures as such.

What Was Important—The Essence of the Described Qualities of the Container

- Inspiration.

Marion Woodman, Ann Skinner and Mary Hamilton have all in their ways had quite a share of life's challenges. It is apparent that they have had to fight for their feeling values; have met resistance, jealousy, and dismissal on their way in the outer world; and they have been confronted with difficult encounters in the inner world as well. The fact that they have stayed committed and focused, kept doing what was important to them from a soul perspective, and

---

jointly lived experience is mentally shared—each intuitively partaking in the experience of the other. This intersubjective sharing of mutual experience is grasped without having to be verbalized—becomes part of the implicit knowledge of their relationship. The sharing creates a new intersubjective field between participants, which alters their relationship and permits them to take different directions together. The moment enters a special form of consciousness and is encoded in memory. It re-writes the past. (It is bad therapy when it confirms past!) Changes in psychotherapy (or any relationship) occur by way of these non-linear leaps in new ways-of-being-with-another. They are based on a lived experience in the presence of another.

144 Stern, *The Present Moment in Psychotherapy and Everyday Life.*

continued to do their work, is inspirational. The knowing of this becomes motivating for the individual according to the interviewees—it becomes a kind of role model and a shared story of connecting to the heroic feminine—not heroic in an outgoing aggressive way, but heroic in the steady, continuing doing of what is aligned with the Self.

I would like to comment on the issue of idealization and the inspiring other. I think this can best be understood seeing the connection between the idealization and the inspiring other as a continuum where the projected idealizations gradually are replaced by an inspirational relation. Naturally all variations of this continuum will be seen in the group of BSR participants (as it is seen in any training groups and analytical relationships).

In terms of understanding our human needs for role models, ideals and motivation, I find Mario Jacoby's work on individuation and narcissism inspiring.[145] In this context I would like to emphasize Kohut's description of the developmental maturation process from the idealized object to balanced inspiration from others. Referring to the analytical setting, the need to fuse with the idealized self-object is a constellation where the analyst or, in the context of the BSR work, the leaders become an ideal model for the participants. Jung called this form of idealization "disciple fantasies."[146] As a transitional phase, this type of idealization sometimes plays an important role in the process of individuation. In the Jungian perspective it involves the analyst embodying the highest values of the analysand that is, carrying the projection of the Self. This allows the analysand to experience her or his own potential wholeness.[147]

Naturally, if the person stays in this phase of what in Jungian terms would be archetypal projection, there is a risk that his or her own individuation will be compromised. "Becoming who you are" is transformed to, "Becoming who your analyst is."[148] Because of the group dynamics in the BSR and the short periods of encounter which do not so easily allow for the natural gradual disappointment from the idealized object that usually happens in analysis where the just human aspect of the analyst gradually is taken in, there is a risk of these "disciple fantasies" in the BSR context never gets resolved.

I do think that there is a conscious awareness of this risk among the leaders. To my awareness they don't feed idealization, and their sharing of their vulnerability and shortcomings help to counterbalance the tendency to idealization; as does their capacity to look at themselves and their own shortcomings with humor; and so does the space given to express the frustrations and disappointment with them. This all facilitates the process of the gradual withdrawing of the archetypal projection and gives rise to a 'just so' human inspiration.

---

145 Mario Jacoby, *Individuation and Narcissism: The psychology of Self in Jung and Kohut.*
146 C.G. Jung, *Two Essays on Analytical Psychology, CW 7,* ¶ 263.
147 Jacoby, *Individuation and Narcissism,* p. 217.
148 Jacoby, *Individuation and Narcissism,* p. 217.

In conclusion, there is a process of maturation that takes place over the time for the participant in the leadership program who might initially experience a strong idealization of the leaders. This is a process in which the idealized projections gradually give rise to ideals formed, which to the individual seem to be worth engaging in oneself and where the leaders serve as inspiration.

Having addressed the phenomenon of idealization, I do think that inspiration and role models are important in the context of psychic work. This is stressed in several of the interviews: to meet the fear of going beyond whatever inner or outer force that prevents one from expressing oneself; to be able to live authentically, to stand up, to face and go through what seems to be unbearable pain. For this we need role models to inspire, encourage and motivate the heroine within: the part of ourselves that acts according to the Self. To hear the stories of others, to hear that it is possible to encounter the inner struggles and find a way forward makes it possible to imagine oneself doing it. Several of the interviewees describe that the three leaders' personal stories as having been inspiring and hope-creating for them—that their actually living through it has been the thing that gave it authenticity.

- The visible love, care, joy and considerations that the leaders have for their own body.

How we ourselves act towards our own body, how we attend to it, and how we speak about it has a huge impact on the receiver. As elaborated on in the section on mirror neurons later, we learn new ways of being by watching others. Equally we impact on others deeply through our own living reality—who we are and how we are in the world.

- Expressing delight—the joy and humor in the work—finding the laughter at the heart of things.

In self-development and in many therapeutic frames there is naturally a tradition to focus on what is not functioning[149]—what needs to be deconstructed and reconstructed. This focus can often dominate to the degree that we lose sight of what is functioning, what gives us delight and joy, and we neglect to share that in the encounters as well. In the BSR approach an equally deep value of giving space to what feels good, delightful, fun, nourishing, humorous and playful is fostered. By embodying that, one shows a way of being in the world that in itself feels life-confirming and is a place of resource. The place of joy and humor is a place that is energy giving and helps to hold the dark or difficult aspects as well.[150]

---

149 This is rooted in the Western medical model of eliminating the pathology as opposed to the holistic approach where supporting and increasing the health is the focus.

150 This is not to neglect the seriousness of the psychic pain. Naturally each encounter must be taken seriously but that does not exclude humor.

Women with low-self-esteem, who enter therapy, especially have a tendency to focus on their shortcomings. If the therapist's frame of theory is focused on that as well, there can be a collusion that feeds the self-devaluating tendency which in effect is anti-therapeutic.[151] The Jungian approach, in equally valuing the prospective and the causal points of view, gives in itself a growth-facilitating perspective. Metaphorically the image of the gardener who tends the plants to facilitate their growth, moves away the stones that hinder this growth, and who can see the oak tree in the acorn counterbalances the image of the detective finding the cause of the crime.

THE ESSENCE OF INTERVIEW 3: "BEING MET WITH UNCONDITIONAL LOVE, OVER AND OVER AND OVER"

The Essence of the Subjective Lived Experience:

- Finding one's creative expression.

In the interview the woman describes how the feeling of being met with unconditional love enabled her to connect to her own creative expression. She tells how her father used to say, "You are made for service." The responses and sharing with Ann Skinner seemed to be fostering the transformation from being made for service to moving into establishing a feeling of agency in herself. An agency that can give rise to a creative expression and a trust that something inside of herself—an impulse from the unconscious, can come forth to express itself and that it has value.

The concept of sense of agency comes from the field of object relation and attachment theory. It is of great therapeutic interest to consider how to facilitate the development of a sense of agency.[152]

The sense of agency is the basis for the feeling that we can actively act in our world and co-create our world—that we can create an imprint and have influence (including to create in the outer world what we feel is aligned with the inner world). Without the sense of agency we are left only with the capacity to respond, often feeling helpless or without influence on what happens. The sense of agency is created by the environment's response to the infant's impulses to express itself, actively doing something with 'its world' and having mirrored back the trust that it can do this, and, having mirrored back to itself by a caring other, that what it

---

151 Polly Young-Eisendrath and Florence L. Wiedemann, *Female Authority: Empowering Women through Psychotherapy.*

152 Fonagy, Gergely, Jurist, & Target, *Affect Regulation, Mentalization, and the Development of the Self.* Jeremy Holmes, *John Bowlby and Attachment Theory* and Jean Knox, *Archetypes, Attachment, Analysis: Jungian Psychology and the Emergent Mind.*

is doing has value. Creative impulses, which are stopped or hindered by the surroundings and criticised, undermine the sense of agency.

To be creative a person must have a feeling of existing as a full being and owning the agency to create. This feeling is not just a conscious awareness but also a sense of having a basic core to be active from—a core sense of self being in the world (see the later section on the core sense of self).

'*Creativity is then the doing that arises out of being.*'[153] In order to be and to have the feeling that one is, one must have a predominance of impulse-doing over reactive-doing (doing based on an inner impulse, as opposed to doing based on a reaction towards an outside stimulus[154]).

The creative expressions in the BSR work are symbolic expressions. They are manifestations of the transcendent function, emerging into consciousness from the unconscious. These expressions enhance the dialogue between consciousness and the unconscious and this puts us in contact with the creative potential of the unconscious.

But the process of symbolic expression in itself has a deeply therapeutic value too—a value I would like to emphasize here. It moves the sense of agency back to the person and re-creates the trust that they themselves, within themselves, have potential; something that can become something that can be expressed in the outer world. They don't have to be passively fixed from the outside, something inside can grow, reinforcing them from the inside.

The description of how that is experienced, and what that gives rise to in the individual is expressed in the phrase "growing a spine."[155] It is a beautiful metaphor for the process.

• Being met with unconditional love—counterbalancing introjected vicious voices.

This statement illustrates how the power of the introjected vicious voices gradually can be transformed. It is the repeating of experience—over and over—to meet a person with acceptance and a loving attitude. Slowly this leads to a deconstructing of the old expectations around meeting with the other. Through the new experience of self-with-other, molecule by molecule a lived experience of a feeling of being lovable and received by the other is being

---

153 Winnicott, "Living Creatively," *Home is where We Start From: Essays by a Psychoanalyst*, p. 39.
154 Winnicott, "Living Creatively," pp. 39 -54.
155 Note: I worked with a child who was referred to me because he could not play. From infancy, all his explorations of the world had been blocked or stopped. He had not been allowed to play with food, to put toys in his mouth or to become dirty. Later, when playing with him, his mother found him boring and would end the play. Thus every impulse in him had been blocked to a degree that it no longer came forth. During the twenty hours we worked together, he gradually grew confidence in sensing, trusting, expressing and sharing his impulses. He grew in the trust that it could be sharable—that he could make and express something in the world.

constructed (see also, the chapter on the links between BSR and neuroscience and developmental psychology).

- Growing a spine.

Growing a spine is the symbolic expression for the felt sense of having a central supporting inner structure—a skeleton—that enables one to stand in the world. Without a spine there is no established support of one's core. A symbolic spine is like a psychic holding structure that is needed so one is able to stand up for oneself. The psychic spine is the structure we rely on to support our centered being. Without this structure we collapse when we try to stand up in the world psychically.

Relating this experience to developmental psychology, the processes of building a spine—vertebra by vertebra—resembles to a great extent Stern's description of the formation of the core sense of self.

Stern uses the word self for the organizing subjective experience of whatever it is that later will be verbally referred to as self.[156] He describes the development of four different senses of self, which all continue to grow and co-exist throughout life. They are the emergent sense of self, the core sense of self, the intersubjective sense of self, and the verbal sense of self. These four senses of self are referred to as four different domains of the development of self. Throughout life they continue to develop. The adult person who enters therapy can, for example, have a very developed verbal sense of self but struggle in one of the other domains. The therapeutic task, according to Stern, is to support the development of the domain wherein the person struggles. Growing a spine centers the focus on the core sense of self.

Stern describes that when the infant grows a sense of core self, the infant approaches us in a way that make us feel as if they have an integrated sense of themselves as distinct and coherent bodies with control over their actions, ownership of their own affectivity and a sense of continuity and a sense of other people as a distinct and separated interactions. And we response to the infant by treating them as a distinct person.

The sense of core self relies on four self-experiences and the experiential integration of them: self-agency, that is self-initiated action; self-coherence, that is experiencing oneself as a dynamic physical entity; self-affectivity, the experience that affects belong to the self not to the person who may elicit them; and self-continuity, the sense of going-on-being; the continuity of experience.[157]

In the process (vertebra by vertebra) invariants [i.e. constants] of self-experience are integrated, forming islands of consistency, resulting gradually in the sense of core-self. The sense

---

156 Stern, *The Interpersonal World of the Infant.*
157 Davis & Wallbridge, *Boundary and Space.* Stern, *The Interpersonal World of the Infant.*

of core self with other is formed as a subjective event through the social experiences of being with someone such that self-feelings are changed.

Development according to Stern requires a constant, usually silent, dialogue between two.[158] This seems to be what is beautifully described in the interview, this dialogue and silent interactions with Ann. It is this being with 'someone' who is meeting her with love and holding her as a distinct other person that is supporting the gradual growing of the feeling of self-agency, and which enables her, vertebra by vertebra, to grow a spine.

WHAT WAS IMPORTANT—THE ESSENCE OF THE DESCRIBED QUALITIES OF THE CONTAINER

- Meeting the other with unconditional love.

To appreciate what it means to be met with 'unconditional love,' I would like to go to its opposite, which is conditional love. Conditional love is love that often implicitly is holding an unvoiced agenda: "you are only loved if…" Answering the "if…." illuminates the assumptions and adapted ways of being that the individual seeking love lives by in order to gain love (or rather acceptance) and to prevent being rejected. It also shows that for the person who has only received conditional love, that love was experienced within the context of a power-constellation: the power to give or withdraw love. Jung stated that where love rules, there is no will to power, and where power predominates, love is lacking. The one is the shadow of the other. The degree of adaptation and the receiving of unconditioned love create the proportional relation between the true and the false self.

For psychic survival mode, the false self can be dominating to the degree that the person herself has lost the feeling connection to the true self.[159] To enhance that person's capacity to re-establish connection to her own true self and to gradually be able to express more of the

---

158 Stern, *The Present Moment in Psychotherapy and Everyday Life*.

159 Winnicott, *Through Paediatrics to Psycho-Analysis*, pp. 296-297. "In the cases on which my work is based there has been what I call a true self hidden, protected by a false self. This false self is no doubt an aspect of the true self. It hides and protects it, and it reacts to the adaptation failures and develops a pattern corresponding to the pattern of environmental failure. In this way the true self is not involved in the reacting, and so preserves a continuity of being. However, this hidden true self suffers an impoverishment that derives from lack of experience."

true self, meeting that person with an attitude of un-conditional love and acceptance seems essential.[160, 161]

- Being active resonating the other—balancing being and doing- nourishment and agency.

As described so beautifully in the interview, it is the containing other who is holding the trust and the hope that the person herself often loses in the process (identifying with the voices of the complexes, robbing her of the trust and the hope). Actively resonating seems to be a position that both supports the other and facilitates the development of a feeling of agency. (Like kindling a fire Ann, according to the interviewee, feeds the small flames of impulses and strengthens them.)

THE ESSENCE OF INTERVIEW 4:
"AUTHENTICITY—ARE YOU GOING TO BE REAL?"

- A space to live through the gradual transformation of the inner constellation and a space to reflect on it—which often let the person to sense a meaningful pattern within the unfolding development.

As it becomes visible in the interview, this experience of a pattern within the unfolding development gives meaning to the past and trust in the future. It grounds the person and moves them from what can feel like meaningless difficulties, struggles or pain, into a 'sense-giving pattern' that gradually develops towards increasing coherence. This coherence arises from a felt experience, lived through over time, rather than an intellectual reflection and understanding, and it is thus grounded in the body, that is, it is 'incorporated.' Jung said:

> The most intense conflicts, if overcome, leave behind a sense of security and calm which is not easily disturbed, or else a brokenness that can hardly be healed. Conversely, it is just these

---

160 There seems to be a difference in different analysands as to their need of closeness and distance in the intersubjective field including the loving container (the need of emotional closeness or distance). I propose this need is to be understood in relation to their attachment pattern. When there has been a pattern of secure attachment, the need of a repairing experience in the therapeutic relation is not an issue. For an insecure avoidant type too much intimacy feels threatening or suffocating; for the ambivalent type, the need for distance and closeness moves back and forth; and for the disorientated disorganized type, it rapidly shifts without the person's own inner awareness and both needs can be present at the same time.

161 The components of the core sense of self have parallels to the conditions that presuppose expression of the true self.

intense conflicts and their conflagration which are needed in order to produce valuable and lasting results.[162]

- A space for exploring and being playful.

The transitional space between inner imagination and outer reality is combining the two in a creative meeting: the playing attitude. To create a safe space for the individual to explore, to play with its own images and allow them to develop; to explore and create new ways of being is the fuel for a creative approach to life—including a creative approach to the challenges of life. Jung said:

> The creation of something new is not accomplished by the intellect, but by the play instinct acting from inner necessity. The creative mind plays with the objects it loves.[163]

Winnicott, in exploring the potential in playing and its value for inner growth, stated:

> The place where cultural experience is located is in the potential space between the individual and the environment (originally the object). The same can be said of playing. Cultural experience begins with creative living first manifested as play.[164]

In the interview, the interviewee is expressing that this space of playing, highly empowered by the mask-work, became a place to engage with and embody new ways of being—a place to discover creative ways of looking at her story, and a place to find the prospective view of her pain: having a sense that *The Explorer* grew out of the same source as her pain. By living the characters of the mask to their extremes, she got to know them, to a degree where she could comfortably incorporate these aspects in her everyday life. In her story one gets a feel for the richness that the space and the world of the masks provides in terms of practising and creatively integrating new aspects of oneself or new aspects of known inner characters as they gradually transform through one's inner work. The transformation of the interviewee's mask became a mirror of the transformation in herself reflecting back to her in all its visibility.[165] The space to play became an area of creative "Formation, transformation, / Eternal Mind's eternal recreation."[166] The space of transformation and play in the BSR work seems to be a widening, a deepening or a multidimensional expansion of the transitional space described by Winnicott, including a wider range of areas of meeting than the imagination and reality.

---

162 Jung, *The Structure and Dynamics of the Psyche*, CW 8, ¶ 50.
163 Jung, *Psychological Types*, CW 6, ¶ 197.
164 Winnicott, 'The Location of Cultural Experience." Published in the *International Journal of Psycho-Analysis*, Vol. 48, Part 3 (1967).
165 It is fascinating to read the interviewees' descriptions of the transformations of her masks.
166 Goethe, *Faust*, Part II, Act I, in Jung, *MDR*, p. 221.

It seems to be a space equal to Jung's playing in the sand.[167] A space where the transcendent function 'plays' with and unites previous opposites, adding created meaning and purposes to her experiences, and over time, to her life as such.

- Someone who has lived it herself.

In analytical psychology, different archetypal representations of the healer are referred to, such as the wounded healer or the shaman. Both terms are encompassing a metaphor that moves beyond the parental field of holding, extending to the archetypal level of the struggles in life.

The shaman, having travelled into the 'underworld' and come back, is the archetypal representation of the healer who has confronted her own darkness in the unconscious without losing herself in it. The shaman is initiated through her own lived experience and that becomes part of her healing power.

The wounded healer is represented in the myths of Asclepius and Chiron. This myth gives rise to the understanding, that having wounds, and knowing one's own wounds, is what enables the empathic understanding of the wounds in others, which in itself can be a remedy. However it also implies that if one's own wounds are not brought to consciousness, they can be impairing for the therapeutic field. They will come between the healer and the patient, infecting the field.[168] In his autobiography *Memories, Dreams, Reflections,* Jung describes his own confrontation with the unconscious:

> In order to grasp the fantasies which were stirring in my "underground" I knew that I had to let myself plummet down into them, as it were. I felt not only violent resistance to this, but a distinct fear. …
>
> I saw that there was no other way out. I had to take the chance, had to try to gain power over them; for I realized that if I did not do so, I ran the risk of their gaining power over me. A cogent motive for my making the attempt was the conviction that I could not expect of my patients something that I did not dare to do myself. The excuse that a helper stood at their

---

167 Jung, *MDR*, pp. 197-199.

168 Working in the psychiatric field I have become aware that this perception of the healer is one of the key attitudes in the approach to the patient that generally differentiates analytical psychology from the medical model (with exceptions in both fields). The Western medical model favors the objective stand and a sharp division between pathology and health (the shadow being a fear of having pathological traits oneself and a strong need to identify with the persona of "normality"). The objective stand can become a defense against being impacted by the struggles of the patient and emotionally stirred by him or her and, for self-reflection on one's own difficulties. And the defense against being impacted can be blocking for empathic understanding of the patient's subjective experience. (Naturally there is an equally danger of falling too deeply into the empathic stand, losing one's footing which is of no help to the analysand).

side would not pass muster, for I was well aware that the so-called helper—that is, myself—could not help them unless he knew their fantasy material from his own direct experience, and that at present all he possessed were a few theoretical prejudices of dubious value.[169]

This way of thinking of the analyst's role is paramount for the attitude with which we meet the other. The attitude is formed by a willingness to try to understand what it means and feels like, from the position of the subjective world, to struggle with the issues the analysands are struggling with. There is a readiness to enter and accompanying them in their inner world and at the same time hold the balance. That is, accompanying but not being overwhelmed by it.

In developmental psychology, Stern describes how the toddler exploring the world constantly uses the parent as reference, checking whether or not it is safe to proceed. He describes an experiment where two pieces of carpet are separated by a black piece of glass that looks like an abyss. On the carpet furthest away is the toddler's favorite toy. The toddler sets out to get it, but becomes aware of the abyss. It looks at the mother to check with her. Now, if she looks scared and her body language implies to hold back, the toddler does not proceed. If she looks encouraging and her body language implies trust, the toddler proceeds. This is independent of the verbal signals that the mother gives.[170]

In terms of meeting and overcoming one's internal fears, having a guide who herself has met not the exact same fears, but equal types of fear, is communicated on all levels. The body picks up the other body's subtle communication testing: "Can I go there too?"—and the other becomes the confirmation that it is liveable in reality.

The metaphor of the shaman and the wounded healer refers to one's own lived experience. Connecting this aspect of the healer to neuroscience, I would like to emphasize the value of Jung's concept that we cannot take the analysand beyond where we ourselves have gone.[171] I propose this is parallel to Pat Ogden's and Allan Schore's description that we cannot go beyond our own window of tolerance. The work done in training is extending the window of tolerance, facing one's own fears and knowing where one's limits are. This work is what builds up a trustworthy companion.

In developmental psychology the containment is done by the parents and, if this was not good-enough, later the therapist will, for a while, do the parental holding.

One could say that the analyst is somewhere between the parental container and the shaman. The shaman's holding expands beyond the parental holding, including standing by the person when the issues extend to the adult's development, encountering the collective unconscious.

---

169 Jung, *MDR*, pp. 202-203.
170 Stern, *The Interpersonal World of the Infant,* p. 132.
171 Jung, *MDR*, pp. 202-203.

To embody the authenticity of someone who has lived it herself; there must be enough common ground in the life story between the one who has lived it and the one going through it to give this level of resonance and the feeling that parts of it are shared. That is what is conveyed in the concept of the wounded healer. One analysand said to a colleague of mine, "When my wound touches your wound, I am healed." Implicit in this statement is the feeling, "I know that you know how it is to feel what I feel." "It gives me the trust that you know what I have to 'crawl through' and that you think I can do it."

That is why therapeutic training needs to be a lived experience of working with one's own material, exploring more and more of it consciously (becoming familiar with the territories of carpets, toys and black holes), combined with theory that also becomes containing too.

I propose this is one of the deep values of the BSR work. Through this approach, there is an expansion of areas where one has gone oneself, and through the shared exercises, a broadening, widening, and a strengthening of one's familiarity with different psychic landscapes. This strengthens one's capacity for containment, including the embodied containment of a broad field of psychic landscapes and the emotional familiarity of it as well as the cognitive knowledge of them.

What Was Important—The Essence of the Described Qualities of the Container

- Being in touch with one's own playfulness, being playful and ready to play.

The playfulness of the leaders models a bringing in of the humor, of the imagination, and a fostering of a creative approach to meet the outer challenges. The lightness in the dark and the darkness in the light are equally adding depth to the other. Marion Woodman emphasizes the archetype of the clown, which can hold the full spectrum of the opposites of comedy and tragedy.[172]

- Being in the unpredictable now.

All three leaders have a background of being in touch with improvisation: Mary Hamilton in the field of dancing, Ann Skinner in the field of theatre, and Marion Woodman in the field of creative drama. This might account for their radiating familiarity with improvisation—a capacity that allows them to stay open to whatever the now brings, and to respond to the now in a creative way. They go into the seven days of the intensives with some structure, but they don't know what will happen. It is exactly that openness that they meet one with, that allows oneself to be open to not knowing what will happen and thereby becoming deeply receiving of oneself, the way one is, in the moment—to allow that which wants to come forth from the unconscious to come forth. The story of the unravelling of the yarn is an exquisite example.

---

172 Woodman, *The Ravaged Bridegroom*, p. 57.

- Space for ongoing soul time.

The BSR week-long intensives allow the participants to let go in a way that is not possible within the one-to-one hour, because in the intensive, participants do not have to go "back up" to their adult persona and be responsible for work, family, etc. after each hour. Thus the intensive provides a space of a whole week of tending and focusing on the inner life. As expressed in the interview it allows for soul time, mythic time and unbroken submersion. This is not to diminish the deep value of the rhythm of personal analysis, but rather to highlight the difference in the experience, when there is a space and a time of this length to focus on the inner process. A space that, due to its length, has a greater chance to provide time for the soul's expressions to come to their natural completion, including plenty of time for hovering.

Due to the embodiment, what comes forth comes forth through the body, in the body, or it has a chance to be worked with in the body. The participants get to encounter these aspects in a safe setting (meaning that the work is contained and that the facilitators are there to help if the material worked with becomes too overwhelming). In this way, the different psychic dynamics are given a form in which they can be experienced, related to, and brought to consciousness, so that the participants later in their everyday lives, can actually draw on this lived insight as a strength, knowing what is behind their feelings, patterns of behavior, and ways of making meaning of things or what resources in oneself hold and support one, or what needs a deeper integration.

- To give space for the participant to live through a gradual inner transformation.

Circumambulated from different perspectives in the interviews, the importance of being given space is stressed in several interviews. The quality of the space stresses the qualities of a containing other who can be with and accompany one in the process without interfering. This quality of growing into a transformation and gradually understanding it is stressed by both Jung and Winnicott.

Jung said:

Understanding is clearly a very subjective process. It can be extremely one-sided, in that the doctor understands but not the patient. In such a case the doctor conceives it to be his duty to convince the patient, and if the latter will not allow himself to be convinced, the doctor accuses him of resistance.

When the understanding is all on my side, I say quite calmly that I do not understand, for in the end it makes very little difference whether the doctor understands or not, but it makes all the difference whether the patient understands. Understanding should therefore be understanding in the sense of an agreement which is the fruit of joint reflection…. The patient, that is to say, does not need to have a truth inculcated into him—if we do that, we only reach his head; he needs far more to grow up to this truth, and in that way we reach his heart, and the appeal goes deeper and works more powerfully.[173]

Winnicott said:

> ... it is only in recent years that I have become able to wait and wait for the natural evolution of the transference arising out of the patient's growing trust in the psychoanalytic technique and setting, and to avoid breaking up this natural process by making interpretations. It will be noticed that I am talking about the making of interpretations and not about interpretations as such. It appals me to think how much deep change I have prevented or delayed in patients in a certain classification category by my personal need to interpret. If only we can wait, the patient arrives at understanding creatively and with immense joy, and I now enjoy this joy more than I used to enjoy the sense of having been clever. I think I interpret mainly to let the patient know the limits of my understanding. The principle is that it is the patient and only the patient who has the answers.[174]

THE ESSENCE OF INTERVIEW 5: "FINDING MY FEMININE VOICE"

The Essence of the Subjective Lived Experience:

•   Finding my feminine voice.

What is individually expressed in the interview seems to be reflected in a broader group of the collective as well; a longing for women to find their own feminine voice. The interest in Marion Woodman's writings on the conscious feminine and the body-soul connections is central in the BSR work and I believe the interest in this type of work reflects this longing.[175]

Whatever that feminine is, I believe it is a concept that cannot be exactly defined and that will vary according to the individual's own experience of it.[176] It seems to be characterised by the feeling attached to its emergence, more than the actual content.

---

173 Jung, *The Practice of Psychotherapy*, CW. 16, ¶ 314.

174 Winnicott, 'The Use of an Object and Relating Through Identifications,' based on a paper read to the New York Psychoanalytical Society, 12 November 1968, and published in the *International Journal of Psycho-Analysis*, Vol. 50 (1969) and later published in Winnicott, *Playing and Reality*, p. 116.

175 I think there is an equal longing in men to find their own voice. In my awareness there has been a growing interest from men to encounter the BSR work, which is moving into offering this type of work to men as well. Marion explains that they in the beginning offered the workshops to both men and women but it was hard to reach the depth of the work because of cultural patterns of relating in mixed groups. There has been a change in this since the BSR work was started and there is now openness and a wish from men to engage with this approach according to Marion.

176 Here I am not aligned with the general view conveyed in the BSR approach, and the classical Jungian approach. Marion Woodman will describe the content of the feminine, (albeit, not in absolutes),

In the interviews it seems to be related to something created out of oneself—a one-self that is rooted in the woman's own body. The longing to find this feminine within oneself seems to move along with the emergence of an inner masculine as well, and where the relationship between the masculine and the feminine is one of mutual support, or what is described in the interview as "a falling in love."

There seems to be a longing, both in the individual as well as intra-psychically, to live a relation between the masculine and the feminine that is not based on dominance and repression, neither on attack and defence, but on a mutual respect.[177] The interviewee's description of the development between the masculine and the feminine in her seems, in her story, to be reflected in the collective development as well. She describes a journey moving through the women's development, being competent both in the academic field and as mother. And she describes a search for the feminine voice that grows out of this development, superseding the polarisation, coming to a full expression in its own right. An expression that in itself is whole but enriched through the love connection to the masculine.

Thus it seems that the seeking for the feminine voice seems to be the search for something aligned with the whole of one's nature—aligned with the body too—not something that one is striving towards but something that seems to grow out of oneself, nurtured by the process of listening on a deeper level inside.

The emergence of the feminine seems often to be spoken about as something growing forth from inside through a process characterised by listening, following hints or intuitions, often unclear at the time, holding on, carrying inside, relating to it without not quite knowing its complete form, until "it" itself seems ready to be born. There are some shared motives that can be talked about, but I think the essence of it is that it transgresses definition—it is what it is because that is what it is. It is also possible to define it parallel to Stern's definition of the self; the feminine is what the woman herself verbally refers to as her feminine self. It is

---

and the description will be given as being opposites of the masculine. I personally think that the content of the concepts of the masculine and the feminine in the Jungian field have a tendency to be influenced by Jung's personal psychology as well as the cultural content belonging to (in my opinion) too narrow window of history. Belonging to a generation and a country where the cultural definition of masculine and feminine is much less confined, I believe it to be less stereotyped in the individual. I equally think that there is a danger in holding on to definitions that might not fit the individual's inner experience. (There is a saying that Jungians have Jungian dreams, Freudians have Freudian dreams, indicating the tendency to adapt to concepts within the theory we feel attached to.)

177 Being quite inspired by Iain McGilchrist's work on the right and the left hemisphere and their connection I cannot help thinking that maybe what in Jungian terminology is described as masculine and feminine has some relatedness to the neurobiological description of the two hemispheres way of processing the world. See Iain McGilchrist, *The Master and His Emissary.*

not about defining it but about finding it, listening to it, and voicing it. It does emerge not through defining it but through listening and following its voice.

In the interview, this process initially takes place beyond words and needs to be related to in a more subtle way. It seems to have to be searched for through other ways of expression such as dancing, painting, poetry making, images, and clay work.

What seems to be voiced in the interview is that, as oppose to feminism, the conscious feminine is not defining itself in opposition to the masculine. It is not relating to the masculine through fighting, but through a mutual enriching relationship possible because each aspect is validated in its own right and therefore is not in a power relation to each other.

There is an oscillating and dialectic movement of development described in the interview, including the description of how the masculine masks moves and transforms parallel with the transformation of the feminine masks. A relation that is gradually coming into being through the process where the masculine is transforming from dominance, and one could say a tendency to monologue with a loud voice, to a more receptive and interrelated appearance, including a capacity to see the feminine and fall in love with her. The feminine process transforms from being mute and depressed without capacity to express itself, to gradually finding its own expression, its own voice and becomes visible. A visibility that makes interrelation possible and is opening the heart of the masculine.

Marion uses the image of the caduceus—the two serpents intertwining to describe the oscillating development of the masculine and the feminine. The areas where they touch are the moments of meeting in the living relationship between the two.

- A space for something being born the right way up.

Again this metaphor is poignant for the healing process. It's not the doing itself that is stressed but the space and the readiness to receive what is born, when it is born. This includes not blocking the labour.

The interviewee's story reflects a point of crucial importance. Before the current work (the BSR intensive attendance), a long process of individual analysis has taken place, and a long process of lived life, working with the difficulties of the first birth has taken place. This precious work is what gives rise to the readiness to receive what is ready to be born.

To receive what is ready to be born may sound easy but the story tells exactly how difficult and sensitive this process is. A slight misattunement, just for a brief moment can threaten to undo the healing that has just happened. It makes one humble in the work and it highlights what is stressed in the interview: the body-psyche is so precise, when we work with sensitive material.

- Adding tools to her toolbox as therapist.

This very practical aspect highlights a quality around the BSR approach that will be made more visible in the chapter that relates the BSR work to neuroscience and developmental theories. The exercise gives concrete ways of working with the aspect of the importance for change, both from the Jungian, the developmental and the neuroscientific view. Jung described how there can be no general method for psychic work based on developing the individual.[178] A new method must be invented with each encounter. The greater the toolbox and flexibility, the greater the readiness to attune oneself to the individual needs.

What Was Important—The Essence of the Described Qualities of the Container

- Opening of the voice channel.

Many of the exercises in the BSR work focus on connecting to and expressing repressed or unlived psychic energy that is blocked in the body. The voice work and the bodywork are unblocking the 'body-voice' so that the energy can come to expression. It is like working with clay; molding, warming, and making the clay flexible, before attuning to create its form, enables, enhances, and refines the expression.

The opening of the voice channel seemed to take place both literally and metaphorically. The opening, the freeing and the deepening of the work with the voice enable the feminine voice to come through.

- Being able to enter cycles of repair after misattunement.

In the interview, the interviewee describes examples where her inner reality did not match some of the exercises proposed or themes discussed. She described how this mismatch at times gave rise to a feeling that the BSR intensives was useless and she felt angry. She also describes the response to her voicing of this disagreement and how the reflected response gave rise to a feeling that the leaders took her serious, reflected on her point and made adjustment. Focussing not on the theme but the process; what seems to be of importance is the container's capacity to repair misattunement and adjust, so the feeling of re-establishing a sharable ground is created.

THE ESSENCE OF INTERVIEW 6: "LIVING METAPHOR"

The Essence of the Subjective Lived Experience:

- Living metaphor—a lived symbolic approach to life.

As described by Whitmont the symbolic approach can:

---

178 Since all scientific methods must be based on the general.

This Symbolic approach can mediate an experience of something indefinable, intuitive, or imaginative, or a feeling-sense of something that can be known or conveyed in no other way, since abstract terms do not suffice everywhere. While to most people in our time the only comprehensible approach to reality lies in defining everything by means of literal abstract, impersonal conceptualizations, it is this challenge to and reliance upon the intuitive and emotional faculties that constitute the fundamentally new character of Jung's approach.[179]

As described in the interview, the encounter with the symbolic approach to life not only provides bridges to the inner world but also creates bridges that establish a sense of wholeness and connection with the outer world as well. A symbolic approach to what happens, relates the inner with the outer, the microcosms with the macrocosms, and it attaches feeling and meaning to the lived context. The outer world is seen in the light of similarities and connections as opposed to separate from the subjective experience.

What does a symbolic approach to life create?

Wilhelm Bitter describes in *Meditation in Religion and Psychotherapy*:

Not only the occidental Western world but the whole of humanity is in danger of losing its soul to the external things of life... Our extraverted forces of the intellect are so much concerned with adequate feeding and hygienic care of the underdeveloped parts of the world, as well as with raising our standard of living. That the irrational functions, the heart and the soul are more and more threatened with atrophy.[180]

Without the soul and the heart we lose touch with ways of orientating ourselves in the world of emotions, ethos and meaning, and we lose touch with a sense of wholeness in the world.

According to Jung, tending to the symbolic approach, as opposed to the traditional symptom-orientated approach, is the means to discover our way out of the unbalanced psychic state again.

Using the language of neuroscience, the symbolic approach describes situations in parallels, analogies and arousal relations, not in defined absolutes. The symbolic approach is parallel to the right hemisphere's mode of processing information (as opposed to the left hemisphere's mode of processing information, which relies on sequential, causal, logical processing more familiar to the symptom-focused / diagnostic approach).

Perceiving our world as living metaphor enables us to re-find the emotional meaning and emotional sense of wholeness reflected in the outer world as well as the inner world. Working with metaphor, we pay attention to the joint meaning as perceived through the senses and intuition. It enables us to understand the outer reality, not only through a factual line of causal

179 E.C. Whitmont, *The Symbolic Quest: Basic Concepts of Analytical Psychology*, p. 16.
180 W. Bitter, (Ed.). *Meditation in Religion and Psychotherapy*, p. 13.

happenings but also through a symbolic approach, creating a sense of meaning and belonging. It enables us to grasp the whole picture. This sense of meaning revitalises the heart and the soul. Marion Woodman says that the soul thrives on metaphor.[181] Perceiving the world as living metaphor is nourishing for the soul.

- The body as living reality.

Research into the body-mind connection indicates that mind and body are not separate, but part of an interwoven network of intelligence. The sensing organs in the body constantly inform the central nervous system of the inner and outer environment and the responses to that are constantly fed back to the body in a continuous loop of exchanging information, regulating and adjusting. Information is stored in the body's perceptions memory. Much of the sensations that the body picks up from our inner and outer environment never reach consciousness. But the processed result of this information may reach consciousness in the form of intuitive knowledge (conscious knowledge based on unconscious perceptions). By attuning to the body, one can begin to listen to its signals. Attuning to the intuitive knowledge of our bodies can become a reservoir of wisdom and guidance, and a source of knowledge about our deepest being. Also one can open the lived reality of the body by tending to this part of ourselves with nourishing images, caring touch and loving attention. It is shown that when we tend to our body with love and care, our body chemistry is changed.

Marion Woodman emphasizes that the body gives us the metaphorical images and messages from the unconscious in the same way as dreams do.[182]

We can interpret these images and messages if we take the time to listen to our body and to the images that come up. The point is that we are flesh and blood and often we don't experience the reality of a psychic image until we feel it in our body.[183]

This parallels the recent paradigm shift in the cognitive sciences, which proposes a mind that is not independent of the body. The mind is an embodied, not a disembodied entity. Rather thinking itself requires and depends upon feelings emanating from the body.[184] In addition, Stern concludes that present moments happen between people with embodied minds, and we react physically as well as mentally to the encounter.[185]

Furthermore, it is reflected in Damasio's model of the interconnectedness between the body perceptions, the image, the feeling and the core-consciousness (see later).

---

181 Woodman, *Conscious Femininity*, p. 15.
182 Woodman, *Conscious Femininity*, p. 118.
183 Woodman, *Conscious Femininity*, p. 118.
184 G. Clark, "The Animating Body: Psychoid Substance as Mutual Experience of the Psychosomatic Disorder."
185 Stern, *The Present Moment in Psychotherapy and Everyday Life*.

THE ESSENCE OF THE PROCESS—EMERGENT SENSE OF THE SELF

> In looking back over the dreams of a considerable period a man may sometimes discover in tiny scraps and fragments, even in single images, meanings to which he was utterly blind at the time. They were parts of a pattern that was slowly being woven...[186]

Holding all the interviews in mind, including the process of interviewing in itself, it felt to me as if the women by witnessing and telling their subjective experience of their inner development over years, were in fact sharing with me how their *inner sense of Self* (with a capital 'S') had gradually emerged. As if those fragments of experiences slowly started to cohere and come into connection with each other, weaving together; and out of this weaving gradually a pattern—a sense of their tapestry came into form. As if they, in the container of the BSR approach, got in touch with an emergent sense of themselves as feminine authentic beings. What at the time seemed more or less isolated or not connected, but yet had been a clear sense or impulse that they felt they had to follow, slowly grew into being a very meaningful part of their greater tapestry and giving rise to a feeling of being connected to the whole as well. They seemed to share the emergent sense of a *weaver*, someone leading, or guiding or providing the next impulses seemed to be what they shared. Their growing experience of trust in the 'weaver' and their own impulses seemed to enrich their lives. It seemed to create meaning in all the things that they had gone through, and were going through. Also they would reflect a trust in the meaning of what they are going to go through in the future; as if the impulse that is followed in the now is linked to a broader feeling of following one's story. It seemed to link the personal story with the broader story too, like a *microcosms* of the *macrocosms*. Out of this process there seemed to grow another way of being in the world—not relying on control and understanding only, but also on a trust in the impulses and a relation to a weaver and their own tapestry. I, as listener, had the feeling of being given a gift to be able to witness a broader patchwork taking form.

Perspective: Linking BSR with Neuroscientific and Developmental Theories

Having looked at each interview and reflected on the subjective lived experience of psychic transformation in the context of the BSR intensives, I would now like to look at the BSR approach from a more theoretical perspective.

---

186 Harold C. Goddard, *The Meaning of Shakespeare*, Vol. 1, p. 16.

It is my aim in the following section to link the BSR approach and the themes presented in the subjective lived experiences with neuroscience and developmental theories in order to show how much the BSR approach has to offer, not only to the Jungian field, but also to the broader field of approaches. Weaving in different aspect of the BSR work I will present it in perspective in relation to the neuroscientific and developmental writings referred to in the introduction. It is a collection of different theoretical directions that I bring. It is not my aim to present them in detail, or to compare the different views in detail, but to show the similarities, the links and the enrichment gained from looking at the same theme from slightly different perspectives. In my view this approach broadens our understanding, supplements our methods and strengthens our container; and it sharpens our awareness of the complexity and layers of interconnectedness that take place in the myriads of interactions, both in the inner and outer life.

I would like to emphasize that soul work can never be reduced to neuroscientific language.[187] I am remembering Marion Woodman speaking to the loss of the metaphorical world and the symbolic language, and what that does to our world. Referring to her time as teacher in creative drama, she tells of her teaching Shakespeare to her students. She quotes Shakespeare's *Macbeth* where death is announced with the words "Out, out, brief candle" One of her students complained, "Why does Shakespeare have to be so complicated? Why did he not just say: 'He is dead!'" Marion's answer was, "It is not big enough for the soul!"[188]

And, yes, there is a marked discrepancy in our responses, body perceptions and evoked inner images and fantasies to the two statements, though they are expressing the same thing. There is a loss in the transitional space where imagination and reality meet. Losing touch with the symbolic language is atrophy of the culture and of our inner world.[189] Marion speaks to why she prefers to convey her points through metaphors, speaking about why she prefers to tell stories to the audience rather than getting her point across by talking theory:

---

187 In my opinion we have to hold in mind the two worlds; the subjective lived experience and the understanding of what moves the soul with the objective vision that can give us the frame in which to work. And when the two come into conflict it must always be the subjective lived experience that has the last word. We need to know the theory and be able to use it in discussion with colleagues and in developing our approach but in the actual encounter with the inner life, in the encounter with the analysand, the objective theoretical viewpoints must be left out, devoting the focus to following the inner life and the subjective lived experience. That is, the reference point in the hour is not the theory but the subjective lived experience.

188 Marion Woodman, *Sitting by the Well: Bringing the Feminine to Consciousness Through Language, Dreams and Metaphor* (Audio Cassette).

189 Woodman, *Conscious Femininity* , p. 54.

So as long as it's theory it's removed from the actual feeling of the audience, and they can get so caught up in the words that they don't realize it's their own body I am trying to address. If I put it in a story form or use images, the mind may not hear it, but the body responds. And if it is reverberating in the body, sooner or later it's going to get through to consciousness. I feel it is more immediate to tell a story or to use metaphor.[190]

Thus it is not possible to limit the understanding of the inner world to neurons and synaptic networks, but it facilitates the communication with other professional fields if we too can speak that language, because these fields' metaphors often are closer to the collective consciousness we are living in. It gives the possibility of describing what we do and why we do it in a language that is used in other fields. In my opinion the Jungian approach has so much to offer that it would be a shame not to learn that language too and maybe create some metaphors that build bridges.[191] We need metaphors that can be shared, but are "sloppy" enough not to pin down the process. All theories about life are in themselves symbols since life cannot be exhaustible or totally explained. There will always be potential for new understanding, new openings and new mysteries.

Having stressed this viewpoint, I would like to continue looking at the following perspectives and links:

1. Positive mothering, implicit healing and non-verbal holding—bridging the positive mothering in the BSR approach with the neuroscientific understanding of implicit communication and its role in therapeutic work, and the developmental aspect of non-verbal holding.

2. Being received, feeling safety and trust, creating secure attachment—bridging the attitude and value of the BSR approach to look with the eye of love with its impact on level of arousal, attachment capacity, and inner work.

3. Being, doing, agency and creativity—how hovering, resonating other, empathic holding and symbolic expression can re-find nourishment in being and re-establish a feeling of agency.

4. Symbolic language—linking body, image, feeling and understanding with creating a global sense of self—bridging the Jungian work and value of symbols and the BSR approach including the reality of the body with neuroscientific understanding of the connection between body, image, feeling and core-consciousness and the developmental understanding of 'global sense of self' and preverbal perception of the world.

---

190 Woodman, *Conscious Femininity*, p. 53.
191 This atrophy is beautifully depicted by Michael Ende in *The Neverending Story*.

5. The symbolic approach and moments of meeting—the transformative power of meetings and symbols—bridging the Jungian understanding of symbols with Daniel Sterns moment of meeting, sloppiness, shared inner landscapes and a feeling of wholeness.

6. Body-knowledge and implicit wisdom and dream knowledge as images of implicit wisdom—bridging dreams, images in the body and body-knowledge with neuro-scientific descriptions of the different modes of processing information in different areas of the brain, linking right-hemisphere processing with body-linked knowledge, intuition, images of feelings and dreams.

7. 'Demo' and new ways of being in life—mirror neurons, procedural leaning and empathic skills—bridging the power of the demo in the BSR approach and the mirroring with the developmental understanding of intersubjectivity, self-with-other, resonance, attunement and mirroring with the neuroscientific description of mirror neurons, procedural leaning, and capacity for following the other's intentions and eliciting empathy.

8. Containing: widening the window of tolerance with the self-regulating other—bridging the value giving to the containing in the BSR work and the understanding that the perceiver and perceived are one, with Allan Schore's writings on the influence of the self-regulating other on psychic arousal, window of tolerance and therapeutic work.

9. Dance of Three: shared feeling voyage, self-with-other, intersubjective field and RIGs—bridging the ways of working in BSR including the many exercises with mirroring through the body and feelings and holding with the body and feelings with developmental psychology's models of RIGs and Daniel Stern's description of shared feeling voyage and moments of change.

10. Non-verbal healing: changes of inner working models through lived experience of self with other, linking non-verbal lived experiences in BSR with transformation of self-with-other, attachment and complexes.

POSITIVE MOTHERING, IMPLICIT HEALING AND NON-VERBAL HOLDING

In this section, I would like to argue for the importance of the non-verbal relation for the growth of a sense of an internal holding center.

Potentially, a sense of a holding center is grown inside through receiving of enough positive mothering.

What do good mothers do and how does the infant perceive good mothering?

When enough good mothering was not provided in infancy for whatever reason,[192] it becomes the task in therapy to seek to provide a repairing experience. The therapist holds the role of the good (enough) mother and gradually this function can be internalized in the individual. (In Jungian terminology the encounter with the therapist has the potential to activate the positive pole of the mother archetype and gradually allow for an inner representation of the archetypal mother to be constellated.)

The understanding of how to foster this growing sense of a 'holding center' intra-psychically is therefore important.

The experience of good-enough mothering takes place from infancy, perceived body to body, implicitly through the senses, through the gaze, the body-holding, the tone of voice, the rhythm of rocking, the feeling that the mother is calm, relaxed and there for the baby. The mother herself is feeling calm and therefore she can give this feeling to the infant. In the BSR work, this level of mothering is brought in consciously and as lived experience, through the positive mothering exercise and its reverberating effect on the field.

It is my hypothesis that any therapy trying to help individuals who lack an inner experience of enough good-enough mothering (Winnicott's terminology) or positive mothering has to provide some experience at this pre-verbal level. The experience must aim at reaching the unmet early need and foster repair on the preverbal level (body and implicit mind, core sense of self) as well as at the verbal level and at the level of procedural relational experience. If touching is used, the analyst most know how to apply it in a non-intrusive way and, if there is a gender difference in the analytical constellation, it might be safer to find another way of reaching the body level or to propose the client to do some work with a same sex analyst or a body therapist.[193] It is very difficult to provide the body with a felt sense of being held and

---

192 This is often the initial situation in therapy. This is not to blame mothers or fathers, but an attempt to understand how we can repair what initially has gone 'not so well.' When the adult enters therapy he or she takes responsibility for repairing what was not constructed in a "good-enough" way and hence keeps hindering the unfolding of adult life in a fulfilling way.

193 Especially for people who lacked enough good mothering or have experienced early trauma (impacting core sense of self and body boundaries) touch can be very healing or very intrusive. Infants or children who have had their boundaries invaded somatically or psychically will be at risk for experiencing re-traumatization. With different gender, intimate boundaries as well as early boundaries come into play, simultaneously increasing the risk.

supported if it does not have an idea of what that feels like from a lived experience.[194] When such an experience is lived, it is possible to recall the feelings and the body state in connection to that in a later situation. The memory has been stored in the body.

The knowledge of the importance of the sound of voice, the gaze, the body posture and the emotional quality radiating from the other is emphasized in the neuroscientific perspective[195] as well as in Marion Woodman's work (the perceiver and the perceived are one). This quality of the emotional field of the other, how they are in the world is implicitly perceived. If the analyst does not love her own body, her own 'inner child,' her own 'feminine being' this is picked up in the field and the words are not coherent with the implicit message.

In conclusion, I propose that BSR has a lot to offer in terms of understanding and healing on the preverbal level which include the general attitude to soul work, the awareness of the impact of presence, the loving gaze, the tone of voice, the implicit communication from body to body, the mutual influence between the perceiver and the perceived. Also the BSR approach offers ways to work with the preverbal level and create implicit healing through dream work, bodywork, working with images in the body, movement, art work, breath work, dance, and mask-work. And in all the preverbal sharing made possible through the mirroring and containing.

BEING RECEIVED: SAFETY AND TRUST—SECURE ATTACHMENT

In the recent years there has been a lot of focus on attachment theories and research on early attachment patterns (see the references in the introduction). The theories describe how our perception of the world is formed by our early relations. How we make meaning of what we experience in the world is deeply influenced by how we learned to make meaning of it in our early relations.

According to attachment theory, the models of meaning that we create in infancy depend on the quality of bonding with our caregivers. The emotional quality of the bond is reflected in individual's attachment pattern. Mary Ainsworth developed procedures for observing children's internal working models in action.[196] Later, a structured clinical interview was

---

194 I recall in my early therapy with a psychologist that she kept saying to me that I needed to be a good mother for myself. I often left her consulting room trying to figure what she meant and how I could do that. I had no idea. We cannot teach that through the cognitive mind. Love travels from one body to another body. One could say that it takes a non-verbal bodily experience to establish a somatic representation of the positive mother archetype—a feeling in the body of being held and loved.

195 Schore, *Affect Dysregulation and Disorders of the Self* and *Affect Regulation and the Repair of the Self.*

196 M. Ainsworth, M. Blehar, E. Waters, & S. Wall, *Patterns of Attachment.*

developed named the Adult Attachment Interview[197] which categorises four basic patterns of attachment relationships. Basically these relationships can be divided into two main categories: secure attachment and insecure attachment. Secure/ autonomous attachment makes us trust the world, trust others and believe that we will be relatively all right; that bonding with others is a source of nourishment and support. Secure attached individuals come to expect that they will be received by others and can ask others for help if it is needed (this is very close to the positive mother complex in Jungian theory). Secure attachment is a buffer and a resource in life when we encounter difficulties.[198] Insecure attachment is described in three sub-categories: insecure/ preoccupied (the individual is moving back and forth in the attachment feeling, seeking it, but feeling invaded or feeling they have to be as the caregiver wants them to be, feeling too close or too separate); insecure/ dismissing (the individual is avoiding intimate attachment as way of protecting oneself from invasion from others); and insecure/ unresolved, or disorganized (the individual's attachment is unpredictable. Bonds of attachment create immense fear, rage or pain or elicit dissociated defence as projection for overwhelming, unregulated, intense, distressing emotions. Predictability is absent and there is no pattern. The need for distance and closeness can exist simultaneously.[199] The insecure attachment corresponds to the negative mother complex in the Jungian terminology but the models from attachment theory give a more differentiated understanding including the level of impact, self-regulation, width of window of tolerance and level of arousal (see later).

When the attachment is insecure, fear will arise in relationships and a lot of psychic energy will go into trying to regulate the attachment. Patterns will develop in order for the individual to feel more secure or to cope with fear, thus shaping the behavior of the individual.

When we look at this perspective, the main initial precondition for psychic transformation is establishing a feeling of being safe (or at least relatively safe) and secure in the attachment. This can potentially, if the therapy goes well, develop into what is called learned secure attachment. That is, a secure sense of attachment is formed in relation to the therapist and becomes a parallel inner model to the previously formed insecure attachment model.[200]

Looking at the interviews, a main premise mentioned for psychic transformation taking place was the sense of feeling safe, of feeling secure, of feeling that there was enough time within the container, and that the container was to be trusted; and, if misattunement happened, that the container could initiate repair.

---

197 C. George, N. Kaplan, & M. Main, *The Adult Attachment Interview*, unpublished manuscript referenced in Fonagy, Gergely, Elliot, & Target, *Affect Regulation, Mentalization and the Development of the Self*.
198 Gerhardt, *Why Love Matters*.
199 Fonagy, Gergely, Elliot, & Target, *Affect Regulation, Mentalization, and the Development of the Self*.
200 Jeremy Holmes, *John Bowlby and Attachment Theory*.

In conclusion, I propose the BSR approach fosters an environment and an attitude in the container that resemble the premises for secure attachment. It is my assumption that when the participant feels that the container, as such, is safe and they can trust the attachment, it makes the level of fear and defence mechanisms go down and sets more psychic energy free to explore their inner world. Thus being received with a loving attitude lessens the anxiety and opens to exploration of the inner world.[201]

BEING, DOING, AGENCY AND CREATIVITY

If a person's feeling of having agency has been impaired by the mother or significant other, who has been ' taking over' and 'imposing' her agency on the infant, so that the infant had to mirror her, the therapist's capacity to attune, to leave space and to encourage the impulse to come forth without taking over, is crucial.

How crucial it is, is mirrored in several of the interviews. Several of the interviewees have talked about the impact of having the space, of the hovering, allowing for the waiting for the new impulse to come forth.

It seems to have something to do with feeling simultaneously that the witness holds the trust that something will emerge and yet the feeling of the acceptance that, if nothing is emerging, it is completely all right, too. It is as if the witness holds the trust in the non-doing. The resonating other holds that space of being without imposing the doing. This seems to be what conveys the sense that the person does not have to *do*. It is allowing enough being so that the *doing* arises of its own *being*. It is the process of waiting for some kind of impulse growing which is experienced as an inner agency coming forth by itself.

For some of the women, it has felt like a huge relief to discover this inner impulse rather than having to rely on their will power to do something. A doing not rooted a reaction but arising from an inner impulse.[202]

This process of holding described by Winnicott[203] is what enables the infant to grow a strong connection to its 'true self.' It is the resting in the 'going on being' that gives birth to the authentic doing. If the mother cannot hold the 'going on being' for the infant, the infant's doing will not be born out of itself but will be a reaction to mother. It becomes a doing imposed to keep the bond to mother. It is a shift of the root of the doing, a shift in its origin. It is not a doing arising out of the being, but a doing to adapt to impingement from the en-

---

201 When a person is "outside of the window of tolerance" no integration can take place (Ogden, 2006). The psyche is in alarm and survival mode and, like with a house on fire, security doors are blocking the usual linking pathways. It is a situation of damage control, not growth.
202 Woodman, *Addiction to Perfection*.
203 Davis & Wallbridge, *Boundary and Space*.

vironment—an impingement that at the same time breaks the 'going on being' and calls for an adaptation to the other. (This naturally happens in life all the time; the crucial point here is that when it has happened too much, too early, in the 'going on being,' the nourishment in the 'going on being' is not established and the doing out of an inner impulse is impaired. This results in too much adaptation and too little capacity to tap into the 'going on being' as a source for nourishment.[204]

There is a parallel set of dynamics engaged in the individuation process.[205] Here the gravity of the center of doing gradually moves down the ego-Self axis. As the ego gradually becomes more attuned to the Self, the doing increasingly arises out of deeper center of impulses, potentials, and new life.[206]

If a person has not had that experience of going on being: the capacity to be, to trust the inner life and to trust that something is holding them can be impaired.[207] The encounter with an analyst who can hold that being can repair and provide them with a revealing experience that something does come forth from the inside, if they just wait and hold the being. An experience, which when it happens may feel as a total revelation, because what felt like inner emptiness due to a lack of holding, suddenly is no longer empty.[208] Something emerges from that inside; and a feeling, an impulse or an insight is created.

In my view, this is one of the healing experiences that analytical psychology uniquely can provide, partly because of its embracing of the archetypal level and numinous dimension in its model of the psyche, partly because of the way the new life is received, and partly because of the fundamental trust in the being and the impulses from the unconscious.

Thus, through the mirroring and the holding, the trust in the inner life can gradually emerge through following the impulses and slowly provide the person with a sense of being embedded in something holding them and moving them (in the case where this sense has been impaired in the early development due to lack of mirroring and holding).

This is referred to in several of the interviews where the work and the process over time gradually give rise to some sense of a pattern being woven, and by some sense of a weaver. As described, borrowing the phrase from Daniel Stern but bringing it into the Jungian developmental model, this could be phrased as an "emergent sense of the Self" (see the essence of the interviews sections).

---

204 Davis & Wallbridge, *Boundary and Space*.
205 What Winnicott would describe as a shift of size or influence from the false self to the true self is, in Jungian terms, close to the individuation process.
206 Ann Belford Ulanov, *The Functioning Transcendent: A Study in Analytical Psychology*.
207 Ulanov, *The Functioning Transcendent*.
208 Ulanov, *The Functioning Transcendent*. The experience that being can be a place of tapping into the nourishment of the Great Mother Archetype.

THE "FEAR OF BEING": CREATING SAFETY AND TRUST

As described in the interviews, gradually over time, emerging through dream images, art work etc., the inner life reveals itself in a form that consciousness can relate to. This process is nourished by the space and the attitude of "the resonating other." The value of the space of holding without interfering is emphasized in several of the interviews.

As described by Marion Woodman,[209] there is in Western culture a rather one-sided relying on "control and doing" and a loss of trust in "being" and in the process of letting things happen (as previously described in part 1). This seems to intertwine with an impairment of an embodied sense of safety and holding and trust in the state of being. If we have nothing to rely on in our beingness, it is terrifying because whenever we stop doing, we face non-being.[210]

In this sense, the doing becomes a defence against the non-being and therefore holds a quality of possession. The source of doing is not the being but the fear of being. Many self-help books rely on activating other ways of doing. But frequently it is a matter of listening and being quiet enough, so that one can hear what is being communicated from a deeper place. Due to the fear of being and the relying on doing, it can be frightening to enter a space of hovering because it potentially puts the individual in contact with a fear of being.

It seems important to establish an experience of being without fear and helping the person to release inner fear locked in the body and relax into being in the body. This is fostered in the BSR in the deep relaxations and breath-work. Gradually the body learns to relax into its own being and relax through guidance from a self-regulating other, the images used in the guidance become potentially images that can induce self-regulation or relaxation. The body learns to relate being with a pleasurable feeling of relaxation and support (literally on the floor).

If a person is experiencing a fear of being, I propose the value of safety and trust in the analytical relationship has a special importance in terms of rebalancing the doing with the being.[211] It seems important to focus initially on building enough safety and trust, so that the analysands can gradually allow themselves to stop doing and slowly grow into trusting being. Only through enough being can a feeling or experience arise that there is something holding them, containing them and witnessing them. This is first held by the analyst and, gradually, as the trust deepens, it can be experienced from inside.

Living in a culture where transformation takes place at a speed which allows for very little room, time and space to keep going on being, a culture which to a great extent is los-

---

209 Woodman, *Addiction to Perfection*, pp. 11-25.

210 Marion Woodman describes the being as the feminine and the doing as the masculine. I have chosen here to stay with the words "doing" and "being" to keep the emphasis on the body's experience of it.

211 As mentioned, I do think this is quite a common feeling in our culture, albeit, often unconscious.

ing the old sense of holding by religious containers on the collective level and the mothering container of the individual level, this emerging lived experience of some sense of Self (with a capital 'S') become a feeling of finding an inner ground that can hold and contain oneself.

In conclusion, both the body and the Self become sources for the experience of being re-nourished by tapping into being.

SYMBOLIC LANGUAGE: LINKING BODY, IMAGE, FEELING AND UNDERSTANDING WITH THE GLOBAL SENSE OF SELF

The most basic hypothesis about the human psyche with which we deal here, then, is that of a pattern of wholeness that can only be described symbolically.[212]

Four different theoretical fields refer to the symbol's connecting function.

The Processing Mode of the Right Hemisphere

Symbolic language appears to be the language of the right hemisphere of the brain. As described the left and the right hemisphere of the brain process information in two different modes. The right hemisphere plays an important role in processing non-verbal communication, including emotional and corporal information. It is particularly involved in grasping the general feel of things, the whole picture, and is involved in visual, spatial and emotional responses.[213] Its mode of processing is symbolic, parallel linking, connecting information by association.

Symbolic language (including dream language) seems to be the closest verbal language of this right brain, but also other ways of expression that Jungians are very familiar with such as art work, clay work or authentic body movement gives access to this right-brain world. The right brain has everything to do with our emotional well-being.

Marion Woodman emphasizes Jung's notion that the symbol speaks to the mind, the body, and the imagination and therefore is healing because it creates a sense of wholeness. Symbolic language seems to be closer to enveloping the global experience and therefore seems more appropriate in describing this inner perceived world by speaking both to the body perceptions and the cognitive grasping of meaning.

Developmental Psychology: Exploring the Global Sense of Self a Sense of Wholeness

Daniel Stern speaks of the preverbal world of the infant which is predominant up until the emergence of the verbal sense of self at around the ages of three to four years (the verbal sense

---

212 Whitmont, *The Symbolic Quest,* p. 15.
213 Schore, *Affect Dysregulation and Disorders of the Self* and *Affect Regulation and the Repair of the Self.*

of self is emerging when the child starts to use language to tell narratives about her or his world). Up till this age, the experiences of the world are perceived as *wholeness in the now*. Stern describes it as a global experience of oneself in the world. He describes how language itself always is a compromise between the lived experience and that which can be verbalised. Stern explains that the global sense of self, capable of capturing and holding myriads of sense-inputs at the same time, always feels verbal description to be an offence. The verbal account of the lived experience can never fully embrace the myriads and myriads of perceptions experienced in the now. Reading Stern's description of the subjective account of the experience of the global sense of self is like entering a dream. The quality, the linking, the feelings, flow as if in a dream.[214] Talking about the global sense of self, the perception of the world as well as of the effect of state, resembles the symbolic world. Equally the global sense of self can be evoked through living the symbol in the body.

WORKING WITH SYMBOLS: THE NEUROSCIENTIFIC ASPECT— BODY, FEELING AND CORE-CONSCIOUSNESS

This central connecting capacity of the symbol, described by Jung and its embodied anchoring emphasized in Marion Woodman's work, is strikingly similar to the description of the neuroscientist Antonio Damasio's work.[215] Damasio speaks of "the feeling of what happens" and explains the fundamental link between the body perceptions, first-order maps, second-order maps, linked with the feeling response to the object and the conscious awareness of this feeling. Damasio thus describes the body and the feelings as a base for core-consciousness.

Damasio's work gives way to explain to non-Jungians the essential value of the symbolic work, which is at the core of the Jungian approach, in terms that appeal to colleagues coming from the scientific field. Damasio uses other words, coming from the scientific approach, explaining the connection between the body, feelings, images and consciousness. What in the Jungian field would be the unconscious, Damasio refers to as non-conscious. The outer things that we see are referred to as "the object," the inner image of it is referred to as "maps" (maps appear in a three-layered process: first-order map, second-order map, and image). In his work, Damasio describes the central function of feelings and images (first- and second-order maps) for core-consciousness. Though it is rather technical, I will provide a brief outline of Damasio's thoughts and hope that the reader will be able to grasp enough to see the similarity with the Jungian theory.[216]

---

214 Stern, *The Interpersonal World of the Infant.*
215 A. Damasio, *The Feeling of What Happens: Body and Emotion in the Making of Consciousness.*
216 Jung, *MDR,* p. 201. Including Jung's statement: "To the extent that I managed to translate the emotions into images—that is to say, to find the images which were concealed in the emotions—I

According to Damasio, consciousness first arises in the form of a feeling—the roots of this feeling are the body perceptions of changes in internal milieu attached to the object presented (the object approaching us which we see or hear)—the information in the body's response gives rise to an immediate sketch of the situation—a first-order map, which consists of neural patterns of object and organism; that is, the representation in the brain of the thing we see and of our self in relation to that. This gives rise to an immediate evaluation: has the object been encountered before? Is it dangerous for the organism? This is all taking place very quickly, the main purpose being whether to illicit a reflex survival response of fight or flight. If the object is not immediately evaluated as dangerous, further processing takes place. A second-order map is formed depicting the relationship between object and organism. That is the image of the relationship between the thing we see and ourselves. The second-order map generates a feeling; the value of the relationship for the organism. That is the feeling that is evoked by the relationship to an object. (Now the interesting thing to grasp here is that the object can be an outer object but it can also be an inner representation of an object that we imagine - an image we see with our inner eye). Thus feelings are generated from our relationship to an image. In short, Damasio's hypothesis is that core-consciousness occurs when the brain's representation devices generate an image (second-order map), which is a non-verbal account of how the organism's own state is affected by the organism's processing of an object (first-order map) and when this process enhances the image of the causative object, placing it saliently in a spatial and temporal context.[217]

This hypothesis outlines two mechanisms: first the generation of the image is the non-verbal account of the object-organism's relationship—which is the source of the sense of self in the act of knowing, and secondly the enhancement of the images of an object (parallel to Marion Woodman's emphasis on the image of a thing rather than the thing itself).

According to Damasio the sense-of-self component is grounded in the following premises: consciousness depends on the internal construction and exhibition of knowledge concerning an interaction between the organism and an object. The organism, as a unit, is mapped in the organism's brain, within structures that regulate the organism's life, and signals its internal stages continuously, the object is also mapped within the organism's brain. In the sensory and motor structures activated by the interaction of the organism with the object, both organism and object are mapped as neural patterns; in first-order maps, all these neural patterns can become images. The sensorimotor maps pertaining to the object cause changes in the maps pertaining to the organism. (This parallels Marion Woodman's statement that our images change our way of being in the world, our sense of self and our body states.)

---

was inwardly calmed and reassured."
217 Damasio, *The Feeling of What Happens.*

The neural patterns transiently formed in the second-order maps can become mental images no less so than the neural patterns in the first-order maps. We thus form inner images of ourselves, objects and the interaction or relationship between ourselves and the object. Because of the body-related nature of both organism maps and the second-order maps, the mental images that describe the relationships are feelings (feelings are describing the quality of relationships—the value for the 'organism').[218]

Damasio, Panksepp, Bull and others have demonstrated that each particular emotional state automatically activates distinct action tendencies: a programed sequence of actions. As explained above, when the body-mind processes incoming perceptions, the new information is interpreted by comparing it with prior experiences. And, on the basis of this comparison, the body-mind predicts the outcome of the different possible actions and forms a physical response to the incoming stimuli.[219] Damasio states:

> Physical actions are creating the context for mental actions; bottom-up processes are affecting upper level processes. [This is] the feeling of what happens.[220]

When we traditionally work with symbols within the Jungian frame, we take the dream symbols, areas of psychic stuckness or pain, and explore them with our verbal sense of self, relating them to our narrative story, to our conscious life, to our past and our future, and to the story of humankind—to the archetypal dimension. These are all dominantly working from the right to the left hemisphere, integrating the world of the right hemisphere (symbolic) with that of the left hemisphere (verbal) through the corpus callosum, working with the emphasis on what Allan Schore refers to as horizontal right to left axis.[221]

In the BSR another dimension is emphasized as well, working with the symbol through the global sense of self, amplifying the symbol through the reality of the body by working with the energy of the symbol in the body as it is experienced in the moment. That is a deep, concentrated way of working with movements, sensations, perceptions, feelings, and their corresponding motions. It is sharable on the non-verbal level through the witnessing and the mirroring.

Using Damasio's model of core-consciousness, this work is very much working with a more vertical axis, moving from body perceptions in the peripheral nervous system to perceived sensations in the lower brain, to reactions to these sensations evoking emotions leading to pre-images (first-order maps) processed to feeling-responses in the middle brain, to images

---

218 Damasio, *The Feeling of What Happens.*
219 Ogden, Minton, & Pain, *Trauma and the Body.*
220 Damasio, *The Feeling of What Happens*, p. 27.
221 Schore, author's notes from Schore's lecture at the following conference: *Psychological Trauma and the Body*, London, 15–17 September 2007.

(second-order maps) that can be processed, including the right brain and then, through the horizontal axis, can be verbalised.

This way of framing, of thinking of the work as moving along two axes rests on my way of conveying the neuroscientific understanding in a simplified metaphor, expressing something that is much more complex in order to facilitate the practical use. Also, when we explain what happens from a neuroscientific perspective we are trying to explain interconnected parallel processes, happening on many levels of the neural network, connected by similarities across modalities at the same time (the processing mode of the right hemisphere). The models and explanations will therefore always be a compromise, since verbal explanations rest on serial, logical, connected sequences of explanations (the processing mode of the left hemisphere).[222] Expressing something symbolically or metaphorically seems better for grasping the multi-connected parallel processing of the right hemisphere.

Margaret Wilkinson describes how symbolic information is the type of information that lights up the most areas of the brain at the same time, engaging much broader areas of processing than non-metaphorical language that just lit up (that is, activated) the language-processing area of the left brain.[223] This seems to support the Jungian perception that the symbol has a wholeness-creating capacity since it speaks to the mind, the heart and the imagination.[224]

Staying with this understanding, is it possible that some of our dreams are the images of feelings, portraying our relationship with objects that evoke these feelings? Dreams could be how nightly, we work through relations to inner and outer objects, their internal, relation and the feeling value in relation to the dream-ego. These are objects coming into our minds, evoked through perceptions from our sense-organs or recalled from stored memory. And could it be that we, in the process of sorting through these images, become more conscious? Could we by tending to dreams and accessing this core-conscious knowledge, an intelligence speaking in images through association and body perceptions, add feeling value to our world? And is it likely that we can gain access to earlier patterns of experiences of self-with-other that we draw upon to orient ourselves and make sense of our world unconsciously? Is it possible that we, by tending to our dreams and body, can gain access to these levels within and draw on their understanding of our world? And is it possible that these levels of our understanding of our world are highly attuned to our emotional well-being, the area that is often suffering when people enter therapy? And is it possible that this area has much higher attunement as to how to rebalance our lives to recreate emotional well-being, because emotional well-being is

---

222 Damasio, *The Feeling of What Happens*.
223 Margaret Wilkinson, *Coming into Mind*, p. 9.
224 Woodman, *Conscious Femininity*.

a global experience of a connection between our body, our mind and our imagination or our body, our feelings and our world-in-the-now? These are questions to ponder.

In Conclusion

Damasio's work emphasizes the role of body perceptions, images and feelings for core-consciousness. Stern emphasizes the preverbal world capacity to create a sense of wholeness.

I suggest that BSR work with the body, the images arising in the body, the feelings and the understanding of it, are intuitively aligned with the findings of Stern and Damasio. I, too, suggest that working with the symbols in the body is aligned with the natural formation of images. The work is raising core-consciousness and it unfolds the feeling-relation in the symbol, and it is creating a consciously felt link between the body perceptions, the image and the feelings, related to the symbol.

SYMBOLIC APPROACH AND MOMENTS OF MEETINGS

There is a paradox for the logical mind in the symbolic approach. The symbol can never be fully described, yet the trying is what builds the relationship to the symbol and what creates relation in 'talking about' the symbol. The symbol builds relation. A relation that is impaired if we move to define it in absolutes, thinking we know what it is. There has to be certain sloppiness in the way we approach it. "Sloppiness" is a word used by Daniel Stern which allows for moments of meeting and makes it possible to co-create a shared world—an intersubjective meeting. Stern refers to this in the context of moments, of meeting between two persons, where two subjective worlds are shared. These moments of meeting are the moment of meeting of two minds and a process of hit-miss-repair-elaborate. Because it is the interaction of two "living systems," it is in itself unpredictable.

When the symbol is alive, it carries in itself a certain unpredictability and capacity to reformulate and transform. This is so vividly expressed in the interviews describing the maskwork, which indeed is work with living symbols. Engaging with the mask is always initiated by having to find "where the energy is now" and it moves and transforms continuously.

When we talk about symbols with others, this openness to 'find' where the symbol is, how it can be described, is like looking at a rich piece of art work that really moves us. We can keep seeing new aspects, new angles and new dimensions. It does not make sense to discuss which description is the right one. There can be a description that speaks more to the shared experience of the picture and therefore is resonating with more people but that does eliminate other descriptions and it never really 'captures' the picture. If the people looking at the piece of art start to discuss who is right, the focus moves from the picture and into all kinds of discussion. If they instead focus on the process of sharing what they see, they open their eyes to the picture. Hearing other people's reflections keeps opening our own eyes and we too become aware of what resonates with us (consciousness-creating). The sharing of what we see is in itself a meeting—a meeting with the image, the other person and the resonating place in ourselves.

I propose that the work we do in Jungian analysis, moving along, working with dreams and symbols belongs to the type of psychic change described as moments of meeting (in the light of the findings of *The Boston group of Change Process Study Group*[225] describing two types of change: 1. a gradually growing transformation through consistent moments of meetings and 2. transformation happening in quantum leaps sparked by a now moment (closer to the impact of a big dream).[226]

In the process of moving along, the symbol allows for movements of meeting—of sharing worlds. The sharing or the moments of meeting can be experienced as meetings between the unconscious and the conscious, between one's own inner images and the images of mankind, between the analyst and the analysand, between past and the present. These moments of meeting, moments of shared worlds, connect and join us with our world. They are moments of meeting with 'other' that change our feeling about ourselves.

BODY-KNOWLEDGE: BEING IN THE BODY, THE REALITY OF THE BODY, PROCESSING BODY MEMORY

The attunement to the body and awareness as to how the energy affects the body, opens to a whole new way of being in one's body. It opens to a consciousness in the body and it makes one become highly alive in the body.

Any work with the body brings us into the now, because the body lives in the now. It moves the focus of attention from being "out there" to being "in here," thus centring oneself in one's own body, one's own reality. Integrating working with the body and the symbols in the body is individuating the body-soul. Integrating the body in the Jungian work is individuating through the body or embodied individuation in the here and now.

Studying medicine, I was always amazed by the intelligence of the living body. An intelligence that the conscious mind often was not even aware of and so, had a hard time in explaining. I would like to give an example of the implicit knowledge stored in the body. It is about

---

225 The Boston group of Change Process Study Group (BCPSG) was created in 1995. It consists of a small group of practicing analysts, developmentalists, and analytical theorist who share the view that knowledge from the bourgeoning field of recent developmental studies as well as dynamic systems theory can be used to understand and model change processes in psychodynamic therapeutic interaction (for more information see www.changeprocess.org). Daniel Stern was part of this group which inspired him to write *The Present Moment in Psychotherapy and Everyday Life*.
226 Stern, *The Present Moment in Psychotherapy and Everyday Life*.

finding balance.[227] When we look at a glass of milk that is tilting we know how to rebalance it, because we know the lived experience of our body tilting, knowing how to rebalance it. We don't think about it. We draw on our body experience and stored body-memory of a similar condition and immediately know what to do, to rebalance and our hands reach out for the glass and do it. Maurice Merleau-Ponty states that we form our capacity for abstract thinking based on these concrete body-stored experiences and memories.[228] Asking people how they know how to rebalance a tilting glass, they often will say, "I just know." But if you ask them to explain, and then follow their directions, the glass still tilts! The verbal mind does not know. Our bodies have implicit knowledge stored outside the explicit field.

Could it be that our dreams arise from this knowledge? And could it be that we can gain access to this type of implicit knowledge through bodywork, as well as dream work? Perhaps our body's knowledge can help us reconnect to the type of wisdom that restores balance in our inner world in the same way that dreams do.

Also, the work with the body is attuning to the stored memory in the body. These are memories of perceptions and episodes that for some reason have not been processed by consciousness, but are a part of the reservoir of prior experiences that we use to orient ourselves with in the now, as described by Damasio and referred to earlier. The reason why they have not been processed consciously can be that they did not carry enough intensity to pass the threshold, compared to the rest of the information processed at the time: that the focus of consciousness at the time was 'focused' on something else,[229] or that the perceived stimuli were too overwhelming to "hold in mind" and therefore were blocked out from consciousness, staying unprocessed. This is the case of traumatized individuals[230] who have experienced overwhelming impacts that could not be processed and made sense of at the time of the trau-

---

227 From Merleau-Ponty descriptions; source: handouts, philosophy lecture, January 1994, University of Aarhus.

228 "Taking the study of perception as his point of departure, Merleau-Ponty was led to recognize that one's own body (le corps propre) is not only a thing, a potential object of study for science, but is also a permanent condition of experience, a constituent of the perceptual openness to the world. He therefore underlines the fact that there is inherence of consciousness and of the body of which the analysis of perception should take account. The primacy of perception signifies a primacy of experience, so to speak, insofar as perception becomes an active and constitutive dimension. Merleau-Ponty demonstrates a corporeity of consciousness as much as an intentionality of the body, and so stands in contrast with the dualist ontology of mind and body in René Descartes" (http://en.wikipedia.org/wiki/Maurice_Merleau-Ponty, Wikipedia, 7. Of July 2008).

229 We continuously perceive millions of sensori-stimuli. The great function of the threshold of consciousness is to sort what is passing the threshold; that is, what is of primary importance for the organism in that moment. Without that capacity, consciousness would be flooded with stimuli.

230 Trauma is to be understood here as including early relational trauma (exemplified by Interview 5).

LOVE MATTERS FOR PSYCHIC TRANSFORMATION

matising experience. These unprocessed fragmented body sensations and overwhelming emotions keep on intruding in the person's life, split-off from the context of the primary experience, but re-evoking the body-psyche state at the time of the trauma, in the person's daily life.

Thus, working with the body enables a working with those previously unprocessed perception-memories—sensorimotor memories—and gradually processing them and integrating them in the conscious mind. This means linking the sensorimotor part with the emotions, with the cognition, and placing the episode in time and place. The actual working with the body movement in this process is potentially allowing for what Ogden refers to as an "act of triumph"[231] completing the instinctive physical response to the emotional impact of the trauma that at the time of trauma was blocked by the conscious mind to secure survival.[232]

This means that sensorimotor information, affect and cognition that previously was outside of the window of tolerance, and therefore could not be processed or integrated through this work, can be processed gradually in the company of a self-regulating other who is there to help and to balance the process, so it does not exceed what can be tolerated. This means that the work is to proceed at a pace attuned to the amount that can be tolerated and processed without exceeding the window of tolerance[233] and balanced with resource-building work as described previously. It also means that the process has a spiralling movement, as the person grows in strength and, as the window of tolerance is widened, more and more of the material can be integrated.

The importance of separated focus on and working with the body's sensorimotor processing is essential according to Pat Ogden.[234] She describes that individuals who are struggling with the effects of overwhelming emotions, often have little awareness of how body perceptions participate in creating and sustaining these emotions. By separately attending to the sensorimotor processing (movements and sensations), the processing of the sensorimotor part of the trauma can take place (including the experiencing, articulating and integrating physical-sensory-perception, body sensation, physiological arousal, and motor functioning).

I propose that this relates to what can take place in the exercises in the BSR, especially in the symptom in the body exercise following the body's movement with the symptom. The

---

231 "Act of triumph" is a concept first described by Piaget. It refers to the natural survival response as action in a threatening situation. This can be suppressed by consciousness or blocked (a freeze-reaction or numbing-out response) which keeps the body in an unresolved traumatic place. Completing the act of triumph in therapeutic settings can free the block and the energy kept in it, and lead to the emotion of victory that is evoked when encountering a dramatic situation and managing it.

232 Ogden, Minton, & Pain, *Trauma and the Body*. Author's notes from P. Ogden's lecture at the following conference: *Psychological Trauma and the Body*, London, 15–17 September 2007.

233 Ogden, Minton, & Pain, *Trauma and the Body*.

234 Pat Ogden is a pioneer in somatic psychology and founder and educational director of the Sensorimotor Psychotherapy® Institute.

sharing after the exercises, the art work, the diary writing, the talk with leaders or apprentices and the following work in the participant's own analysis or therapy allows for the emotional processing including experiencing, articulating and integrating the emotions.[235] Also the continuous work in personal analysis parallel with the BSR intensives is building up the ego, providing the cognitive processing, the narrative integration and solidifies the changes over time.

The importance of the personal analysis alongside the BSR intensives is unquestionable, as referred to in the interviews as well. And there can be times where the timing of the intensive does not match the timing of the individual. For example, something can 'come up' just at the end of the intensive. The processing then, can take place in the personal analysis.

Thus, through the working with the reality of the body, the symptoms and symbols in the body and the authentic movements in the body, it is possible to process previously unprocessed memories locked in the body and gradually work towards integration, releasing the energy that previously was used to hold the split-off parts out of consciousness and foster the sense of wholeness that is born when "sensory-motor-affect-cognition" are linked in the mind. That is in Marion Woodman's terminology when the body, soul, and mind are one.

In conclusion, I suggest that it is the reservoir of body knowledge that we tap into through many of the exercises in the BSR approach and that this work gives access to the working through previously unprocessed trauma locked in the body, moving through the "act of triumph" and releasing the resources in the body, creating a greater integration of the body, mind and soul.

"DEMO'—NEW WAYS OF BEING IN LIFE—MIRROR NEURONS, PROCEDURAL LEARNING, EMPATHIC SKILLS

As mentioned in the description of the BSR work, all the exercises are introduced by a demonstration. Why are the exercises not just explained verbally? How can we understand the huge value of the demonstrations and the impact they have both on the qualitative aspect of the exercises and the staying impact on the participants that they refer to in the interview? In the recent years, neuroscience has been researching a special kind of neuron in the human brain called mirror neurons. These neurons are responsible for our capacity to follow another person's acts and then carry out the same act. In addition, an act that is perceived as a lived through procedure of how to do something, can be memorized. We are then able to recall and perform that procedure.

This way of acquiring new knowledge largely extends the form in which we learn how to do something by being instructed verbally or by reading about it. The load of information

---

235 Ogden, Minton, & Pain, *Trauma and the Body*, p. 13.

that can be perceived in a short time when we can use all our senses to receive it is huge. Moreover, most of it does not have to be processed consciously, only the essence. In the learning process we are engaged with our whole being. While gleaning information, we are living through the sequence of procedures and we are able to do the same. It has been shown that that is a fundamental way of how we learn from others, picking up new ways of doing things and being in the world. It is fundamental way by which we communicate and learn new procedures and it is the central tool of communicating how to be in life.[236]

Further, due to the mirror neurons, it is not just 'how to do something,' it is also the form in which it is done, the body movements while doing it, the facial expressions and the emotions evoked in the person while doing it, that are picked up. We are able to pick up what Stern would call the vitality background feelings of the person's state of being while doing it. The most amazing thing is that we can be creative with the procedure that we have picked up, and let it blend with our own vitality background feelings when we conduct the procedures ourselves.

This can best be illustrated by the example of a piece of music. We can have the notes written down and that can give us the sequence of the piece of music, but when the teacher plays it, the sequence is played through her way of being. The shifts, the speed, the pauses, the crescendos and diminuendo, the lightness of pressure, the places that are emphasized or toned down all become an expression unique to that person's way of playing the piece. When we hear it we can pick it up and if we are skilled musicians we can play it like the teacher, or we can pick up the tune of the melody and let it be formed uniquely by our own way of playing it, letting it resonate with our own being. This is an amazing capacity we have as human beings (mammalian animals do the same, but it is unknown if they can become conscious of it in the same way as humans).

Thus, by watching a demonstration of how to do something, we are picking up the procedure and we can play it on our own instrument, giving us a lived through experience of how that is for us with sensations, perceptions, emotions, feelings and cognitive understanding.

The impact of the discovery of the mirror neurons is huge and extends the understanding of procedural learning. It is also the mirror neurons that seemingly are responsible for our capacity for empathy, to feel into another being's feeling state and sense what they are feeling, moment by moment and adjust our response to that. This capacity is the foundation for attunement and our skills for relating to others.

Ann Skinner[237] describes that it is the power of the demonstration that shapes the quality of the following floor work. By this we tap into another layer of the power of demonstra-

---

236 Bauer, *Warum ich fühle, was du fühlst.*
237 Ann Skinner teaching, in relation to apprenticing in the BSR intensive, Grimstone, UK, 2005.

tions, because it conveys not only a procedure but also the background attitude with which we do the procedure. Hence you, in your demonstrations, by being attuned, focused, deeply authentic—not performing but really conveying the space of allowing things to happen, following with complete commitment wherever the energy that you are working with is going—that whole attitude will shape the floor work because the participants who watch the demonstration pick up all these layers and will 'get' what you are expressing.

This way of learning, communicating and picking up what is going on in our surroundings is already established in the late foetus stage and keeps refining through our development. We are from early on attuned to pick up what takes place in our surroundings and making sense of that—we are attuned to pick up what other humans are expressing, doing and feeling and to make sense of that, and to let that information shape our responses, expressions, actions and ways of being. We pick up and learn from our environment from the earliest stages of our lives (including intrauterine sensations). It is a whole field of implicit knowledge available to us, that we often are not conscious of—we 'just do it' or we 'just respond' in that way. The influence of this knowledge is enormous. In terms of the therapeutic field, it adds to the understanding of the importance of how we are, how we do things and how we respond.

The importance of this is well-known and described, but the explanation of why it is so influential has been lacking the physiological dimension that neuroscience now contributes. It might not feel like a revolution in the way we practice in the therapeutic field, but it certainly adds a dimension of the value of therapy that can be explained to a broader community. It helps to verbalise models that can complement intuitive knowledge and validate the whole area of implicit experience in therapy.

In conclusion, learning new ways of being through watching the demo, watching Mary dance, watching Marion touch her hands and face with care, or seeing Ann allowing for a spontaneous impulse to be followed has a powerful influence on many layers of one's being. The "mirror in the body" work develops one's capacity to move into another person's world and get a feel for that world —we get a lived experience of that world, and we get a body-knowledge of it.

CONTAINING, WIDENING THE "WINDOW OF TOLERANCE" WITH THE "SELF-REGULATING OTHER"

One new field of theory that shares some of the psychic landscape with analytical psychology is regulatory psychology. Allan Schore writes about this emerging field, combining knowledge from psychiatry, neurobiology, psychoanalysis, object relations and attachment theory.[238] Supporting his theories with the neuroscientific research about the brain, he explains where the different processes take place and describes how this gives rise to different ways of processing different types of information. This gives a physiological understanding and a scientific description of some of the mechanisms that analytical psychology works with, but to a certain degree, has not been able to communicate to other fields because the metaphors used to explain what takes place are not shared by a broader community.

Thus, regulatory psychology shares much of Jung's thoughts on the self-regulating psyche and the body-psyche as a homeostatic system. However, in regulatory psychology, there is a huge emphasis on the developing brain and its need for other brains to serve as regulators. The developing brain needs a self-regulating other in the developing process as it slowly grows into being able regulate itself. This theory stresses the important role of the self-regulating other and explains neuroscientifically what Stern writes about in the early dyadic relationship.

Pat Ogden describes *containment* through the model of the *window of tolerance*. The window of tolerance is the amount of emotional intensity we can hold and cope with without going into hyper- or hypo-arousal (overheating or shutting down). Self-regulation is learned from others in infancy. The good-enough parent is there for the infant, and having a broader window of tolerance the adult-brain-body can hold what the child-brain cannot yet hold, thus helping the child to cope with the aroused emotional tension, tolerating it, and down- or up-regulating it. Through this process the child gradually grows in a widening of its own window of tolerance.[239]

In regulatory psychology, pathology is seen very much as the system's incapacity to self-regulated intense physic-psychic tension, leading to an extreme position of either hypo- or hyper-arousal. These are states that the organism, as such, cannot cope with constructively because it cannot down or up-regulate itself back into the window of tolerance. These states are activated by early survival mechanisms and the circuits belong to the non-reflective, non-differentiated, survival reflexes in the brain. Access to the slower and more reflective and differentiated parts of the brain is not developed sufficiently, because the survival states were not mediated by a self-regulating other who could mediate them, restabilising the level of tolerable arousal, and helping the infant to cope with them.

According to Allan Schore, the regulating interaction is communicated from right hemisphere to right hemisphere. This stresses a need to understand and develop ways to reach these

---

238 Dr. Allan Schore is on the clinical faculty of the Department of Psychiatry and Biobehavioral Sciences, UCLA David Geffen School of Medicine, and at the UCLA Center for Culture, Brain, and Development. He is author of four seminal volumes, *Affect Regulation and the Origin of the Self*, *Affect Dysregulation and Disorders of the Self*, *Affect Regulation and the Repair of the Self*, and *The Science of the Art of Psychotherapy*, as well as numerous articles and chapters.

239 Ogden, Minton, & Pain, *Trauma and the Body*.

early traumatic coping responses that are preverbal, and to help the person to regulate the arousal, coming back into a window of tolerance and staying within the window of tolerance for the arousal. With the help from the self-regulating other, this can be mediated and the window of tolerance for psychic arousal can slowly be broadened and the person grow his or her capacity to self-regulate.[240]

The understanding of these arousal levels and the implicit communication between two brains—between two living systems, between analysand and analyst, indeed parallels the Jungian model of transference and the communication from unconscious to unconscious. It also touches on the concept that we can only go as far as we ourselves has gone. It is the analyst's capacity to hold the level of tension without fear that is communicated to the analysand, body to body, right hemisphere to right hemisphere, and is helping him or her gradually to tolerate the state without dissociation.[241] This includes sensitivity to feel into the amount of *tension* evoked that is described in *holding the tension of opposites.* To reflect on the window of tolerance might make us sensitive to the amount of tension that can be tolerated and the active need for holding and regulating that the analyst can provide. It especially points to the importance of knowing the special needs of individuals who have experienced early relational trauma when one is working therapeutically.

The description of the state outside the window of tolerance seems to contribute with important knowledge to the Jungian field. It describes the homeostatic psyche as an open system that learns regulation from others and continues to be able to do so throughout life. It highlights the importance of the analyst's active engagement in the regulation process. Ogden and Schore describe that, when dys-regulation happens, the system needs the other to bring it back into the window of tolerance. In states of dys-regulation, no integration or reflection is possible.[242] This puts into question the self-regulating capacity of the homeostatic system in case of trauma. Schore's work seems to imply that the self-regulating psyche only works within the *window of tolerance.* More reflection on the practical implements of this seems important to consider in the Jungian field.

How the BSR Approach Fosters a Widening of the "Window of Tolerance"

Each individual has a different setting for the amount of arousal that is within their zone of comfort, ranging from hyper-arousal to hypo-arousal. The width of one's window of tolerance sets the limits to one's capacity to hold and to be in the position of being the *self-regulating* other for clients.

---

240 Schore, *Affect Dysregulation and Disorders of the Self,* and *Affect Regulation and the Repair of the Self.*
241 Schore, *Affect Dysregulation and Disorders of the Self,* and *Affect Regulation and the Repair of the Self.*
242 Ogden, Minton, & Pain, *Trauma and the Body,* Schore, *Affect Dysregulation and Disorders of the Self,* and *Affect Regulation and the Repair of the Self.*

LOVE MATTERS FOR PSYCHIC TRANSFORMATION

Widening one's window of tolerance means that one can comfortably cope better with one's own arousal, and down- and up-regulate it. It enhances one's capacity to contain and be in the position of regulating the arousal in others. The width of the window of tolerance seems to be extended during training in the BSR work. I propose that the BSR approach with its emphasis on holding and containing is of real value in terms of widening one's window of tolerance, benefitting one's own self-regulating capacity and one's capacity to contain others.

THE DANCE OF THREE, "SHARED FEELING VOYAGE," THE INTERSUBJECTIVE FIELD

Due to our capacity for empathy, understanding of the connection between movements and intentions, and the connection between body language and accompanying emotions, we can become aware of how another person feels through the way she moves and expresses herself. We do it unconsciously all the time. And we especially rely on this skill in therapeutic work (see the section on mirror neurons).

This capacity is enhanced when we put ourselves in the same physical position and let our movement mirror the other person.

This body-mirroring is a part of many of the exercises in the BSR intensive. To illustrate, I will refer to the work with a dream symbol in the body. In the dyadic work with the symbol, the partner is mirroring what the body of the dreamer is expressing when moving with the symbol that she works with. She holds the symbol in her imagination, and lets her body become that symbol. Through embodying the symbol in this way, the symbol is not talked about but becomes a living energy moving both in the dreamer and in the person mirroring her. The symbol is explored and shared implicitly through the reality of the body.

Stern says that psychic healing takes place in movements of meeting, when two psychic landscapes for a moment share common ground, creating an intersubjective shared field. These movements are shared, felt experiences, a feeling voyage and most often implicitly expressed in the knowing, I feel that you feel what I feel.[243] This is precisely what is lived in the embodied mirrored dream work and practiced and experienced in the Dance of Three, symbol and symptom in the body, mask-work and other variations of work in triads and dyads with the mirror, the container, and the dancer.

Naturally, any verbal exchange can be shared when the movement has found its natural completion. As the one working with the symbol, the company of the mirror feels like a validation of one's embodied reality and, when the mirroring is attuned, it creates a deep feeling of being seen and being able to share and communicate one's world in a global embodied

---

243 Stern, *The Present Moment in Psychotherapy and Everyday Life.*

feeling-language. The communication beyond words makes it possible to share what cannot be conveyed in explicit language or does not yet have an explicit expression. The therapeutic effect of this work is apparent.

As mirror, one gets to know the other person's symbol from inside out. One gets a sense of how it feels, how it sees the world, how it moves, how it relates, how it expresses itself. The mirror's reflection back to the mover will be one's body's amplification of that symbol.

In terms of training, empathic skill and being able to move oneself into the world of the other and act in a way that is attuned to that person, I propose that this way of working is remarkable: both as training for one's empathic skills, and certainly in terms of training as analyst. As an analyst one's instrument is opened and expanding from a mostly verbal interaction to a conscious embodied instrument that can attune and find the active resonance with the analysand's being. It opens to ways of working with core sense of self and body sense of self[244] that is much more difficult to reach through the verbal level of interaction.

I too would suggest, that if we are working with analysands who have issues prior to the verbal sense of self (age three), including preverbal or relational trauma, engaging in all the implicit modalities opens the door to share the preverbal stories. The body memory will recall and express itself in movements (as illustrated in the interviews).

INNER WORKING MODELS, RIG AND COMPLEXES

This paragraph will focus on non-verbal healing; changes of inner working models through *lived experience of self with other*—linking non-verbal lived experiences in BSR work with transformation of *self with other*, attachment and complexes.

To meet and adapt to the world around us, we meet the new and make sense of the new, based on our previous experiences. We learn what clues are important in our interactions with significant others, to secure the right response and keep the attachment bond. Our experiences in the past influence how we perceive the now. In terms of intimate relations, the quality of our earlier experiences shapes the inner models of *being with other in the world,* thus influencing how we perceive the now.

Internal Working Models Change Through New Lived Experiences of "Self-with-Other"

These models of unconscious acquired non-verbal patterns and expectations[245] are, within Jungian theory, what give rise to complexes. Coming from the field of infant observation,

---

244 Stern, *The Interpersonal World of the Infant.*

245 These are described in various ways by different schools: in Jungian theory they are known as "complexes"; Daniel Stern (1985) names them "Representations of Interactions that have been Generalized" (RIGs); John Bowlby (1969) named them "internal working models"; Wilma Bucci named

Daniel Stern describes these inner models as *Representations of Interactions that have been Generalized* (RIG).[246] These representations are gradually formed and re-formed in our development. They are like "maps" that guide our ways of being with others. In attachment theory, these inner models are described as *internal working models.* As the reader familiar with Jungian theory will notice, both RIGs and "internal working models" have similarities to Jung's complex theory.[247] In brief, Stern emphasizes the formation of these relational expectations and patterns in the dyad. The attachment theorist emphasizes the attachment patterns that they give rise to; Jung emphasizes the feeling tone and the archetypal core of the complexes.

According to attachment theory, the higher the fear of rejection,[248] the more attuned to signals of possible rejections the person will be, and the more likely the person's behavior will be based on ways of defending themselves from rejection. This can dominate to the extent where the *now* is perceived as the *past*—and the *now* seems a repetition of the *past* (what Stern calls *when the past robs the person from the now*).[249] It is due to those formed inner models, based on our feeling experiences, that our past relations keep being important for the now. By becoming conscious of one's complexes, one's expectations and *meaning creating models of interactions*, one can slowly start to differentiate and separate the past from the now.

Also in relation to a caring other and through the lived experience of being met with love and feeling received, new experiences are formed. Experiences that when repeated can become generalized and grow into new forms of RIGs or remodel old forms. Thus *ways of be-*

---

them "emotional schemas" (1997); and Robert Clyman calls them "procedural memories" (1991). Described in Sue Gerhardt's *Why Love Matters.*

246 RIGs differ from internal working models, as described in object-relations, in the sense that they are based on average expectations of "self-with-other" and thus have a more plastic quality continuously adapting. (For details and other differences, see also Stern, 1985).

247 Gustav Bovensiepen: Attachment-dissociation network: some thoughts about a modern complex theory *Journal of Analytical Psychology* 51 (3): 451–466. In this paper the author revises complex theory in the light of modern infant research, neuroscience and object-relation theory. The author takes up Jean Knox's idea of understanding complexes as analogies to the "internal working models" of attachment theory. The author proposes understanding complexes as dissociated sub-networks in the network structure of the psyche; these sub-networks contain the internal working models, the characteristic affects and unconscious expectations or fantasies. With this network model, one can try to understand severe defensive organizations in some patients as a pathological organization of different complexes. See also Jean Knox, *Archetypes, Attachment, Analysis* and Verena Kast, *Father Daughter, Mother Son.*

248 Fear of rejection or feeling rejected is part of the experience in insecure forms of attachment. It may be more or less conscious and there may be various types of defense patterns to avoid the feelings of rejection, including giving up relating.

249 Stern, *The Present Moment in Psychotherapy and Everyday Life.*

ing with others and feeling accepted and received can gradually lessen the impact of introjected voices from the past or the impact of negative complexes.[250]

Inevitably in this process, old constructions will be triggered. The therapist's understanding of what is going on, and capacity to repair the connection, rather than to repeat the destructive role of past figures, is the healing response. Stern says that it is not the constant attunement from the mother that is crucial for the infant, but her capacity to repair when misattunement happens. It is shown in infant observation that breaks in being together can be repaired (breaks in the interconnected field—meaning not sharing inner landscapes, not meeting in a shared worlds, and a loss of a connection or attachment) The mother's capacity to attune to the infant after a misattunement and to meet the infant in his or her world, repairs the break and re-establishes the intersubjective field. This capacity is creating models of what is sharable and expressible in relation, for the infant. The mother's capacity to repair is resulting in secure attachment and trust. This is equally true for the therapeutic dyad (even more so, since people in therapy often lack experience of possible repair after misattunement).

Emphasis on Lived Experiences: How Does Psychic Transformation Happen?

A lived experienced gets ordered in a structure in episodic memories, actions, perceptions and affect. The experience of being with a self-regulating other, gradually forms RIGs (Representations of Interactions that have been Generalized). RIGs are the basic units for the representation of the core self: *experience of me in the world with another*. When different RIGs are activated the infant re-experiences different forms of ways of being with the self-regulating other. RIGs are constantly updated. They are building blocks or working models for how to be in the world with others. They embody expectations about any and all interactions and serve as a guiding function. RIGs differ from internalizations—these have a final form and are experienced as internal signals (symbolic cues) rather than as lived or reactivated experiences.

When we look at complexes, focusing on the attachment, the focus shifts from the complex as such and the qualities of it to the relational pattern it constellates and the way one perceives oneself and the world when it is activated. What we select as important in what a person says, and the way it is said, is deeply formed by our previous experiences and the meaning making models that we have created from them.

---

250 When Jung formed his complex theory, neuroscientists thought the neuronal networks in the brain were static—the neuronal networks being the physical aspect of the models we form in our minds. Today neuroscientists know that the brain is 'plastic'—that means it can remodel itself. This might help us to understand why Jung's description of complexes has a greater emphasis on describing the actual content, whereas Stern put emphasis on the forming and gradually changing of RIGs and the relational aspect of the models and how that can be changed, "synapse by synapse" by layers of new interactions.

If we apply this perspective to the Jungian model, it would mean looking not at the complexes as such, but more at how one perceives the intersubjective world when that complex is activated. The work is gradually deconstructing old negative models and reconstructing new positive ones by providing a repairing lived experience of self-with-other and not confirming the past models. (Stern says it is "bad therapy" when the therapist confirms the past.[251])

Summary: Comparing Neuroscience & Developmental Aspects with BSR

Having compared different aspects of the BSR work, bridging it with neuroscientific theories and developmental theories, what can be said in summary? At which point do they meet, and where do the Jungian theory and the BSR approach add unique contributions in the context discussed in this book?

In drawing out the essence, I will emphasize the following:

COMPARING NEUROSCIENCE AND DEVELOPMENTAL ASPECTS WITH THE BODYSOUL RHYTHMS APPROACH

POINTS OF MUTUAL EMPHASIZES AND INCLINATIONS

- Positive mothering, implicit healing and non-verbal holding.

- Being received, safety and trust, secure attachment.

- Being, doing, agency and creativity—how hovering, resonating other, holding and symbolic expression can re-find nourishment in being and re-establish a feeling of agency.

- Symbolic language—linking body, image, feeling and understanding with creating a global sense of self.

- The symbolic approach and moments of meeting the transformative power of meetings and symbols.

---

251 Stern, *The Present Moment in Psychotherapy and Everyday Life.*

- Body-knowledge and implicit wisdom and dream knowledge as images of implicit wisdom.

- 'Demo' and new ways of being in life: mirror neurons, procedural learning and empathic skills.

- Containing—widening the window of tolerance with the self-regulating other.

- Dance of Three—shared feeling voyage, self-with-other, intersubjective field and RIGs.

- Non-verbal healing—changes of inner working models through lived experience of self-with-other.

POINTS OF ASPECTS UNIQUE TO THE JUNGIAN THEORY AND THE BSR APPROACH

What do the Jungian model and BSR approach complement that is not included in the neuroscientific and developmental models?

- Continuously to combine the somatic realm, the imaginative realm, and the cognitive understanding, body-perceptions, symbolic expressions and the understanding of it in relation to the personal, cultural and archetypal level; continuously working with the axis—bottom up and top down, and left and right hemispheres integrating the levels.

- The transcendent function and the ego-Self axis.

- The collective dimension; the containment in the group.

- The archetypal dimension.

- The spiritual dimension.

- The emergent sense of Self and a sense of a meaning with the process.

- The developmental perspective of adult life.

- The prospective dimension of the unconscious manifestations.

- A concrete practical approach for applying the knowledge of science and developmental theory into the therapeutic setting of healing soul-work.

- Values and symbols that can help hold the implicit and unconscious processes that take place in the therapeutic field.

- Emphasis on the reality of the psyche.

I propose that these points illustrate themes of unique value in the Jungian model of the psyche and in the BSR approach. They illustrate aspects of the psyche that can never be reduced to developmental or neuroscientific understanding alone but show the multi-dimensions of the human universe, thus complementing the scientific views. The Jungian theory thus aims for an all-embracing understanding of the human condition.

In this perspective, I propose the Jungian model of the psyche and the BSR approach has unique contributions to the neuroscientific and developmental theories in what hopefully continues to be a mutual inspiration.

Why Love Matters for Psychic Transformation

I would like to return to the title of the book *Love Matters for Psychic Transformation*. The initial description of the BSR work accounts for the value of love in the work and how it permeates the BSR approach. The interviews are six subjective stories that illustrate and amplify the effect. The perspective links different theoretical aspects, many related in some ways to the matter of being received with a loving, empathic attuned attitude and the impact when that has been lacking in one's past.

The last two paragraphs will bring us back to the beginning: why love matters. Bringing the two dancers of the book together: the Jungian theory and the BSR approach in relation to developmental psychology and neuroscience.

WHY LOVE MATTERS FOR PSYCHIC TRANSFORMATION: THE NEUROSCIENTIFIC AND DEVELOPMENTAL PERSPECTIVE

The Matter of Love for the Baby—Love and Early Development of the Brain and the Body

Sue Gerhardt is a psychoanalytical psychotherapist who has done pioneering work helping parents with their babies. She describes the interaction between the early development of the infant, the development of the neuronal networks in the brain and the regulation in the body.[252] In her work, she explains how the invisible patterns of the early relationship are wo-

---

252 Gerhardt, *Why Love Matters: How Affection Shapes a Baby's Brain.*

ven into the body and the brain from infancy, orientating our lives in particular directions. She says: "The power of the earliest themes in our lives resembles chaos theory. Like in chaos theory, a small difference in the beginning of a process can lead to a huge change in outcome." "These early themes of our lives are built into our organism and inform our expectations and behavior."[253]

Gerhardt states that these "built-in patterns" of bodily function and emotional behavior are shaped by our social interactions (she is here aligned with Stern but opposed to Freud, that argues for a more self-generating and self-made individual. For the relation to analytical psychology see the footnote.)[254]

Like Stern, Gerhardt describes how our early experiences form characteristic ways of relating to other people and of coping with the ebb and flow of emotions, which are not only psychological tendencies but also physiological patterns. She says: "They are the bones of our psychological life, hidden and outside of our awareness the invisible history of each individual."[255]

Thus the unconscious forces that shape our emotional responses through life are patterns of emotional experiences with people, most powerfully set up in infancy. These patterns are not unchallengeable, they are plastic, but like with riverbeds, it takes work to redirect the flow of our feelings, working patiently "molecule by molecule."

Love and Our Capacity to Manage Emotional Stress

Peter Fonagy,[256] who has done a lot of research into early attachment, refers to the brain as a "social organ." It is shown that the quality of the baby's early relationship shapes the developing brain and body (neuronal pathways regulating the muscular tension, heart rate, homeostatic balance etc. in the body). They shape the formation of relational patterns and the baby's capacity to cope with emotional stress. Fonagy says: "We know that a poorly handled baby develops a more reactive stress response and different biochemical patterns than a well-

---

253 Gerhardt, *Why Love Matters*, p. 14.

254 Andrew Samuels, *Jung and the Post-Jungians,* Chapter 1. The Jungian schools range from the archetypal school (emphasizing the inner actualizing system, the concept of the Self and the relation between consciousness and the unconscious) to the developmental school (describing maturation as continual deintegration–reintegration movements where various archetypal elements in the primary self "mate" with the environment). This gives the basis for the true internal object.

255 Gerhardt, *Why Love Matters*, p. 14.

256 Peter Fonagy OBE, Fmed Sci is a British psychoanalyst and clinical psychologist. He is Freud Memorial Professor of Psychoanalysis and head of the department of Clinical, Educational and Health Psychology at University College London, Chief Executive of the Anna Freud Centre, training and supervising analyst in the British Psycho-Analytical Society in child and adult analysis, a Fellow of the British Academy, and a registrant of the British Psychoanalytical Council.

handled baby."[257] In line with this, Gerhardt concludes that "Well-managed babies come to expect a world that is responsive to feelings and helps to bring intense [arousal, MR] states back to a comfortable level; through the experience of having it done for them, they learn how to do it for themselves."[258]

The Impact of Love on the Meaning-Making Models of the World and Expectations for Interactions with Other

The infant is from the very beginning tuned into relating and making sense of its surroundings. Meaning emerges as the infant begins to recognize whether the mother coming towards her or him will bring pleasure or pain. Sue Gerhardt says:

> Early emotions are very much about pushing people away or drawing them closer, and these images will become expectations about the emotional world in which he [or she] is living, that helps the baby to predict what happens next and how to best response.[259]

> Babies need a caregiver who identifies with them so strongly that the baby's needs feels like hers.[260]

In conclusion, we can say that early regulation is about responding to the infant's feeling in a non-verbal way, through face, tone of voice and touch; and the early emotions of the infant are about pushing people away or drawing them closer.

THE DEVELOPMENT OF THE BRAIN AND THE GROWTH OF NEURONAL NETWORK IN RELATION

Orbitofrontal Cortex, Emotional Life and Pleasure

Looking a bit more specifically at different structures of the brain, the prefrontal cortex has been drawing much attention. It is known that the prefrontal part of the cortex has a unique role in the way that it links the sensory areas of the cortex with the emotional and survival-oriented sub cortex. The orbitofrontal cortex plays a key role in one's emotional life and holds an important component of one's story. The capacity to emphasize, to vicariously experience

---

257 Fonagy, Gergely, Jurist, & Target, *Affect Regulation, Mentalization, and the Development of the Self,* p. 15.
258 Gerhardt, *Why Love Matters,* p. 19.
259 Gerhardt, *Why Love Matters,* p. 20.
260 Gerhardt, *Why Love Matters,* p. 23.

what others are experiencing and to have the capacity to enter other people's state of mind requires a developed orbitofrontal cortex.[261]

The orbitofrontal cortex is especially linked to the right side of the brain. As described earlier, the right hemisphere is particularly involved in grasping the general feel of things, the whole picture, and is particularly involved in visual, spatial and emotional responses.[262] Allan Schore describes how the orbitofrontal cortex is the controller for the entire right hemisphere which is dominating throughout infancy (up till year three, which is the same age as the non-verbal senses of selves are dominating as described by Stern[263]). The orbitofrontal cortex is the area involved in rewarding pleasurable feelings of all kinds, having the largest opioids level in the brain. It is deeply involved in managing emotional behaviors and responding to emotional cues in others.[264]

Sue Gerhardt states that if a mother is finding pleasure in her relationship with her infant; that is when the relationship is dominated by pleasurable interactions; the parent and the infant are, without realising it, building up the infant's prefrontal cortex and developing her or his capacity for self-regulation and complex social interaction. Gerhardt further describes that the first sources of pleasure for the infant are smell, touch and sound.

Being lovingly held is the greatest spur to development.[265]

The autonomous nervous system of the mother, in effect, communicates with her infant's nervous system soothing it through touch.

The power of the gaze into a smiling face equals the power of touch.[266]

According to Allan Schore, looking at faces has an even more powerful role to play in human life. Especially in infancy, the looks and smiles help the brain to grow. He explains how the infant reads the pupils in the mother's gaze, which inform it of the arousal of the autonomous nervous system in the mother. This will inform the infant that the mother is experiencing pleasurable arousal, the infant's nervous system in response becomes pleasurably aroused; the heart rate goes up and endorphins are released which make the infant feel good. Also the neuro-transmitter dopamine, which is growth-stimulating for the neuronal network in the orbitofrontal cortex, is released (increased dopamine in the orbitofrontal cortex also induced an increased top-down, 'calming down' of any stressing arousal impulses, arising from

---

261 Gerhardt, *Why Love Matters*.
262 Schore, *Affect Dysregulation and Disorders of the Self* and *Affect Regulation and the Repair of the Self*.
263 Stern, *The Interpersonal World of the Infant*.
264 Schore, *Affect Dysregulation and Disorders of the Self* and *Affect Regulation and the Repair of the Self*.
265 Gerhardt, *Why Love Matters*, p. 40.
266 Gerhardt, *Why Love Matters*, pp. 40-41.

lower parts of the brain and thus stabilises the arousal).[267] Gerhardt concludes that it is shown that lots of positive experiences with loving caregivers early in life produces brains with more neuronal connections (resembling muscles: the more they are used, the more they grow).

> What a small child needs is an adult who is emotionally available and tuned in enough to help regulate his states.[268]

She refers to a study from a nursery home, showing that it was not the mother's absence itself that created increase levels of stress hormones, but the absence of an adult figure "who was responsive and alert to their states moment-to-moment."[269] The value of the attuned caregiver who follows the inner state of the baby and empathically resonates with it moment-to-moment, is paramount for the healthy development of the infant.

In conclusion, enhancing deep, emotionally positive social interactions stimulates the growth of the neuronal network, the capacity to self-regulate, and emotional development.

The Power of the Image

From the age of 18 months, the brain develops the capacity to store images. As explained by Antonio Damasio, these are emotionally loaded images of self-with-other. Commenting on these images Gerhardt says: "It is the sketchy beginning of an inner life—an inner library of images that will be refereed to and will become increasingly complex and loaded with associations."[270] These emotionally loaded images are, according to Sue Gerhardt, close to the psychoanalytical idea of inner object or internalized mother (or the image of mother when recalling RIG with mother).

Sue Gerhardt states that: "The inner images also become an important source of emotional self-regulation. In future situations with similar types of emotional arousal, they can be used as guide to behavior in the absences of the caregiver."[271] But if the infant is deprived of a self-regulating other, the effective internalized parental strategies for soothing and calming of high arousal in the right brain is not established as "good-enough." This makes the individual vulnerable to emotional stress.[272] Emotional stress is easily triggered (the person has a narrow

---

267 Notes from seminar on the effect of dopamine on various brain circuits, Psychiatric Conference, 22 May 2008, Aarhus, Denmark.
268 Gerhardt, *Why Love Matters*, p. 48.
269 Gerhardt, *Why Love Matters*, p. 48.
270 Gerhardt, *Why Love Matters*, p. 47.
271 Gerhardt, *Why Love Matters*, p. 47.
272 Hypo-arousal is a collapse-response proceeded by too long periods of unregulated high arousal. Schore describes this stage as driving full speed with the brakes on, or having the heater turned up and the windows fully open: from the outside the speed or the temperature seems alright, but the situation is consuming a lot of energy (Schore, *Affect Dysregulation and Disorders of the Self* and *Af-*

window of tolerance) and the individual cannot evoke the image of the caregiver and induce emotional self-regulation. She or he therefore stays in a stage of emotional stress for prolonged periods.[273]

Management of Feelings: Comments on the Differences Between the Right and Left Hemispheres' Styles of Processing

The development of the orbitofrontal cortex gives a growing ability to manage feelings. Gradually, the right and the left side of the orbitofrontal cortex start to weave together, connecting the expression and management of feelings. Around the third year there is a shift from right hemisphere dominance towards the development of the left hemisphere. The left hemisphere's mode of operation is dominated by sequential and verbalised processing—that is one message at a time as we know it from verbal conversation. This is different from the right hemisphere's mode of operation. The right hemisphere's processing is characterised by intuitive grasping of meaning and similarities across many modalities, parallel processing, and a feel for the whole picture. This is known from our way of processing images, situations, body language and feelings. It is also the capacity we rely upon for attunement.[274] Also, the right hemisphere's processing is non-verbal. It can be unconscious or implicitly conscious.

The right and left hemisphere exchange information largely through the corpus callosum (a bridging structure linking the two hemispheres with a broad pathway of nerve fibres). When the two sides of the brain can link the information, we can communicate emotions verbally as well as through touch and body language.

The non-verbal form of images based largely on feedback from other people's faces, continues to inform our emotional responses throughout life and they continue to be influenced by networks created early in life. Likewise, the networks continue to be influenced by other people's emotional responses to us throughout life. Thus the quality of the feedback from the other person's face matters throughout life! Attuned feedback facilitates the process of symbolising the emotional response and expresses it verbally, and it fosters the constant update of the network through new feedback reflection.[275]

In the studies referred to by Gerhardt, what seems to be paramount for emotional well-being and health is that the left hemisphere's operations has the capacity to be well connected to the right hemisphere's information. In other words, that we are capable of putting into

---

fect Regulation and the Repair of the Self). Donald Kalsched, speaking about dissociation in trauma, describes it as the last way out of an unbearable situation, a defense mechanism of the Self—a type of encapsulation of the soul, even a feeling of psychic death or retreat, *The Inner World of Trauma*.
273 Schore, *Affect Dysregulation and Disorders of the Self* and *Affect Regulation and the Repair of the Self*.
274 Stern, *The Present Moment in Psychotherapy and Everyday Life*.
275 Gerhardt, *Why Love Matters*.

LOVE MATTERS FOR PSYCHIC TRANSFORMATION

words how we are feeling and to express it. If the connection between the left and right hemispheres is poorly developed, the left hemisphere is able to create a story that is not anchored in emotional reality (and we behave in ways not anchored in our emotional realities. This resembles the true and false self).[276]

Sue Gerhardt concludes that it seems to be the process of putting feelings into words that enables the left and right brain to become integrated.[277]

NEUROSCIENTIFIC PERSPECTIVE ON THE THERAPEUTIC DYAD AND THE BSR APPROACH

Why Love Matters for Development in the Adult's Brain and Body

Most important for therapeutic work is that what seems to be relevant for the early dyad, seems to be relevant in the therapeutic dyad as well.

> [The] mirroring of a healthy early relational experience by the analytical dyad enables the process of affect regulation, first by the analyst and then by the patient leading to change in the nature of attachment both in the inner and outer world.[278]

According to Gerhardt and Schore, helping adults who were deprived of good-enough early relationships to improve their emotional well-being is done by helping them to self-regulate. Like with the infant, this seems to be done by responding to the adult's feelings in a non-verbal way, moment-to-moment—through face, tone of voice, posture and potentially touch (Schore does not include touch. He does not come from a therapeutic tradition including touch. On the matter of therapeutic touch, I refer to the interview: Finding my Feminine Voice).

Schore argues that affect regulations travels from right hemisphere to right hemisphere. If the early environment could not attune and provide enough support for affect-regulation, he emphasizes that this can be provided later in a therapeutic setting by an attuned therapist. Schore states that affectively focused treatment (transformation inducing encounters) literally alter the orbitofrontal system. He suggests that non-verbal transference and counter-transference-interactions that takes place at preconscious-unconscious levels represent right hemisphere to right hemisphere communications of fast-acting, automatic regulated and dysregulated emotional states between the patient and therapist.[279]

---

276 Gerhardt, *Why Love Matters.*
277 Gerhardt, *Why Love Matters*, p. 55.
278 Wilkinson, *Coming into Mind,* p. 10.
279 Allan Schore, "Minds in the Making: Attachment, The Self-Organizing Brain and Developmentally-Oriented Psychoanalytic Psychotherapy," p. 315. *British Journal of Psychotherapy*, 2001; 17 (3):

To summarize, by attuning to the fast-acting emotional realm concerned with regulating emotions, the therapeutic relation through the non-verbal communication can gradually enhance the capacity to self-regulate.[280]

BRINGING IN THE JUNGIAN THEORY AND BSR APPROACH: SOME CONSIDERATIONS

Due to the cognitive development of the adult who enters therapy, there are more strings to play on than in the baby. Parallel with the therapeutic relation, an inner relation to images can be fostered. Images that arises through working with the body and from dreams. Images that can help us to self–regulate (as described in the previous paragraph on the internalization of the image of the mother).[281]

In Jungian terms, the symbols become the containers and by active imagination of what we could call supporting symbols—or archetypal representations of the good mother, the wise women, etc., these inner figures holds potential as self-regulating other. (They have from a Jungian perspective other potentials as well, here I argue for this specific quality.)

In my opinion, this is a huge benefit of the Jungian approach that meets with the field of developmental psychology, regulatory psychology and neuroscience. Because the images that arise from our dreams are born of our own body, they are part of us. They are linked with our bodies' perceptions. I suggest that their healing or regulatory potential reaches not only the conscious mind, but also the unconscious body-soul-mind or the preverbal body-soul-mind. This is opposed to the conscious suggestion to a client from a therapist to try to imagine a specific image. Thus our own images carry strong healing capacity. The work with our own images in the body is at the center of the BSR approach.

DREAM-SYMBOLS AS SELF-REGULATING OTHERS

I have talked about the self-regulating other in terms of the early dyad where it is the qualities of the positive mother that are stressed. I too have suggested that the BSR approach offers potent ways of fostering constructive relations to our inner images; relations that can be a source of self-regulation. Finally, the BSR approach fosters establishment of inner representations of positive mothering or, in Jungian terminology, constellates an inner representation of the positive mother archetype through the lived experiences of positive mothering. The

---

pp. 299-328.

280 It takes time, adult brains are plastic but they are not as fast in developing as the fast growing and forming brain of the infant.

281 Wilkinson, *Coming into Mind*.

positive mother is the base and the foundation—the ground we start out from and return to for soothing and nourishment.

Now other aspects of the self-regulating other, I propose, is what can be personified in dream symbols and in mask-work—aspects that when integrated, balance the personality as a whole, as well-known in Jungian theory.[282]

THE INTERACTION WITH THE SELF-REGULATING OTHER CHANGES PATTERNS OF EXPECTATIONS

It seems from the large amount of studies done in the field, that the earlier and more prolonged the interpersonal trauma, the more the need for a self-regulating other that extends to the somatic unconscious realm communicating through preverbal modalities. The care radiating from an attuned empathic other stabilises the bodily felt stages of tension and enables the person to tolerate their emotional world. It enables them to move from the evoked stage of distress and overwhelming pain or anger, characteristic the hyper-aroused stage, or the numbing characteristic of the hypo-aroused stage, to a stage where the emotional and physical intensity can be tolerated and coped with. This regulation enables a shift from distress to more comfort, from pain to more pleasurable feelings, and enables a state where processing and integration can take place.

I propose that the BSR approach, including the exercises in pairs and triads, provides an excellent opportunity to interact with the self-regulating other, both in terms of inner symbols and in terms of the partner in the exercises.

HOW THE BSR APPROACH ENHANCES RELATIONAL SKILL

Sue Gerhardt outlines that good relationships depend on finding a balance between being able to track your own feelings, at the same time as you track other people's feelings. Good relationships also depend on being able to tolerate uncomfortable feelings whilst they are being processed with another person. I suggest that both aspects are enhanced through the exercises in the BSR approach. The caregiver's capacity to handle uncomfortable feelings such as anger and hostility without being overwhelmed by distress or feeling too uncomfortable is paramount for her capacity to help the child to regulate them. The same is true for the therapeutic relation. In the context of the BSR intensives, I suggest that the lived experience of being with another, exploring their feelings, mirroring and containing them, fosters this

---

282 Naturally many other aspects can be personified in dreams and mask-work including "dys-regulating others," as is exemplified in the interviews where the participants created masks with "negative" energy, and so can other aspects.

capacity in the person who is mirroring. Since it takes place in a larger containment of the BSR work, the skill can be practiced in a secure setting.

Regarding to early relational trauma, I think it is important to comment on dys-regulated states. For the infant, anything that threatens the regulation is stressful and is experienced as putting survival at a risk.[283] The infant cannot self-regulate and, if not helped to do so by a loving other, he or she remains stuck in a state of hyper-arousal or hypo-arousal. If we understand this as an emotional reality, the need for an emotionally available and attuned other becomes obvious. This is also true if the states of dys-regulation are evoked in an adult working with early relational traumas. If the attuned other does not help to restore the state of arousal, the traumatized infant part remains stuck in a state of overwhelming arousal. (See the example of being attended to when crying in bed, in Part II).

MANAGEMENT OF FEELINGS: COMMENTS ON THE DIFFERENCES BETWEEN RIGHT- AND LEFT-HEMISPHERE PROCESSING

In the Jungian approach, symbolic work is very much fostered. A particular feature of the BSR approach is the active engagement of the body's reality, the bodily mirroring and containing and the shared feeling voyages that are possible through the exercises. The experience, that the symbol has a healing power because it speaks to the mind, the body and the imagination may be due to its capacity to relate to the reality of the body, the right brain and the left brain at the same time bridging all modalities of expression.[284] This synthesis is nurtured in the BSR approach, through focusing on the bodily felt senses, the emotional reality anchored in the body, the expression of these emotions and feelings in movement, including images and other creative modalities and the careful linking of it with expression to be communicated verbally. Altogether there is a linking of the right brain's felt sense with the left brain's verbal account.

This work I propose has deep significance in terms of a gradually growing capacity to manage feelings, constantly bridging the right hemisphere's experience with the left hemisphere's expression of it.

---

283 The infant needs to evoke attachment to the mother, being depending on her for life. Misattunement is a break in the bond or the shared field. Stress responses from the baby elicit attention and renewed attachment to mother in a healthy mother-child relation.

284 Levin's and Modell's work shows that more brain centers light up in response to metaphor than any other form of human communication, thus indicating the formation of new pathways arising from and in response to the symbolic (Levine, *Waking the Tiger* and Modell, *Reflections on Metaphors and Affects* cited in Pally, *The Mind-Brain Relationship*, p. 132.

IN CONCLUSION: THE FIELD OF LOVE—THE NEUROSCIENTIFIC AND DEVELOPMENTAL ASPECT OF LOVE IN RELATION TO BSR

The neuroscientific and developmental aspect of love emphasizes the importance of the quality of the emotional field that surround us. It stresses the huge effect of being met with a feeling of being received, loved and cared for. It also stresses the growth-stimulating aspect of the attuned caring other who is attuned to and who responses to one's emotional state moment by moment. And it emphasizes the non-verbal dimension of this: the impact of face, gaze, voice, posture and touch.

As explained, a feeling of being responded to by a loving attuned other reduces stress-responses related to survival at the attachment level. When the attachment feels secure—not only in the now, but also in a way that it feels as if it will also stay secure in the nearest future,[285] the person can move into exploring her or his inner world, and can engage with creative impulses. She or he can start to feel herself/ himself more, both in relation to the inner and outer world.

I suggest this lowering of the stress-response on the attachment level is also what gives enough security to allow previously repressed or unthinkable feelings of distress to emerge (or unthinkable distress responses in the body). Feelings that before had been dissociated because there was no way of dealing with them in relationship.

The possibility to express these feelings, to allow the physical responses to emerge and to have a containing other who can help to regulate them, and who is there if it becomes too overwhelming, allows for conscious exploration of these affects, including their somatic expression, the emotional expression, the images that the feelings give rise to, as well as the verbal expression. This quality of the container therefore allows for the integration of previously disintegrated aspects, which fosters a feeling of increased wholeness. The circle of repair can take place—including repair related to past experiences.

The concept of the prospective view of psychic material also opens up to a direction of energy into the future—conveyed in a feeling of exploration and curiosity. The feeling that there is a healing process taking place, and the trust that it will continue to take place, gives birth to hope and solidifies the trust. It shifts the attitude which becomes open to transformation (whereas anxiety gives rise to an attitude that fears transformation).

---

285 Conveyed by the attitude of welcoming the soul in all its aspects, which means the person does not have to use a lot of energy to figure out when they are not accepted—behavior breaking the attachment.

WHY LOVE MATTERS FOR PSYCHIC TRANSFORMATION FROM THE BSR PERSPECTIVE

In developmental psychology the theories are founded on the basis of careful observations of the developing infant and its interactions with the mother.[286] In neuroscience the theories are based on careful observation of the brain through picturing the areas of activity mostly through MRI and through observations of neurological patients.

The BSR approach and its development are based on careful observations of the inner world and the world of dreams. The idea of inner work focused on the dream images in the body originates from dreams where this approach was dreamt. So does the being looked at with the eye of love—which appeared in a dream of Marion Woodman's.[287]

The reality of the inner life is at the foundation of Jung's theories. Just as our inner images can give a precise account of the situation as it is, and can give images of what is needed for healing. It is the trust in these images—which are often very precise, that is the vehicle for this work. The value of listening to the body-soul's needs in order to heal, and the experience of psychic transformation that takes place when the body-soul is reflected in the eye of love, was the observation through this inner listening.

The BSR approach developed from these observations and the combined knowledge and skills from the three professional fields of the founders. As described, the emphasis is on the verbal and non-verbal holding and mirroring of the new life, the importance of the gaze, receiving with an attitude of love, containing, active resonance, hovering and presence. So are authenticity, reflecting the soul, relating to and working with the reality of the body-soul and the awareness that the perceiver and the perceived are one.

This approach is remarkably aligned with Gerhardt's, Schore's, Fonagy's, Stern's, Ogden's, and Wilkinson's description of what matters for the brain-body-mind to develop and gives rise to social, emotional and physical well-being.

Also, it puts in perspective the value of the wisdom of inner knowledge, intuition, body-knowledge and subjective feeling value and it evokes in me an admiration for the three BSR founders' capacity to distil the essence of this knowledge, to develop an approach founded on this knowledge, embodying it and in the practical conducting of it including the development of the exercises, the rhythm of the work, and the structure of the intensives.

---

286 The interactions with the father have not yet been studied to the same extent.
287 Woodman, *Sitting by the Well.*

THE MATTER OF LOVE FOR THE BODY-SOUL, THE INNER LIFE AND THE INDIVIDUATION PROCESS

In conclusion on the matter of love in the BSR approach, I will draw together the observation from the interviews. As described, what is mirrored to us affects us physically and emotionally in our meaning-creating minds. It affects our inner images and our way of being in the world.

THE EFFECT ON THE BODY'S STATE OF BEING WHEN RECEIVED WITH "THE EYE OF LOVE"

When the women in the interview describe what the loving container did to them, they express that they felt something getting more fluent, flowing freer, and expanding. These are words for vitality background feelings that give contours to the way we are in life,[288] but it is also real physical happenings: the motor neurons fire in different ways, some muscle fibres that were held in tension relaxes, the blood flow to the periphery of the body increases, hormone levels and neuropeptide levels change and breath- and heart-rates are influenced.[289]

THE EFFECT ON THE SUBJECTIVE LIVED EXPERIENCE: THE FELT SENSE OF THE TRANSFORMATION TAKING PLACE IN THAT CONTAINER

As described in the perspective on the interviews, the felt sense of the transformation taking place in that container, in essence, was the following:

> Being held in the mist of despair. Receiving validation of who one is, as being and the quality of that in relation to the whole. Being part of the community open to explore deeper values of life and spiritual reflections. A growing capacity to contain. A freedom to dance—an invitation to embody one's passion. A love for the body, the instinctive act "seeing the loneliness"— "Now! Moments" in the group. Bringing healing into the collective field. Finding one's creative expression. Being met with unconditional love. Counterbalancing introjected vicious voices. Growing a spine. The courage to step into one's own truth. A space to live through the gradual transformation of the inner constellation and a space to reflect on it, which often lets the person perceive a meaningful pattern of this unfolding development. A space for exploring and being playful. An encounter with someone who has lived it herself. Finding one's own feminine voice. A space for something being born the "right way out." Adding tools to one's

---

288 Stern, *The Present Moment in Psychotherapy and Everyday Life.*
289 The organism as such does not separate the physical and psychic realms. That is only an illusion of the mind (Damasio, *The Feeling of What Happens: Body and Emotion in the Making of Consciousness*).

toolbox as therapist. Living metaphor—a lived symbolic approach to life. Experiencing the body as living reality.

All these statements express the subjective lived experience.

WHAT WAS IMPORTANT?—THE ESSENCE OF THE DESCRIBED QUALITIES OF THE CONTAINER

Equally, the felt sense of what qualities of the container supporting this transformation were in essence:

> Giving validation of the participant's way of being, of her uniqueness, without judgement. Providing community with openness to discuss life values and approaches to the spiritual dimension of life. Embodying being the "Self-regulating other." Reflecting the person's essence back to her. Inspirational. The visible love, care, joy and consideration that the leaders have for their own bodies. Expressing delight—the joy and humor in the work—finding the laughter at the heart of things. Meeting the other with unconditional love. Being active resonating the other. Balancing being and doing—nourishment and agency. Re-establishing a feeling of agency. Being in touch with one's own playfulness; being playful and ready to play. Being in the unpredictable now. Providing space for ongoing submersion. To give space for the participant to live through a gradual inner transformation. Opening of the voice-channel. Being able to enter cycles of repair after misattunement.

In conclusion, what gradually emerges through the process of being received with the eye of love is that one starts to meet oneself with the attitude of love, allowing the soul's expressions with growing courage and living in a way that is more aligned with one's true nature.

CONCRETE METHODS FOUNDED IN NEUROSCIENCE, DEVELOPMENTAL THEORIES, AND JUNGIAN THEORIES

Looking at the Jungian model of the psyche and the BSR approach from the perspective of neuroscience and developmental psychology, and describing it with the metaphors of these fields, what seems to take place could be expressed as follows:

Working consciously with images, symbols, symptoms and feeling states, letting the content express itself in the body and voice, letting it develop and transform. Working with mirroring and containing, providing a self-regulating other. Working with a partner who is attuned—moment-to-moment—to the emotional state of the one working. Enhancing the integration of the self-regulating other through the paired work and through the work with dream images and masks. Allowing for somatic as well as emotional processing of traumatic experiences locked in the body. Creating an environment that provides secure attachment, safety and trust. And providing metaphors that can hold the process and serve as a container as well.

RECEIVING SOUL

How do we create a facilitating environment? How do we hold the new life? How do we look at it, mirror it, and respond to its needs? How do we understand the good-enough therapist who holds a space where development can take place where there is enough frustration to create the tension that moves it forward, but not so much that it is broken?

My reply would be that the metaphysics of analytical psychology has great potential in offering a philosophy and psychological theory that answers these questions, and that the BodySoul Rhythms approach offers important perspectives, solid foundation and practical implementation of providing a growth-facilitating container on all levels. The stories of the women who have shared their experiences with me seem to effect an environment that is now a living reality in their inner world: a lived body memory they can draw on for themselves as their process continues to unfold.

Gathering the Essence: Love Matters

> … to arrive where we started
> And know the place for the first time.
>
> ….
>
> A condition of complete simplicity
> (Costing not less than everything)…[290]

I have presented an insight into what seems to matter for the soul to feel received, and to start to unfold—an insight given through the accounts of the subjective lived experience of psychic transformation as it is referred to in the six interviews with the women who have done the BSR leadership training.

I also have linked the BSR approach with the new neuroscientific and developmental theories and shown how much the BSR approach has to offer, not only in the Jungian field but also in a broader field of approaches.

The mirroring, the containing, the empathic attunement, the active resonating, the welcoming of the soul's expressions, the devotion, the trust, the reflecting, the giving space are all building blocks to the concept of love.

Love is also an attitude—an attitude with which we meet and receive the other.

Who is *the other*…?

This perspective opens to *the other* as our own body, our soul, our inner life, our heart, our struggles. It opens to our loved ones, the lonely woman in the circle, the partners in the dance, the analysand in the seat in front of us, the colleague next to us, the inner masculine, the morning forest, the gaze we meet as we reflect ourselves in the eye of *the other*.

---

290 T.S. Eliot, *Complete Poems and Plays: 1909–1950*, *Four Quartets*, 'Little Gidding,' p. 145.

To meet the other with "the eye of love" is a creating act. As the interviewees describe, this creates a sense of safety and security, and a sense of being. From the neuroscientific point of view, this way of being met regulates inner arousal. There is a non-verbal meeting between two right hemispheres, and a lowering of the heart rhythm. Feeling into the body, some of the interviewees describe how their bodies became more fluid and relaxed. From developmental psychology, we know that being met with a loving gaze is the most powerful stimulation for development. It enables new representations of 'self with loving other' as Daniel Stern would put it. A present moment of meeting is formed. Finally, from a Jungian perspective it creates a sense of the soul feeling received.

"To arrive where we started—and to know the place for the first time"... Arriving at the point that neuroscience and developmental perspectives describe as "moments of meeting" and which Marion Woodman, Ann Skinner and Mary Hamilton describe and create as a lived experience of receiving the soul in the BSR approach.

That the two important fields of wisdom that I am founded in have a mutual meeting point in the importance of love, I find satisfying. The still-point in the dance.

I hope this book has provided the readers with insight into why love matters for psychic transformation.

> The soul needs love as urgently as the body needs air
> All the possibilities of your human destiny are asleep in your soul.
> You are here to realize and honor these possibilities.
> When love comes in to your life,
> Unrecognized dimensions of your destiny awaken and blossom and grow[291]

---

291 John O'Donohue, *Anam Cara*, p. 9.

Postscript: On Love - A Moment of Meeting—Receiving Soul

Is love a feeling, an act or an attitude? Is it a blessing? Is it a connectedness to a kindness that dwells deep down in things? While writing the manuscript, I often thought the need to define love, at least to make an attempt since I wrote so much about it. But it never quite seemed to make sense or to fit when I tried to define love. There is always something more to it, another kind of love to be added and the words already sounded too distant to capture what it is. The best one can do, I believe, is to describe what it is for us. What we sense in our body and what images come to our mind.

Love has myriads of places to be felt in, myriads of variants of expressions, myriads of sounds and forms.

In the context of working to midwife psychic transformation, my best attempt is that love is the *emphatic presence in love with soul*. Here comes my description of that feeling:

The feeling changes my body posture. I become relaxed and attuned. My gaze feels more focused, ready to meet the gaze of the other. When my focus is on the other as the whole person, I feel a care in my eyes and I have a feeling of a gaze, embracing the body of the other, the whole person. When my focus shifts to that little spot on my retina, where we perceive the image, my gaze become more centered. It feels even more focused, searching, looking into the eye of the other and deeper—looking for the soul. And when I see glimpses of the soul in there, my heart and my body feel it. The muscles around my eyes relax, my face creates a smile and there is this quick arriving wash of joy and excitement that resonates in my body: "Oh there you are... hi, there." My hands start to feel bigger, as if all my present-ness flows into my hands and they are reaching out. They feel as if they are ready to support a birth or to hold and greet something arriving. And when that moment of meeting arrives, it's like the gift of an old friend and a newborn baby. There is a sense of rest arriving in the meeting. A shift from searching to being ready to receive. My heart sinks back in a soft red welcoming armchair. My hands find their resting place on the sides of the chair; my gaze is a mixture of curiosity, a smile and care. My mouth seems silently to form the question "... tell me how you are... tell me your story... and out of the silence a voice emerges.

Appendix

THE RAINMAKER OF KIAU-TCHOU

[Jung said:]

As an example of being in Tao and its synchronistic accompaniment I will cite the story, told to me by the late Richard Wilhelm, of the rainmaker of Kiau-Tchou:

"There was a great drought where the missionary Richard Wilhelm lived in China. For months, there had not been a drop of rain and the situation became catastrophic. The Catholics made processions, the Protestants made prayers, and the Chinese burned joss-sticks and shot off guns to frighten away the demons of the drought, but with no result. Finally the Chinese said: 'We will fetch the rainmaker.' And from another province, a dried-up old man appeared. The only thing he asked for was a quiet little house somewhere, and there he locked himself in for three days. On the fourth day clouds gathered and there was a great snow-storm at the time of the year when no snow was expected, an unusual amount, and the town was so full of rumours about the wonderful rainmaker that Wilhelm went to ask the man how he did it.

In true European fashion he said: 'They call you the rainmaker, will you tell me how you made the snow?' And the little Chinese said: 'I did not make the snow, I am not responsible.' 'But what have you done these three days?' 'Oh, I can explain that. I come from another country where things are in order. Here they are out of order; they are not as they should be by the ordinance of heaven. Therefore the whole country is not in Tao, and I am also not in the natural order of things because I am in a disordered country. So I had to wait three days until I was back in Tao, and then naturally the rain came.'"

From 'Interpretations of Visions,' Vol. 3 of seminars in English by C.G. Jung (new edition, privately multigraphed, 1939), and page 7 in CW, Vol. 14, *Mysterium Coniunctionis*, paragraph 604, note 211.

References

Ainsworth, M.; Blehar, M.; Waters, E.; & Wall, S. *Patterns of Attachment*. Hillsdale, NJ: Erlbaum, 1978.

Alistar, I. & Hauke, C. (Eds.). *Contemporary Jungian Analysis: Post-Jungian Perspectives from the Society of Analytical Psychology*. London, England: Routledge, 1998.

Allan, J. *Inscapes of the Child's World*. Dallas, TX: Spring Publication Inc., 1988.

Auden, W.H. *Another Time*. New York, NY: Random House, 1940.

Bauer, J. *Warum ich fühle, was du fühlst*. Hamburg, Germany: Hoffmann und Campe Verlag, 2005.

Bitter, W. (Ed.). *Meditation in Religion and Psychotherapy*. Stuttgart, Germany: Ernst Klett Verlag, 1958.

Bovensiepen, G. Attachment-dissociation network: some thoughts about a modern complex theory. *Journal of Analytical Psychology*, 2006; 3: 451–466.

Buirski, P. *Practicing Intersubjectively*. Maryland, MD: Rowman and Littlefield Publishers Inc., 2005.

Campbell, J. *Myths to Live By*. New York, NY: Viking Penguin Inc., 1972.

Clark, G. The Animating Body: Psychoid Substance as Mutual Experience of the Psychosomatic Disorder. In *Landmarks: Papers by Jungian analysts from Australia and New Zealand*, Ed. Formaini, H. Manuka, Australia: Australian and New Zealand Society of Jungian Analysts, 2001.

Damasio, A. *The Feeling of What Happens: Body and Emotion in the Making of Consciousness*. Florida, FL: Harcourt, 1999.

Davis, M. & Wallbridge, B. *Boundary and Space: An Introduction to the Work of D.W. Winnicott*. London, England: Karnac Books, 1991.

Douglas, C. (Ed.) *Visions: Notes of the Seminar Given in 1930-1934 by C.G. Jung*. Princeton, NJ: Princeton University Press, 1997.

Eliot, T.S. *Complete Poems and Plays: 1909–1950*. Orlando, FL: Harcourt, 1952.

Ende, M. *The Neverending Story*, Hardcover edition, New York, NY: E P Dutton & Co Inc., 1997.

Fried, E. *Es ist was es ist (It is what it is)*. London, England: Calder Publications, 1983.

Fonagy, Peter; Gergely, György: Jurist, Elliot; Target, Mary *Affect Regulation, Mentalization, and the Development of the Self,* New York, NY: Other Press, 2004.

George, C.; Kaplan, N.; & Main, M. (1985) *The Adult Attachment Interview,* Berkeley, CA: University of California at Berkeley, Department of Psychology, 1985. Unpublished manuscript referenced in Fonagy, Elliot & Target *Affect Regulation, Mentalization and the Development of the Self).*

Gelder, M.; Mayou, R.; & Geddes, J. *Psychiatry,* Oxford, England: Oxford Medical Publications, 2005.

Gerhardt, Sue. *Why Love Matters: How Affection Shapes a Baby's Brain,* East Sussex: Routledge, 2004.

Gide, André. *The Counterfeiters: A Novel,* New York, N.Y.: Vintage; First Edition, 1973.

Goddard, Harold C. *The Meaning of Shakespeare,* Volumes 1 and 2, Chicago, IL, The University of Chicago Press 1951.

Goethe, Johan Wolfgang von. *Faust, Part Two,* (Philip Wayne, Trans.), London, England: Penguin Classics, 1959.

Graves, Robert. *The White Goddess: A Historical Grammar of Poetic Myth,* New York, N.Y: Farrar, Straus and Giroux, 1948.

Harding, Esther. *Woman's Mysteries,* Boston & Shaftsbury, MA: Shambhala, 1971.

Henderson, Joseph L. *Shadow and Self.* Chiron Publications, 1990, in Sabini, Meredith (Ed.) *The Earth has a Soul: C.G. Jung on Nature, Technology and Modern Life,* p. 279.

Holmes, Jeremy. *John Bowlby and Attachment Theory,* London, England: Routledge, 1993.

Jacoby, Mario. *Individuation and Narcissism: The psychology of Self in Jung and Kohut* (M. Gubitz, Trans.). London: Routledge, 1991.

———. *Jungian Psychotherapy and Contemporary Infant Research: Basic Patterns of Emotional Exchange* (R. Weathers, Trans.). London, England: Routledge, 1999.

Jarret, James L. (Ed.). Nietzsche's Zarathustra: Notes of the Seminar Given in 1934-1939 by C.G. Jung. (Bollingen Series XCIX), Princeton, NJ: Princeton University Press, 1988.

Jung, C.G. *The Collected Works, Second Edition.* (Bollingen Series XX; H. Read, M. Fordham, & G. Adler, Eds.; R.F.C. Hull, Trans.). Princeton, NJ: Princeton University Press, 1953-1979.

———. *The Practice of Psychotherapy, The Collected Works Vol. 16, Second Edition.* (Bollingen Series XX). Princeton, NJ: Princeton University Press, 1966.

———. *Two Essays on Analytical Psychology, The Collected Works Vol. 7, Second Edition.* (Bollingen Series XX). Princeton, NJ: Princeton University Press, 1967.

———. *The Structure and Dynamics of the Psyche, The Collected Works Vol. 8, Second Edition.* (Bollingen Series XX). Princeton, NJ: Princeton University Press, 1969.

———. *Civilization in Transition, The Collected Works Vol. 10, Second Edition.* (Bollingen Series XX). Princeton, NJ: Princeton University Press, 1970.

———. *Mysterium Coniunctionis, The Collected Works Vol. 14, Second Edition.* (Bollingen Series XX). Princeton, NJ: Princeton University Press, 1970.

———. *Psychological Types, The Collected Works Vol. 6, Second Edition.* (Bollingen Series XX). Princeton, NJ: Princeton University Press, 1971.

———. *Memories, Dreams, Reflections* (A. Jaffe, Ed.; R. & C. Winston, Trans.). London, England: Collins & Routledge & Kegan Paul, 1962, paperback edition, London, England: Fontana.

Kalsched, Donald. *The Inner World of Trauma: Archetypal Defences of the Personal Spirit,* London, England: Routledge, 1996.

Kast, Verena. *Father Daughter, Mother Son,* Dorset, Great Britain: Elements Books Limited, 1997.

Klein, Josephine. *Our Need for Others and its Roots in Infancy,* London, England: Routledge, 1987.

Knox, Jean. *Archetypes, Attachment Analysis: Jungian Psychology and the Emergent Mind,* London, England: Routledge, 2003.

———. Author's notes from Jean Knox's lecture: *The Unbearable Nature of Meaning, on the Impact of Relational Trauma on the Meaning-Making Process and the Loss of Self-agency;* talk given at Society of Analytical Psychology, Cambridge, England, March 2008.

Levine, Peter. *In an Unspoken Voice: How the Body Releases Trauma and Restores Goodness.* Berkeley, CA: North Atlantic Books, 2010.

———. *Somatic Experiencing Manual,* 2007.

———. *Waking the Tiger,* Berkeley, CA: North Atlantic Book, 1997.

Luke, Helen. *The Way of Women, Ancient and Modern*, Three Rivers, Michigan, MI: Apple Farm, 1975.

————. *Such Stuff as Dreams are Made on*, New York, NY: Belltower, 2000.

McDougall, Joyce. *Theaters Of The Body: A Psychoanalytic Approach to Psychosomatic Illness*, New York, N.Y: W. W. Norton & Company, 1989.

McGilchrist, Iain. *The Master and His Emissary: The Divided Brain and the Making of the Western World*, New Haven, CT: Yale University Press; 2010.

Modell, A.H. *Reflections on Metaphors and Affects*, Annual of Psychoanalysis, 1997; 25: pp. 219-233.

O'Donohue, John. *Anam Cara: A Book of Celtic Wisdom*, New York, NY: Harper Perennial, 1997.

————. *Eternal Echoes: Celtic Reflections on Our Yearning to Belong*, New York, N.Y: HarperCollins, 1999.

————. *To Bless the Space Between Us*, New York, NY: The Doubleday Broadway Publishing Group, 2008

Ogden, P.; Minton, K.; & Pain, C. *Trauma and the Body: A Sensorimotor Approach to Psychotherapy*, London, England: W.W. Norton and Company, 2006.

Ogden, P. Author's notes from P. Ogden's lecture at the following conference: *Psychological Trauma and the Body*, London, 15–17 September 2007.

Oliver, Mary. *West Wind: Poems and Prose Poems*, Boston, MA: Mariner Books, 1998.

Pallaro, P. (Ed.), *Authentic Movement: Essays by Mary Stark Whitehouse, Janet Adler, and Joan Chodorow*, London, UK: Jessica Kingsley Publishers; 1999.

Pally, R. *The Mind-Brain Relationship*, London, UK: Karnac, 2000.

Rich, Adrienne. *The Dream of a Common Language: Poems 1974–1977*, New York, N.Y. : W. W. Norton & Company, 1993.

Rilke, R.M. *Selected Poems*, (J.B. Leisman, Trans.), Middlesex, England: Penguin Books, 1964.

————. (Albert Ernest Flemming, Trans.), *Selected Poems*, London, England: Routledge, 1986.

Robinson, Roxana. *Georgia O'Keeffe: A life*, Boston, MA.: University Press of New England. 1999.

Rothschild, Babette. *The Body Remember: The Psychophysiology of Trauma and Treatment,* New York, NY: Norton and Company, 2000.

Rumi, Jelaluddin (Coleman Barks, Ed.). *The Essential Rumi,* San Francisco, CA: Harper, 1995.

———. *Love is a Stranger,* Boston, MA: Shambhala Publications, 2000.

Sabini, Meredith (Ed.). *The Earth has a Soul: C.G. Jung on Nature, Technology and Modern Life,* Berkeley, CA: North Atlantic Books, 2007.

Samuels, Andrew. *Jung and the Post-Jungians,* London and New York, NY and UK: Routledge, 1985.

Schore, Allan N. "Minds in the Making: Attachment, The Self-Organizing Brain and Developmentally-Oriented Psychoanalytic Psychotherapy. *British Journal of Psychotherapy,* 2001; 17 (3): pp. 299-328.

———. *Affect Dysregulation and Disorders of the Self,* New York, NY: Norton Professional Books, 2003.

———. *Affect Regulation and the Repair of the Self,* New York, NY: Norton Professional Books, 2003.

———. Author's notes from Schore's lecture at the following conference: *Psychological Trauma and the Body,* London, 15–17 September 2007.

Sidoli, Mara. *When the Body Speaks,* London, England: Routledge, 2000.

Sieff, D.F. *Understanding and Healing Emotional Trauma: Conversations with Pioneering Clinicians and Researchers.* Routledge, London, UK: 2015.

Spring 72, *Body & Soul: Honoring Marion Woodman,* New Orleans, LA: Spring Journal, 2005.

Spring 81, *The Psychology of Violence,* New Orleans, LA: Spring Journal, 2009.

Stern, Daniel N. *The Interpersonal World of the Infant: A View from Psychoanalysis and Developmental Psychology,* London, England: Karnac, 1985.

———. *The Diary of a Baby,* Basic Books, New York, NY: 1990.

———. *The Present Moment in Psychotherapy and Everyday Life,* New York, NY: Norton, 2004.

Ulanov, Ann Belford. *The Functioning Transcendent: A Study in Analytical Psychology,* Asheville, NC: Chiron Publications, 1996.

Van der Hart, O.; Nijenhuis, E.R.S.; Steele, K. *The Haunted Self: Structural Dissociation and the Treatment of Chronic Traumatization*, New York, NY: W.W. Norton and Company, 2006.

Von Franz; Marie-Louise. *The Golden Ass of Apuleius,* Boston, MA: Shambhala, 1992.

————. *The Feminine in Fairytales.* Boston, MA: Shambhala, 1993

————. *The Interpretation of Fairytales*, Boston, MA: Shambhala, 1996.

Whitehouse, Mary S. Physical Movement and Personality. In Pallaro, P. (Ed.), *Authentic Movement: Essays by Mary Starks Whitehouse, Janet Adler, and Joan Chodorow* (Vol. 1. pp. 51-55) Philadelphia, PA: Jessica Kingsley Publishers,1999.

Whitmont C. Edward. *The Symbolic Quest: Basic Concepts of Analytical Psychology,* Princeton, NJ: Princeton University Press, 1991.

Wilkinson, Margaret. *Coming into Mind: The Mind-Brain Relationship: A Jungian Clinical Perspective,* London, England: Routledge, 2006.

Winnicott, D.W. *The Location of Cultural Experience*, Published in the *International Journal of Psycho-Analysis*, Vol. 48, Part 3, 1967.

————. The Use of an Object and Relating Through Identifications, Published in the *International Journal of Psycho-Analysis*, Vol. 50, 1969.

————. *Home is Where We Start From: Essays by a Psychoanalyst,* London, England: Penguin Books, 1986.

————. *Playing and Reality*, Harmondsworth, Middlesex, England: Penguin Books Ltd., 1971.

————. *Through Paediatrics to Psycho-Analysis.* New York, NY: Basic Books, 1975.

————. *Playing and Reality*, Oxon, England: Routledge, 2005.

Woodman, Marion. *The Owl was a Baker's Daughter*, Toronto, Canada: Inner City Books, 1980.

————. *Addiction to Perfection: The Still Unravished Bride,* Toronto, Canada: Inner City Books, 1982.

————. *The Pregnant Virgin: A Process of Psychological Transformation*, Toronto, Canada: Inner City Books, 1985.

————. *The Ravaged Bridegroom: Masculinity in Women,* Toronto, Canada: Inner City Books, 1988.

———. *Leaving My Father's House,* Toronto, Canada: Inner City Books, 1992.

———. *Empowering Soul Through the Feminine, Interview with Marion Woodman* by Michael Bertrand, 1992, quoted from Marion Woodman's homepage.

———. *Conscious Femininity: Interviews with Marion Woodman,* Toronto, Canada: Inner City Books, 1993.

———. *Sitting by the Well: Bringing the Feminine to Consciousness Through Language, Dreams and Metaphor* (audio cassette) Louisville, CO: Sounds True, 1998.

———. *Bone: Dying into Life,* New York, N.Y.: Penguin Group, 2000.

Woodman, Marion & Dickson, Elinor *Dancing in the Flames: The Dark Goddess in the Transformation of Consciousness,* Boston, MA: Shambhala, 1997.

Woodman, Marion & Mellick, Jill. *Coming Home to Myself, Reflections for Nurturing a Woman's Body and Soul,* Berkeley, CA: Conari Press 1998.

Yalom, Irvin. *Theory and Practice of Group Psychotherapy,* New York, NY: Basic Books, 1985.

Yeats, W.B. *The Countess Kathleen and Various Legends and Lyrics* includes *The Lake Isle of Innisfree,* part of public domain, 1892.

Young-Eisendrath, Polly & Wiedemann, Florence L. *Female Authority: Empowering Women Through Psychotherapy,* New York, NY: The Guildford Press 1990.

Permissions

Many thanks to all who have directly or indirectly provided permission to quote their works, including:

Artist and photographer Mary Jo Hoffman, Minneapolis, for permission to use the oak sprout picture that is decorating the front cover. For more information about Mary Jo Hoffman's work please see her blog, STILL at http://stillblog.net/.

Photographer Michael Groen for his portrait photo on the back cover. Michael Groen, Associate in Society of Wedding and Portrait Photographers in 2008, International Glamour Photographer of the Year 2008 SWPP, Supreme Qualified Master 2009, QEP Qualified European Photographer in Federation of European Photographers 2009, QEP Qualified European Photographer in Federation of European Photographers 2013 is owner of 'Billedmageren* together with his colleague Laerke Johanne Groenborg. For more information please see http://www.billedmageren.dk.

The Permissions Department, Faber and Faber: permissionslicenses@faber.co.uk for the World excluding USA for permission to use the poems of T.S. Eliot.

Excerpt from "Burnt Norton," "East Coker" and "Little Gidding" from FOUR QUARTETS by T.S. Eliot. Copyright 1936, 1940, 1942 by T.S. Eliot. Copyright © renewed 1964 by T.S. Eliot. Copyright © renewed, 1968, 1970 by Esme Valerie Eliot. Reprinted by permission of Houghton Mifflin Harcourt Publishing Company. All rights reserved.

The lines from "Transcendental Etude," from THE DREAM OF A COMMON LANGUAGE: Poems 1974-1977 by Adrienne Rich, Copyright ©1978 by W.W. Norton & Company, Inc. Used by permission of W.W. Norton & Company, Inc.

Extract from the "Song of Amergin," translated by Robert Graves in *The White Goddess*, Copyright © 1948 and renewed 1975 by Robert Graves. Reprinted by arrangement with Carcanet Press Limited, Manchester, UK. www.carcanet.co.uk.

Lines from the poem *A Great Wagon* by Rumi, Jelaluddin. Translated by Coleman Barks in *The Essential Rumi*, Copyright © 1995 by Coleman Barks. All rights reserved. Reprinted with permission from Mr. Coleman Barks.

The poem "The Root of the Root is Your Self," by Rumi, Jelaluddin translated by Kabir Helminski, from *Love is a Stranger*, © 1993 by Kabir Edmund Helminski. Reprinted by arrangement with The Permissions Company, Inc., on behalf of Shambhala Publications Inc., Boston, MA. www.shambhala.

The lyrics to *Weaver Weaver*. The lyrics are from an old folksong adapted by Starhawk, author, global justice activist and a respected voice in modern earth-based spirituality who generously has allowed me to quote it. For more information please see www.starhawk.org.

Apart from the permissions that were so generously granted, I would like to give my deepest appreciation of the work quoted from authors who have been of deep inspiration to me:

Sue Gerhardt, C.G. Jung, John O'Donohue, Allan Schore, Daniel Stern, Margaret Wilkinson, and D.W. Winnicott.

BIOGRAPHICAL BACKGROUND

WENDY BRATHERTON BSC.

Wendy Bratherton, a Jungian Analyst, integrates BodySoul work, trauma work and Craniosacral Therapy into her practice. She facilitates Infant Observation seminars for The Society for Analytical Psychology in London. She has trained in trauma work with Babette Rothschild. www.wendybratherton.com

MARIAN DUNLEA MSC.

Marian is a Jungian analyst and core faculty member of the Marion Woodman Foundation. She is the director of the Ongoing Professional Development Program. She is currently researching and writing a book on BodyDreaming,™ her innovative approach to working with the interface between psyche and soma. Her trainings in psychotherapy include Jungian Analytical Psychology, Psychoanalytic Psychotherapy, Psychosynthesis, Somatic Experiencing and Infant Observation. She facilitates groups internationally, working with BodyDreaming,™ BodySoul Rhythms, mask, myth, and the Celtic seasonal cycle. www.mariandunlea.com.

DANIELA F. SIEFF, D.PHIL.

I am a writer with roots in evolutionary anthropology and an active interest in the dynamics of the psyche. The question that engages me is: 'What makes us who we are?' I have explored this question in relation to (1) our internal psychological and emotional world (2) our external physical, social and relational world, and (3) our evolutionary heritage. My exploration has taken the form of both scholarship and personal experience. I have a doctorate in biological anthropology from the University of Oxford. My research took me to a wilderness region of Tanzania to live with a traditional cattle-herding people. I studied what families needed to survive, as well as how evolutionary processes contribute to shaping social behavior. For the last 15 years I have focused on the dynamics of the wounded psyche. My understanding has emerged through bringing together my own personal experience with knowledge that comes from psychotherapy, neurobiology, anthropology and evolution. My book, 'Understand and Healing Emotional Trauma: Conversations with Pioneering Clinicians and Researchers' was born out of this process, and was published by Routledge in 2015. For more information see www.danielasieff.com.

MARLENE SCHIWY, PHD.

Marlene Schiwy is a workshop leader and author, and does Jungian work with individual clients. A former professor of literature, women's studies, and creative writing, with a background in music and psychology, soul-work has been the essence of Marlene's personal life and vocational calling. She completed the first Leadership Training Program in 2004 and teaches Affiliated Workshops in Canada, the US, and Europe. From 2005 to 2007 she studied at ISAP Zurich. Marlene has had a lifelong love of creative process and finds great fulfilment in helping others to explore their own buried creativity and make contact with the deep archetypal images that carry their life energy.

Along with Jung's depth psychology and Marion Woodman's exploration of the conscious feminine, Marlene's approach is influenced by James Hillman's love of the image, and Helen Luke's work on story. The author of two books and half a dozen articles, Marlene is currently writing a book on the Dark Feminine in women and men today. She has been conducting writing workshops, professional development seminars and Jungian Writing Circles internationally for two decades. In 2003 Marlene created "Body Soul Writing," the first university writing course in Canada to introduce expressive movement into the writing process. In 2005 and 2006 she conducted extensive filmed interviews with Marion Woodman. To all of her creative endeavours Marlene brings a unique blend of Jungian training and solid academic grounding, a lifelong love of creative process, and her own intense and vibrant engagement with the ongoing alchemy of everyday life.

WENDY WILMOT, M.E.S. AND M.A.

Wendy Wilmot is Canadian and resides just north of Toronto. She is a Jungian Analyst graduated from ISAP, Zurich who has abiding interests in Analytical Psychology and the field of Ecology. She has two children and four grandchildren.

THE MARION WOODMAN FOUNDATION

For information about any of the BSR programs and the faculty, contact the Marion Woodman Foundation Program Office or visit the website at www.mwoodmanfoundation.org and www.bodysouleurope.org.

If you are interested in having a trained BodySoul leader come to your area, also contact the Program Office.

Contact information: Marion Woodman Foundation, 7110 SW Fir Loop, Suite 250, Portland, OR 97223 USA, 503-746-5899.

Program office: Caryn Aman, Program Director, caryn@mwoodmanfoundation.org.

Index

A

active imagination 15, 25, 34, 101, 102, 214

adaptive patterns 29

Ainsworth, Mary 182, 227

alchemical 78, 138

anima mundi 140, 141

animus 108, 114, 134

archetypal dimension(s) 10, 17, 158, 190, 206

archetypal mother 6, 27, 181

artificial love 45

Asclepius 167

attachment patterns xv, 31, 182, 203

Attachment Theory 145, 161, 183, 228

Auden, W.H. 45, 227

authentic being 36

authentic movement 3, 20, 120, 230, 232

autonomous nervous system 210

B

Bealtaine 140

being present 43, 44

birth trauma xii, 110, 114, 120, 124

'blank' face 43

body dreaming 143, 145

body-memory 29, 194

body movement xi, xiv, 22, 25, 187, 195

body-psyche 13, 14, 19, 25, 115, 145, 146, 148, 173, 195, 199

body-states 28

body symptoms 25

body-work 92, 100, 101

Bratherton, Wendy vii, 106, 117

breath-tending 27

Brigid's Day 132

C

Celtic calendar 140

child complex 28, 30

Chiron 6, 167, 228, 231

civil war 55

cognitive development 214

collective unconscious 17, 140, 168

communal healing 55, 57

conditional love 164, 165

coniunctio 135

cranio-sacral (therapy) 115, 119, 120, 121

cranio-work 120, 121, 122, 123, 124, 127

crone xii, 14, 15, 40, 41, 42, 154, 155

crucifixion 105

cycle of renewal 147

D

dance xi, xv, 5, 6, 9, 10, 33, 36, 39, 63, 65, 66, 68, 69, 103, 120, 123, 126, 144, 146, 148, 155, 156, 182, 198, 219, 223, 224

Dance of Three Exercise 10, 25, 26, 35, 37, 38, 63, 65, 103, 108, 109, 120, 124, 180, 201, 206

Death Mother 100

depression 43

Descartes, René 194

despair vii, 16, 51, 53, 59, 150, 151, 219

developmental psychology xii, xiii, xv, 4, 13, 14, 15, 40, 149, 151, 153, 155, 163, 168, 180, 207, 214, 218, 220

development of self 163

Devon mask 102

dissociation 29, 43, 203, 211, 212, 227

Divine Child 105

dopamine 210, 211

dream-ego 191

dreams xi, xiv, 2, 3, 5, 7, 10, 17, 19, 25, 27, 28, 33, 37, 52, 53, 60, 69, 71, 99, 102, 113, 119, 127, 143, 145, 146, 148, 172, 176, 177, 180, 191, 193, 214, 215, 218

dream series 8

dream work 5, 6, 10, 12, 17, 24, 51, 65, 68, 113, 127, 143, 145, 182, 201

Dunlea, Marian vii, 129, 130

E

earth-based spirituality 128, 234

Eckhart, Meister 26, 98

ego-Self axis 36, 185, 206

Eleusinian mysteries 72

Eliot, T.S. 41, 62, 101, 102, 139, 144, 223, 227, 234

emergent sense of the Self 185

energy, holding of the mask 39

envy 45, 56, 138

extroverted 38, 48, 52, 54, 56, 152

F

fairy tales 5, 12, 18, 19, 33, 39

fear of rejection 43, 203

Feldenkrais 3

feminine body xii, 156

Field Theory 141

Freud 131, 208

G

Gide, André 134

God-image 14, 19

'good-enough' mothering 117

good mother 15, 54, 116, 127, 182, 214

good mothering 53, 118, 124, 181

good mothering exercise 124

Gorgon (terrifying) 116

Graves, Robert
The White Goddess 106, 228, 234

Great Feminine 141, 143

Great Mother 16, 140, 185

great mother principle 16

Green Man 116

grief 14, 29, 38, 55, 78, 119, 125, 158

group body 147

group work 28, 57, 152

H

Hamilton, Mary xi, xii, xiv, 2, 9, 36, 52, 63, 72, 80, 91, 109, 131, 147, 156, 157, 158, 169, 224

Harding, Esther 15, 76, 228
  Woman's Mysteries 15, 76, 228

Hecate 15

human relationship xv

I

I Ching 107

Imbolc 132, 140

implicit memory field 137

individuation process 13, 14, 18, 42, 55, 156, 185, 219

inner child 26, 29, 182

International School of Analytical Psychology xi, 62

introverted 38, 48, 51, 52, 54, 56, 81, 135, 139

intuitive 48, 54, 114, 120, 126, 175, 176, 198, 212

J

Jacoby, Mario 159
  Individuation and Narcissism 159, 228

Jung, C.G. xiii, xiv, xv, 2, 3, 5, 6, 10, 12, 13, 16, 24, 49, 107, 140, 159, 171, 226, 227, 228, 231, 235
  Memories, Dreams, Reflections xv, xvii, 7, 8, 18, 166, 167, 168, 188, 229
  The Practice of Psychotherapy 171, 229
  The Structure and Dynamics of the Psyche 13, 141, 166, 229

K

Kalsched, Donald 21, 96, 102, 115, 212, 229
  The Inner World of Trauma 21, 96, 115, 212, 229

Klein, Melanie 131, 229

Kohut, Heinz 159, 228

Kore 28, 102

L

Lacan, Jacques 131

Levine, Peter 21, 143, 145, 147, 216, 229

limbic system 143

linear mythology 23

living metaphor 133, 134, 144, 145, 150, 151, 175, 176

Loubert, Candace 145

love for the body 84, 156, 157, 219

Luke, Helen 4, 48, 75, 154, 230, 237
  Such Stuff as Dreams are Made On 48, 230
  The Way of Women 154, 230

Lunasa 140

M

Marion Woodman Foundation ix, 2, 3, 107, 130, 237

mask-work xiv, 5, 6, 11, 25, 26, 37, 38, 71, 83, 88, 96, 97, 99, 100, 101, 102, 126, 135, 136, 143, 166, 182, 192, 201, 215

McDougall, Joyce
  Theaters Of The Body 131, 230

McGilchrist, Iain 44, 172

meditation xi, 7, 10, 43, 89, 132, 145

Medusa 19, 71, 100, 105, 116

Merleau-Ponty, Maurice 193, 194

metaphor vii, 5, 19, 23, 32, 33, 40, 48, 63, 78, 79, 133, 134, 142, 144, 145, 151, 156, 162, 167, 168, 173, 174, 175, 176, 179, 191, 216, 220

midwife 36, 150, 225

mirror neurons 135, 137, 148, 180, 196, 197, 201, 205, 206

modern woman 19

Moon Goddess 116

mother archetype 15, 27, 28, 181, 182, 214

mother-child complex 30

mother complex 28, 183

mother-daughter relation 28

mother-infant relationship 118

Mother Nature 16

mother (negative) 56, 118, 183

mother (positive) 15, 27, 29, 31, 56, 77, 124, 182, 183, 214, 215

mother's reflection 155

Mother Teresa 111

Movement 3, 20, 120, 193, 230, 232

myth(s) xi, xii, xiv, 10, 12, 18, 19, 28, 102, 104, 105, 118, 134, 138, 140, 167

N

native mythologies 23

neo-cortex 143, 148

nervous system 100, 143, 148, 190, 210

neural pathways 135, 137, 142, 144

neuroscience vii, xii, xiii, xiv, xv, xvii, 13, 40, 125, 126, 135, 136, 137, 143, 145, 149, 151, 163, 168, 174, 175, 178, 196, 198, 203, 205, 207, 214, 218, 220, 224

neuro-transmitter 210

New Physics 141, 145

Nietzsche, F. 13, 24, 88, 104, 107, 140, 228

Thus Spake Zarathustra 104

Now Moment 94, 102, 104

now movements xv

O

O'Donohue, John xviii, 140, 235

Anam Cara 140, 224, 230

Eternal Echoes xviii, 230

To Bless the Space Between Us 49, 230

Ogden, Pat xv, 34, 168, 195, 199

old memories 29

orbitofrontal cortex 209, 210

P

Pacifica Graduate Institute 80

Palestine 55

paradox xii, 16, 27, 40, 41, 44, 192

paradox, holding the 44

patterns of adaptations 29

personal mother 27, 30, 31, 54, 55

Pert, Candace 144

Phase 1 workshop 37

Phase 2 workshop 3, 37, 38, 111, 113

place of activation 143

place of resource 143, 160

poetry xii, 5, 74, 104, 125, 126, 132, 173

positive feminine 114

positive mothering xi, 6, 11, 25, 26, 27, 28, 29, 30, 31, 121, 123, 124, 179, 180, 181, 205, 214

positive mothering exercise xi, 6, 11, 25, 26, 27, 30, 31, 121, 181

prayer 61, 66, 67

Psyche and Eros myth 105

psychic transformation vii, xiii, xiv, xv, xvi,
    4, 48, 150, 157, 177, 183, 204, 207,
    218, 223, 224, 225
psychosomatic 33, 35, 227
psychosomatic realm 35

Q

Qi Gong 113, 114, 120
Quantum theory 137

R

rainmaker 75, 226
Reeves, Paula 72, 138
right brain-to-right brain interaction xv
Rilke, R.M. 61, 90, 96, 230
role-models 19
Rothschild, Babette 121
rubedo vii, 62, 78, 150, 151, 155, 156, 157

S

sacred feminine 72
sacrifice 39, 67, 93, 112, 113
sadness 29, 53, 59, 61
Samhain 140
Schore, Allan N. xv, 154, 168, 180, 190,
    235
    *Affect Dysregulation and Disorders of the
    Self* 11, 32, 182, 187, 198, 199, 200,
    210, 211, 212, 231
    Affect Regulation and the Repair of the Self
    32, 182, 187, 199, 200, 210, 211,
    212, 231
sensate 48, 116, 120
sense-organs 191
sensorimotor psychotherapy xv
shadow work 45, 88, 89

shaman 167, 168
shame 43, 55, 59, 60, 83, 93, 95, 179
Sidoli, Mara 35, 231
Sieff, Daniela F. vii, ix, 90, 96, 100, 231,
    236
silent agendas 29
Skinner, Ann xi, xii, xiv, 2, 63, 81, 91, 131,
    143, 147, 154, 158, 161, 169, 197,
    224
soul-mirror 25
stereotypes 44
Stern, Daniel N. xv, 26, 122, 180, 185,
    187, 192, 202, 235
    *The Present Moment in Psychotherapy and
    Everyday Life* 4, 16, 32, 40, 94, 157,
    158, 164, 176, 193, 201, 203, 205,
    212, 219, 231
Sun God 116
sword of discretion 93
symbiotic sameness 45
symbol, living 37

T

Tai Chi 3, 113, 114, 115, 120
Tarot 107
tension of opposites 144, 200
the perceived are one 43, 182, 218
thinking 26, 27, 48, 49, 52, 60, 66, 67,
    71, 76, 93, 100, 138, 139, 146, 148,
    152, 168, 172, 176, 191, 192, 194
transcendent function 142, 144, 162, 167,
    206
transitional object 8, 9
trauma xii, xv, 11, 21, 88, 95, 96, 105, 110,
    114, 117, 120, 121, 124, 155, 156,
    181, 194, 195, 196, 200, 202, 211,
    212, 215, 216

Trauma work 145

U

unconditional love vii, 52, 77, 150, 161, 162, 164, 219, 220

un-mothered child 24

V

Vagus nerve 21, 143

virgin xii, 14, 15, 36, 40, 41, 42, 76

voice channel 21, 22, 174

von Franz, M-L 18, 19, 41, 79, 86, 155

W

White Goddess 106, 117, 228, 234

window of tolerance 11, 154, 168, 180, 183, 184, 195, 199, 200, 201, 206, 211, 212

Winnicott, D.W. xi, 8, 9, 36, 125, 126, 154, 155, 162, 164, 166, 170, 171, 181, 184, 185, 227, 232

Playing and Reality 125, 171, 232

wise woman 42, 110, 116

Woodman, Marion ix, xi, xii, xiii, xiv, 2, 3, 5, 9, 12, 13, 14, 15, 16, 32, 33, 36, 41, 44, 49, 50, 80, 91, 100, 107, 130, 131, 152, 154, 155, 158, 169, 171, 176, 178, 182, 186, 187, 188, 189, 196, 218, 224, 231, 233, 237

Addiction to Perfection 2, 13, 44, 49, 131, 152, 184, 186, 232

Conscious Femininity 2, 32, 33, 44, 176, 178, 179, 191, 233

Dancing in the Flames 2, 13, 78, 131, 233

Sitting by the Well 178, 218

The Pregnant Virgin 2, 62, 91, 232

The Ravaged Bridegroom 2, 13, 169, 232

Y

Yeats, W.B. 140, 233

yoga 3, 7, 63

This publication was made possible by a grant from the

Marion Woodman Foundation

The Marion Woodman Foundation is a nonprofit organization established to ensure the continuation of BodySoul Rhythms® in the world.

Created and refined over three decades by Marion Woodman, Mary Hamilton, and Ann Skinner, BodySoul work grew from C.G. Jung's deep psychological insights and Marion Woodman's passionate commitment to articulating the sacred feminine and bringing embodied consciousness into our lives.

The Marion Woodman Foundation is now a vibrant community of women and men dedicated to practicing and broadening the reach of BodySoul Rhythms®. We continuously draw on the insights of C.G. Jung and Marion Woodman bringing the unconscious to consciousness and embracing the unlived life while enhancing, deepening, and making this work accessible in the world.

Marion Woodman Foundation
7110 SW Fir Loop, Suite 250
Portland, OR 97223
+1-503-746-5899
office@mwoodmanfoundation.org
www.mwoodmanfoundation.org

Printed in Great Britain
by Amazon

40581839R00150